OUTLIVING THE WHITE LIE

OUTLIVING THE WHITE LIE

A Southerner's
Historical,
Genealogical,
and Personal
Journey

JAMES WIGGINS

University Press of Mississippi / Jackson

The University Press of Mississippi is the scholarly publishing agency of
the Mississippi Institutions of Higher Learning: Alcorn State University,
Delta State University, Jackson State University, Mississippi State University,
Mississippi University for Women, Mississippi Valley State University,
University of Mississippi, and University of Southern Mississippi.

www.upress.state.ms.us

The University Press of Mississippi is a member
of the Association of University Presses.

First printing 2024
∞

Library of Congress Cataloging-in-Publication Data available
LCCN 2023053698
ISBN 9781496848086 (hardback)
ISBN 9781496850355 (trade paperback)
ISBN 9781496848109 (epub single)
ISBN 9781496848116 (epub institutional)
ISBN 9781496848123 (pdf single)
ISBN 9781496848130 (pdf institutional)

British Library Cataloging-in-Publication Data available

Contents

Part 4. How the White South Was Persuaded to Shackle Itself

Part 5. Constitutional Constructions, Reconstructions, and Deconstructions

Part 6. The Second Deconstruction of American Democracy

OUTLIVING THE WHITE LIE

The Boy Emperor's New-Old Clothes

"Why ya'll got dog hair?" he asked. "He" was black, about six years old, and named Danny.

"What?!" I blustered. I was white and about sixteen.

"Yeah, you know," he answered, "we got people hair," pointing to his own hair that was distinctly undoglike, "but ya'll white folks got hair like dogs . . ." pointing at my dog Sam and then to my own suddenly mongrel locks, "Why that?"

I retorted with righteous racial indignation. "Uhhh . . ." I said, looking at his hair, feeling my own, looking at Sam's.

I sat and contemplated this conundrum atop the mountain built up by fifty-pound sacks of soybean seeds piled in the back of the bob truck. It was planting time in late spring on my father's farm. My job was to drive the truck along the turnrow, tracking the planter as it slowly progressed across the field, reloading the hoppers with seeds as needed. Danny and Sam were riding along to keep me company. Between reloads, there was always time for pseudoscientific discussions on curveballs and curved girls—each representing a wizardry surpassing our understanding. But on that day, there was also time to discuss the paradoxical "physics" of race.

Rendered speechless by his challenge, I started to grow self-conscious. And I wasn't supposed to be self-conscious. Not in this way. After all, I was an American born into the post–World War II "American Century." I was male in a male-chauvinist society, a heterosexual in a homophobic society. But most to the point here, I was white in a white-supremacist society, descended from an exceedingly lengthy line of southern ancestors on both sides of my family, many of whom owned black slaves, many of whom served in Confederate armies defending that ownership, quite a few of whom died doing so. And this was not just the South, but Mississippi. But not just Mississippi, it was a farm on which Danny's black father worked for my white father, a farm in a place called Longshot in the Yazoo-Mississippi Delta. And it was at the time when, whatever recently enacted laws said, Jim Crow remained something of a lived reality.

For all that, I wasn't some sort of aggressive racist. I didn't use the *n*-word. I wasn't White like those crude Klanish types. No, I wasn't White; I was just normal. Which, in the South, in America, meant being white. All others, those who didn't share my skin tone and hair type, had always been clearly abnormal. In other words, I had had the luxury of taking it all for granted. Of being as unaware of this ever-present white superiority as I was of the daily working of gravity. I didn't have to consider it, so I could be blithely inconsiderate. Thus, armored in utter unmindfulness, I didn't have to premeditate my insults, I could blunder through life stomping on toes in unthinking ways and remain blissfully free of guilt.

In sum, it was a time and place in which I was the standard by which all else was to be measured—measured and found wanting. I and my ilk were the black hole of whiteness around which all and everyone else in the galaxy revolved—as it was in the beginning, is now, and ever shall be: white world without end. Amen. Amen.

I bestrode my world like a pimply colossus.

At least, until this moment, I had. Already reeling, I was then hit with yet another blow to the solar plexus. "And why ya'll got dog skin?" Danny persisted, pulling back Sam's dog hair to show me his white dog skin. "We got people skin, see?" He helpfully held his arm next to mine. It was true, of course. Dogs have white skin on those parts of their bodies protected by their mammalian hair, which is most of their bodies. And so, people with white skin are more like their canine brethren. Black people, though, have skin over their bodies that is unlike Sam's or Fido's or Rover's. It is distinctively human skin, nicely matched with their human hair.

That may have been a fine analysis, but for me, the stars had broken from their courses. The polar axes had reversed. Like in an anxiety dream, I felt exposed before the world's mocking eyes—but not due to the horror of mere pantlessness this time. As the individual strands of my wavy brown hair danced in the breeze, like an arhythmic white man, I was fully naked while still fully clothed. I had lost my cloak of superiority. I had become the outsider looking in, the specimen under glass. Still squatting on my mountaintop, gasping for breath in the rarified air, I felt a touch of vertigo.

"Errr . . ." I added, beginning to feel mangy.

And thus, as a white teenager, I floated for one brief moment in what the great black scholar W. E. B. Du Bois famously described as "double consciousness." As explained in his seminal *The Souls of Black Folk* (1903), it was a "peculiar sensation" felt by blacks living in a white man's world, a "sense of always looking at oneself through the eyes of others, of measuring one's soul by the tape of a world that looks on in amused contempt and pity." Here and now, though, it was my white soul that was being measured and found inferior, measured and found to be bestial in fact. And, though Danny's remarks weren't contemptuous, there surely was a tone of pity in the child's voice. He wanted to help me cope with the stigma of my very unhuman nature, but we both knew it was hopeless. Nothing could be done to hide the evolutionary waywardness that was joyfully wallowing atop my head like a dog-haired dog on a day-old dead possum.

Danny stared at me, squinting in the relentless Delta sun, patiently waiting for an answer. But no more words were needed. He had peaked behind the veil. The jig was up. Du Bois, the "singularly clairvoyant scholar," spoke again through his silent, knowing gaze to dismantle the pretense of white boys like me. "I see in and through them," Du Bois had said. "I see these souls undressed and from the back and side. I see the workings of their entrails. . . . And yet they preach and strut and shout and threaten, crouching as they clutch at rags of facts and fancies to hide their nakedness, they go twisting, flying by my tired eyes and I see them ever stripped—ugly, human." In his innocently honest six-year-old way, Danny had asked what Du Bois called the eternally "unasked question" for blacks, posed as, "How does it feel to be a problem?" Only now, in this Feast of Fools atop the soybean sacks, it had been turned upside down and inside out and put to me.

In defense of embattled white folk everywhere, I reiterated, "Uhhh . . ."

Don't worry, though. The moment of dumbfounding illumination passed fairly quickly. Ultimately, I responded to Danny's questions by muttering about it long enough for it to dissipate into the ether, and we moved on from curveballs to knuckleballs to spitballs. In short order, by default, I was rightly—and whitely—restored to my perch at the center of the universe. The still-white-supremacist society in which I lived made sure of that.

I had learned one important, new lesson, however. Not, though, that racial norms were entirely arbitrary and that the whole idea of "race" and of race consciousness—the notion that skin color or hair type is a marker for innate traits of character—is utterly meaningless and is, in fact, a lie. Not that our illusions about racial superiority and about race itself seriously distort our understanding of the past. And not that a society built on these falsehoods is and always has been seriously flawed. No, I had learned that I needed to avoid such unsettling "dog-hair moments" in the future. Quickly, like with every old southern family's mad relation locked in the basement of its genealogy, I locked the embarrassing episode away in the back of the bottom drawer of the filing cabinet of my memory. Out of sight but still, deeply lodged in my mind, it survived on the bugs and stale bread crusts of my psyche. It was the ghostly voice that naggingly kept asking me, *How does it feel to be a problem?* Because, as it turned out, Danny—black, poor, few prospects in life—was not the problem; I was the problem. I was the Great Pretender. But just one among the millions of other counterfeit emperors promenading through life in our "rags of facts and fancies," in the finery of our oblivious whiteness.

Historian Peter Parish observed that, in the antebellum South, "decent" people had "learned to live with slavery by learning to live a lie." They "divided their lives into compartments," he said, and thereby "evaded rather than confronted the inherent contradictions of slave society." This world, in which illusion was normalized and reality rendered strange, lived on long after abolition. Long, long after. America learned to live with the aftermath of slavery by adapting its well-practiced lies to the new reality, first by dividing the Republic into racially segregated compartments, then by using racially coded dog whistles to evade rather than confront the persistence of systemic racism in our much-ballyhooed "postracial" age.

On the subjects of slavery and race, self-deception remains the nation's default position—on both minor issues and major. We offer pro forma laments over the venal sin of slavery but then hastily recommend that it be "gotten over" and "moved past." Susan Neiman—an American scholar who grew up in the South but has lived and worked in Germany for many years—points out that there are more Holocaust museums in the United States than in Germany, Israel, and Poland (the site of Auschwitz) combined.

That in and of itself is not a problem except that there are also far more Holocaust museums in the United States than there are museums devoted to slavery and Jim Crow. With our choices of commemoration and noncommemoration, we "outsource evil," Neiman says. She calls our fixation on the Holocaust "a form of displacement for what we don't want to know about our own national crimes."

In that displacement, I have been as out of kilter as any. I am a southerner by birth, breeding, and education. And I am a historian but one who spent decades in the study of modern Europe, not of the South. I had always told myself I was drawn to the study of France and Germany out of sophistication. In fact, I spurned the study of the South out of fear. In studying the South, I would be studying myself, my parents, my ancestors, and the crushing force of slavery and race. It would cut a bit too close to the bone. Best to furrow my brow over the plight of oppressed coal miners in the Ruhr Valley rather than oppressed cotton pickers in the Mississippi valley. The ones right outside my window.

So it remained for nearly forty years, until Mad Uncle Rufus apparently made his escape from my mental basement to wreak havoc on my complacency. In time for the Civil War sesquicentennial, I began a deep dive into my forbidden history, a project that has now spanned a dozen years. To be sure, I don't pretend to have given myself the equivalent of an advanced degree in the history of the South. I have done only limited reading in primary sources and certainly have not made astonishing new finds in previously unexplored archives. I have instead relied heavily on the works of many of the best academic scholars of the past fifty years and more, men and women who have spent decades engrossed in the topic. Those scholars' works are commendable; they deserve a wider audience. I should also acknowledge that my reading in these secondary sources has been extensive but not exhaustive. For every one of the many insightful books I've read, its bibliography has pointed me toward countless others that I still should read. Ten or so years of independent study does not make up for thirty years of studied indifference. On these subjects, I am well informed, but not the best informed.

What, then, can I bring to the topic that others have not? If I have stumbled upon any original insights along the way, they have come from my perspective—one that is hardly unique but is distinctive. My interest in the South is scholarly and objective but is also deeply personal and familial, with each side informing the other. This work began as "straight history" but expanded to include genealogy and, as we have already seen, a bit of autobiography. I and my ancestors are part of the story. Also, though, as it turns out, my decades of studying everything except southern history have been, at least, some sort of an advantage. To tap the old cliché, I had to leave home—intellectually speaking—in order to come home; I needed to look away from the South first so that I could then see it. But I assert that no one can truly grasp the enormity and peculiarity of racial slavery and its resulting racism in the South without a comparative perspective. Accordingly, I have read books about slavery in Brazil and the Caribbean, in ancient Greece and Rome, in the Islamic world and in premodern Africa. On the topic of race, I have read about the North as well as the South, about apartheid in South Africa and the era of racial fascism in early twentieth-century Europe. I come at the history of the South from multiple perspectives.

Academic historians' necessarily more narrow approach also means that they primarily teach history majors in their classes and author books read primarily by other historians in their fields. That is not a shortcoming; it is the nature of their job. Scholarship is not born only of long hours of research and writing, but of the give-and-take of peer review among highly knowledgeable and highly critical scholars within those narrow disciplines. That painstaking process is essential to finding the truth as we can know it. There are surely professors who embrace the role of public intellectual and engage with the community accordingly, and I have great respect for those who do. But the task is enormous. And the gap between mainstream scholarship and the general public's knowledge of that scholarship remains vast. Particularly on the most difficult, controversial topics—like slavery and race.

This is where I think that I can play a useful role. Maybe some academics will read and benefit from this book, but I am not writing for a scholarly audience; I am, instead, translating scholars' findings to a general audience. I have not spent my years as a historian expounding for other scholars at academic conferences, but neither have I spent my time evangelizing to the already converted. I have taught history to nonhistorians in for-credit classes on the college level, in noncredit continuing-education classes created for the public, for the educational/travel Roads Scholars Program, which draws in well-educated participants from coast to coast, and in a column written for my local newspaper. I am not the one who has blazed new paths of understanding through original research in primary sources, but I am well suited to lead nonspecialists out of the wilderness of misinformation and down those enlightening paths created by others.

And I have done all this in my home of over forty years, Natchez, Mississippi—in which "Where the Old South Still Lives" was the town's slogan up until a few years ago. I have taken on the moonlight-and-magnolias legend and the Lost Cause myth at their source. I have expounded the scholars' message at the grassroots, before members of the Sons of Confederate Veterans and of the garden clubs that sponsor the Natchez Pilgrimage of antebellum mansions. Therefore, I know the history of slavery and race, but I also know what the general public knows and does not know about these topics. I know the questions they ask, the misconceptions they harbor, the perspectives that impress them. From this experience, I know better than to expect epiphanies of conversion; I do fully expect, though, to provoke thought.

After introducing myself and my homeplace, part 1 of this book will deal with the topics of the moment that tend to dominate public attention, such as flags and monuments, "black Confederates," Robert E. Lee's alleged abolitionism, Abraham Lincoln's bigotry, etc. But then, in part 2, I will use the limited scope of these discussions as gateways through which to dig more deeply into the brutal nature, enormous scale, and importance of slavery in southern and American society. Part 3 will explore the reality that, besides the extreme exploitation of the enslaved, the South's system of slavery also disadvantaged those white southerners—the majority—who owned no slaves. Part 4 will then explain how those non–slave owners were nevertheless persuaded to support slavery through the deliberate creation and propagation of racial identities. Part 5, then, will deal with the continued promotion of racism after the end of racial slavery through the century after the Civil War. And part 6 will discuss the backlash against racial justice and the accompanying backlash against genuine democracy since the 1960s up until the present.

Rest assured that in the history of slavery and race in America, I am not trying to cover every topic nor to cover any one of them comprehensively. The academic works cited in the bibliography fill those purposes nicely. Instead, my aim is more focused. I am trying to provide a greater understanding of certain aspects of that difficult history to those who are most likely to lack it. Maybe blacks will read and benefit from this book, but let me be plain in saying that I am a white man writing primarily for a white audience about the tortured historical relations between white and black people. Because, even amid the turmoil and ferment of fall 2022, it is here that the gap between what is known and what should be known is widest and of greatest consequence.

To prepare ourselves for this labor, we will all need some "dog-hair moments" of awkward revelation. Looking at this country's racial reality plainly in the eye is not easy. It is history that challenges us. It can bite, filling our society's need for a gadfly. It will rattle both the callous complacency of conservatives and the smug complacency of liberals. It most certainly rattled me. To any who take offense at something I have written, I assure you that, in writing it, I have offended myself more often than I have offended you.

Inevitably, there will be those who question my love of the South and will try to cast doubt onto my standing to criticize our self-destructive racial habits. For any who do, I will remind them that I'm a white man, born and raised smack-dab in the middle of the Mississippi Delta. For the past forty years, I have lived in the royal seat of King Cotton himself. I am descended from whole cadres of slave owners and entire corps of Confederates. For any who think to challenge my Dixie bona fides, hang your heads in shame. . . . Ain't nobody more southern than me.

Which is where we must begin.

CHAPTER 1

Race and Me and Mississippi

So then we come to Longshot in the Delta, in Mississippi, in the South of my youth. For most, it would seem to be the deepest, darkest exotica. But while William Blake challenged us "to see a world in a grain of sand," I hold that we can see the world in a clod of that southerly, Mississippily, Deltan dirt.

In his meditation on "the South as mirror," historian Howard Zinn makes this counter-intuitive but sharp observation: the South, he says, "far from being utterly different, is really the essence of the nation. It is not a mutation born by some accident into the normal lovely American family. . . . It contains, in concentrated and dangerous form, a set of characteristics which mark the country as a whole. It is different because it is a distillation of those traits which are the worst (and a few which are the best) in the national character." Yes, distillation does make a difference. From the corn cob shucked in the sunshine comes the corn whisky refined in the moonshine. One, sweet to the tooth; the other, a kick to the head. The genus and species, though, remain the same. Other historians have echoed Zinn's judgment.

The South, in other words, is America's America. And if the South is America's America, Mississippi is the South's south, double-distilled, industrial strength. And within Mississippi, yes, the Delta is Mississippi's Mississippi. This is the point historian James Cobb makes in calling the Delta "the most southern place on earth." Extending Zinn's thoughts, he calls it "a mirror within a mirror, capturing not just the South's but the nation's most controversial traits in mercilessly sharp detail." Rather than a perversion of the American dream, it was "its ultimate realization in a setting where human and natural resources could be exploited to the fullest with but little regard for social or institutional restraint." But, he continues, casting his interpretive net more broadly, "the same economic, political and emotional forces that helped to forge and sustain the Delta's image as the South writ small may one day transform an entire nation into the Delta writ large." We have been warned.

At first glance, the Delta of northwest Mississippi—where I grew up—is essentially a two-dimensional surface of stark geometries, a flitter-flat swamp-plain, drained long ago. At second glace, most decidedly, the ground does not undulate. Arrow-straight roads pierce the landscape at precisely surveyed intervals. In photographs taken from above, it mimics an abstract painting reduced to the purity of verticals and horizontals. From below, few trees interrupt the horizon line. Open vistas stretch in every direction. Little shade blunts the sun's rays. Everything is apparent; nothing is cryptic. Surely, here, things are exactly as they appear. Certainly, it is a place tailor-made for the family of an eminently rational and practical engineer, like my father, and a mannered and proper schoolteacher, like my mother.

The farm story of my father and mother, therefore, somewhat mirrored that of the 1960s TV sitcom *Green Acres*. Except that my father was not a high-priced Manhattan lawyer—though he did serve as the Bogue Phalia southern district drainage commissioner at one point. And except that my mother was not born into Hungarian aristocracy—though she was a "*W* girl*," a graduate of Mississippi State College for Women, and earlier had been much decorated with honors at East Mississippi Community College. And when the high commissioner of drainage and Miss Scooba conjoin, potentates shudder. Every third yahoo claims descent from Charlemagne, but still-hot aristocratic blood flows in my veins.

In a place characterized by extremes of wealth and poverty, however, they were solidly middle class. They had a statistically middling three children, well provided for in middling comfort and security, with indoor plumbing and air-conditioning, and a collegiate future taken for granted but with a Chevy rather than a Cadillac in the driveway. In a sea of fervent Baptists and Methodists (both black and white), a lake of Cajun and Italian Catholics, and a puddle or two of Episcopalians, we were polite Presbyterians. And therefore, we were necessarily predestined not to drink too much, not to fall victim to an addiction, not to be arrested, not to have marital problems, not to have mental problems. No muss, no fuss, no fizz, no drama. So it appeared at least. But even if reality was otherwise (and it was), we knew "how to seem." Yes, we were surely meant for this sensibly uniform place. We collectively cowered in horror of undulations.

My father had grown up in the Delta town of Merigold but was the son of the town doctor, not a farmer. An electrical engineer by college training, after marrying my mother in 1942, he headed to the Pacific with the Seabees, coming home to a GI Bill home loan and a return to circuitry. After several years, though, he took an ill-considered detour into farming, lured there by his doctor father who had long dreamed of life as a Delta planter. Now, with his son as surrogate/partner, he would transcend the respected "Dr. Wiggins," and blossom into a baronial "Big Daddy."

This turn of events came as quite the surprise to my mother. She was from Shuqualak in east Mississippi, the daughter of a merchant, an English major in college who taught Alfred Tennyson and Charles Dickens to small-town children before marriage to my engineer father—the man who had previously given no hint of an itch to farm. Accordingly, she would be the most reluctant of farmwives. Nevertheless, in 1952, agrarian success was a certainty, as my grandfather had declared to my father, as my father had proclaimed to my mother. The laws of science could not be altered. The advance of progress could not be stayed. The age of sharecropping was ending. Mules were evolving into tractors, hoes into multirow cultivators. The folklore of almanacs was bowing before the science of "progressive" farming. And my father read all the books, subscribed to the most avant-garde agricultural journals.

And thus, my equilateral father set about cultivating his parallelograms in the Delta. The farm shop was put into unfailing order, with shelves and hanging nails each carefully labeled. There was and would be a place for everything, and everything would be in its place. In this world, there were screwdrivers for screws, there were hammers for nails, and each was to be assigned to its own compartment, just as John Calvin and Euclid had decreed.

In this best of all possible clockwork universes in the angular Deltaland— this hierarchical and segregated Deltaland—there was also a place for everyone, and everyone had their place. The society was already in unfailing order, with everything from waiting rooms to cemeteries, movie theaters and drinking fountains carefully labeled. There were whites and there were blacks, and each was assigned to their own compartments. There was to be no commingling in bedrooms, at front doors, or in voting booths. Every day of my father's life had unfolded around a reenactment of the rituals of dominance and subservience. Even in the Seabees, he had been given command of an all-black company of laborers—because, as a white man from the South, it was assumed he "knew how to handle blacks." After the war, he would transfer this "expertise" to agriculture. In his early years on the farm, he installed himself as a colonial overlord. In his Navy pith helmet and khakis, he summoned up visions of the British Raj—a sahib swaying above his peasants atop his rumbling, trumpeting, elephantine red cotton picker.

But despite the impressive display of order, things were not as they seemed. Something was amiss. My father's order was a fiction; his reason a fallacy. There were no cinches. Not here. Not in the 1950s and '60s. His realm of plumb bobs and squared corners was about to go cattywampus. His two-dimensional Flatland contained dimensions of reality undreamed of in his science. Here in Longshot, in the Delta, the effect would be more mind-blowing, more hallucinogenic than anything dropped, snorted, or smoked in beatnik cafés or the halls of high hippiedom. Here in Longshot, in the Delta, should we have expected anything less?

A point of clarification. It has to be stressed that this Mississippi Delta is not that other place often called the "Mississippi Delta." It is not the bird's-foot-shaped delta in Louisiana where the Mississippi River meets the Gulf of Mexico. It is the delta in the northwest part of the state of Mississippi, the Yazoo-Mississippi Delta, the one shaped like the pupil in a cat's eye, wide in the middle, narrowing to a point at the top and bottom. In form, then, it was a convex lens that magnified good but refracted evil into scalding heat on the skin—a more horrifying, more beautiful, more pious, more hedonistic, more hospitable, more violent South. It was the cat's-eye delta that ate the bird's-foot delta and all other deltas for an elegant Sunday brunch and then left their mutilated carcasses on the doorstep as a token of its gently purring affection.

It is *the* Delta.

It is, therefore, defined by its contradictions. As such, its symmetries and sureties were all lies, trickster gods incarnated into this world to vex men of reason like my father, men who failed to realize that boundary lines on maps—no less than color lines in society—are abstractions, not geological or biological realities, that equations and laws did not/could not encompass, much less contain, the world. My father's cherished geometries of precisely tiered races and perfectly square townships had been measured from base lines that were chosen arbitrarily and then laid over a shifting swampland shaped by unpredictable ebb and flow.

Even in its flatness, the flatland deceived. Truth be known, it undulated. And did so sensually, secretly, so unlike whorish hills and dales. At irregular intervals, there were crests and troughs, voluptuous upswells here, downswells there, inswells and outswells obscure to the inattentive glance but apparent to the steady gaze. It posed in the drape of its straight lines, but like a belly dancer heavily veiled and ever poised in agonizing anticipation before the first rhythmic pulse, before the slow-tempo reveal, before the final cataclysmic revelation.

It had come by its curvatures honestly. During floods, ridges of sandy loam had been built up along the banks of the creeks and rivers where the heavier particles of alluvium had been quickly deposited. For the mound-building Native Americans of centuries before and for the earliest planters and slaves in the nineteenth century, these natural levees that the rivers themselves created were home, and those same waterways provided the only transportation. But away from the water courses, there were the bottomlands, the backswamps. Here, the finer, lighter particles of clay had spread more widely at flood tide. These lands were also insanely rich and deep, but their bounty would come at a cost. In the aridity of summer and the deluge of winter, the bottomland went feral. In the high heat of the dog days, it dried into pellets, hard and lead gray as buckshot, and cracked wide along randomly opened fissures. With the rains of winter and spring, it congealed into a glue-like "gumbo" and tried mightily to swallow man and beast. Despite their fertility, then, these buckshot/gumbo lands were the last to be settled. They were contrariness made manifest, formed from the vital humus of pure cussedness.

And so, what of such a place that remained the becalmed eye of wilderness in the hurricane of modern civilization? One such place is twelve miles east of the Mississippi River and twenty-five miles west of the Sunflower River. And six miles east of the nearest railway depot to the west, and ten miles west of the nearest depot to the east. As the twentieth century opened, it was still home to panthers, bears, alligators, and giant ivory-billed woodpeckers, even if not dinosaurs and lost tribes of indigenes. It was the heart of darkness, unseen, unspeakable, incomprehensible, unintelligible, disoriented, and disorienting. It was the awesome, awful, unmasked face of God.

It was Longshot, in utero.

As all the "Longshots" of the Delta were opened up and the wilderness retreated, contradictions were enhanced, not resolved. Even though the swamps had been drained, their mugginess still abounded, malingering like spirits in the air, blurring farsighted vision. Almost all the trees had been cut down, but somehow their shadows remained, shadows that didn't cool but did obscure. The truth was slyly hidden in the middle of the bald, brilliant, broiling light. All logical sense was sun-struck dumb, reduced to quivering mirages formed in the summer heat and dust on every horizon, turned alien and strange as the reflections in funhouse mirrors. Conversations, then, took place in a pidgin tongue mixing a bit of plain English with gracious artifice and vile obscenities, all floating in the encyclopedic hush of things left unsaid.

Here in Longshot, in it but not of it, my insistently average family queued courteously around the rim of the volcano. In this birthplace of the down-and-dirty blues and soaring gospels, where every straight line got sweaty as it navigated between the siren songs of juke joints and honky-tonks, amid a nightly crescendo of lustful frog songs and an ever-rising crescendo of spirit-filled freedom songs in the sixties, my family stood apart, discreetly tapping toes to the canned rhythms of elevator music.

Except for my father. His toes abided no tapping at all. His unschooled black farmhands—infinitely better educated in the whims of Deltaland—thought he was "funny" in his reserved, book-learned ways. But funny peculiar, not funny haha. My father was not at all funny haha. And as the years passed, as the tumultuous sixties unfolded, he failed to see the humor in the futile, fading labels on his farm shop's shelves, the fading labels of "whites" and "coloreds," the painted ruins of his monuments to orderliness. Here, he saw the unnatural amalgamation of bolts, washers, and nuts. There, the prodigal intermarriage of cultivator blades and grease guns. He had been romanced by the image of geometrical regularity; he could not, would not, meander. An empiricist to his core, he trusted his vision and chased after every mirage. He was terrorized by the haints in which he refused to believe, making them all the more terrifying.

The land gave up a nice enough living, mostly, and I grew up in what I assumed to be an utterly stable family, without ever the slightest worry about shelter, abundant food, or access to quality care for every ailment, small or

large. But my father did not "succeed" by Delta standards. He would end
where he began. He never mastered the art of schmoozing with bankers
and bureaucrats, much less the good ole boys down at the Feed and Seed.
He trusted in logic and law in a land of winks and nods.

Over time, he escaped. But not into the time-honored Delta haven of
madness. He drank enough bourbon to worry my grandfather and mother,
but mainly, he retreated into a meticulous daily regimen that insulated him
from the fray. He dispensed morning instructions to the "hands," and he
received progress reports at day's end. But he was invisible in between, keeping a wary distance from the unreasoning vortex lurking, lapping, swirling
just beyond the creak of the back screen door. He marked his triumphs over
unruly nature and integrating society in other ways. He ate his vegetables,
but slowly. And only after they had been separated into discreet mounds
around the rim of the dinner plate, each sternly warned about any offense
against vegetable propriety. No deviant amalgamation of pea and potato here.
No frozen broccoli of his'n dared to spear an ear of garden-fresh corn. He
withdrew into a quiet ennui.

But what becomes of a decent white man in the cat's-eye delta in the wan-
ing days of Jim Crow and the waxing days of the civil rights revolution? I
never heard my father or my mother use the *n*-word—though my father's
pronunciation skirted its boundaries from time to time. Such language was
"crude," said my mother. By reputation, my parents were "good to the help"
and held themselves to a standard of civility when talking to or about them.
They raised me to be proper. I didn't use the *n*-word either. I didn't go out
"n----- knockin'" at night. I had been taught that there were rules of decorum
that transcended race, creed, or color. They were not to be breached. Unless
they were.

I also never heard either of my parents take issue with visiting friends
or family when they loudly, frequently, belligerently used the *n*-word and
far worse. Which happened frequently. Sharing a chuckling, back-slapping
fondness for racial slurs was/is a primary ritual of group bonding for some,
as communal as a shared meal of familiar foods, a retelling of time-tested
tales, a not-so-secret handshake among exclusive members of the club. As
a ritualistic call-and-response, it established baseline solidarity among the

participants. My parents did not respond in kind. They did not, though, refute either.

As uncivil and crude as racial slurs were, they thought it was equally uncivil—not to mention socially awkward—to challenge incivility from a neighbor. It was especially important to go along in order to get along. "Moderation" most often took the form of disapproving of violence—however loudly or quietly—while supporting segregation and disfranchisement that inevitably sparked resistance, which was met in turn by more of those very acts of violence. By mutely participating in the system, my parents mutely perpetuated it. As did many others. As I did, too.

So, what becomes of a virtue when it is used not as a weapon against vice but as a shield to fend off responsibility for vice? It becomes vice masquerading as virtue. And in the South, every day was Mardi Gras. To realize such a feat of pretense, though, a proper morality was needed, along with a theology to legitimize it. Good and decent southerners received just such a revelation. Their religion centered around the worship of a Trinity consisting of an all-powerful Yahweh of self-righteous vengeance targeting others, an all-forgiving Jesus to bless their own flawed souls, and then their wholly Holy Spirit, the Lord God P's and Q's—a deified representation of forms rather than substance, the divine source of social grace, which was the only truly saving grace for good and decent southerners. Above all else, one must mind one's P's and Q's. Once baptized in this spring-fed lake of civility, the initiate was incapable of racial sin—most especially if self-consciously veiled in genetic eccentricity, the figurative hijab of all orthodox southerners. Vile racism was thus reduced to bad manners.

Because some will insist on mischaracterizing my point here, let me assure you that I am wholeheartedly in favor of civility and displays of good will between races. But let's not deceive ourselves about the saving grace of mere interracial courtesy. It is not that it is wrong but that it is not enough. And, by itself, it is pure guile. For too many, to break bread with a black man, to hold a door open for a black woman, to sing hymns together in a show of biracial harmony is miraculous proof of one's personal racial purity. For some, the "show" is no show; it is sincere. But as it happens, with others, the supposedly redeeming incantations of "please" and "thank you" and a virtuous sharing of water fountains have easily meshed with support for blatantly racist policies. Or, in the case of so many self-labeled "liberals," a dismissive disdain for even a discussion of reparations. Baptized in the tranquil pond of our post–Jim

Crow social graces, we proclaim deliverance from the cumulative effects of centuries of injustice. We are like the privileged younger generation of an organized crime family swearing our own blamelessness but still hoarding the loot stolen by our forefathers. And then sputtering our righteous indignation when the injured parties are reluctant to "get over it" and "move on."

In this congregation, I was a dutiful member, always minding my racial P's and Q's. And as a result, it was amazingly easy to feel profoundly moral as I remained blind before injustice, deaf to offense, mute before others' racial slurs. I was a fly on the wall to revolutionary events, but one obliviously nearsighted in most all of its thousand eyes. I have grown since then, but let's be realistic about the scope of my personal transfiguration. I don't believe anyone can grow up in this racially obsessed society and not absorb, consciously or unconsciously, a racial consciousness complete with stereotypes and prejudices. We are then—not by nature, but by historical nurture—a nation of race-aholics. One in which some proudly revel in their disease as a birthright, while others assume a pose of offended denialism. Some admit the problem and begin a program of rehabilitation only to declare themselves fully cured with each single day's right-footed step—inevitably destined therefore for relapse. But some admit the problem and begin rehab fully recognizing it to be a lifelong project of self-examination and self-reformation. And so it should be for us all.

The first step, though, is to accept the truths of our past and our present, both large and small.

PART 1

THE LARGER IMPLICATIONS OF THE SMALL DEBATES OF THE MOMENT

CHAPTER 2

Our Distinguished Error Emeritus

*Doesn't the Confederate battle flag represent "heritage, not
hate" to southerners because the war could not have been about
slavery since most white southern families did not own slaves?*

"It is now law."

With this four-word recital of stark fact—delivered with all the fervor of
a man buckling his belt after a proctology exam—Mississippi's Governor
Tate Reeves announced the signing of a bill on June 30, 2020, to change the
state flag, the one with the battle banner of the Confederacy in its upper
left quadrant. And thus, 155 years after its abject defeat in war and 126 years
after its inclusion in Mississippi's flag, the Rebel symbol surrendered its final
fortress of official status in American governance.

After decades of controversy, it had been a long time coming. As recently
as 2001, by a two-to-one margin in a statewide referendum, Mississippians
had voted to keep the flag as a symbol of regional pride, of "heritage, not
hate." As to how it could be seen this way, a nationwide poll conducted in
2011 revealed that the majority of those with an opinion considered the Civil
War to have been primarily about states' rights (i.e., local self-determination)
rather than about slavery. Again, this was a nationwide poll. For others, however, the flag was a symbol of slavery and white supremacy and, as such, of
hate, not heritage. It was, they alleged, a literally high-flown, loudly flapping
incarnation of the tectonic fault line of race that still divided the people of
the state and the nation. It was a dismal failure at the one job a state flag has,

that of being a unifying symbol for its people. I agree with that judgment and am very much glad "it is now law."

But before further discussion of Confederate flags (or monuments), I should establish my credentials on the topic. As we say down here, I do have a dog in this fight. Nearly a score of them in fact. I know of nineteen of my ancestors from four and five generations ago who served in Confederate armies. Eight of them died doing so. None of my ancestors fought for the Union. Some were slave owners, some not. They were planters, doctors, merchants, yeoman farmers, tenant farmers, and farm laborers. Some were officers (none were generals), though most were privates. To track the sweat and blood spilled by my various grandfathers, uncles, and cousins is to track virtually the entire course of the war east of the Mississippi. Of those who lost their lives, cavalry Lieutenant Henry Oscar Beasley fell first, while poetically "leading a charge at Chewalla" in the maneuverings after the Battle of Shiloh in May 1862. The following month, Andrew Jackson Brock was killed at Gaines Mill in Virginia during the Seven Days Battle. Three months later, Bennet Lawrence died defending the Bloody Lane at Antietam. Captain James Gaston was killed at the Railroad Gap on day one of the Battle of Gettysburg in July 1863. Lewis Wiggins endured the same fate in the charge up Culp's Hill on day two. Captain Hugh Gaston, James's younger brother, died at Ezra Church during the Atlanta Campaign in the summer of 1864. Wesley Anderson died of yellow fever months after enlistment without ever "seeing the elephant." Richard Henderson suffered through bouts of pneumonia and tuberculosis before developing an ulcerated leg wound, dying an old, sick man at the age of twenty-two.

Of the survivors, there was Captain Algernon Sydney Kirk who contracted tuberculosis and resigned his commission but somehow lived until 1914. Martin Van Buren Brock (A. J.'s younger brother) was wounded during the Seven Days in the summer of 1862, then lost a leg at Gettysburg in the summer of 1863. Abner Wiggins (Lewis's cousin) lost an eye at Chickamauga. Timothy Anderson (Wesley's brother) was captured at Perryville in Kentucky, Samuel Henderson (Richard's brother) was taken prisoner at Vicksburg, was exchanged, fought at Atlanta, and finally was captured again at Allatoona, Georgia, at the start of General John B. Hood's calamitous invasion of Tennessee. Samuel McNees "rode with Forrest" (Lieutenant General Nathan Bedford Forrest) at the Battle of Tupelo. Coley Di Rienzi Kirk (Algernon's brother) futilely chased Major General William Tecumseh Sherman across

Georgia and the Carolinas. The soon-to-be "Reverend Moses" Black was called by the Lord of Good Sense to desert in December 1864 from the trenches at Petersburg. This, after two and a half years with the Second Georgia as it had trudged from Malvern Hill in the Seven Days to Second Manassas to Burnside's Bridge at Antietam to the Devil's Den at Gettysburg to the Battle of the Wilderness to the Battle of the Crater. He was the last survivor of my five relations in Lee's Army of Northern Virginia. With four dead and one AWOL, none would be there, then, to represent my battered forebears at the surrender ceremony at Appomattox in April 1865. A bit more than three years had passed since Uncle Oscar's fateful, fatal "charge at Chewalla." The South and the strands of my ancestry were in tatters.

All of the above were my uncles or cousins. Fatefully for me and my direct biological inheritance, though, my line of grandfathers fared comparatively well in the war. A bit too young, a bit too old, or a lot lucky, they missed the worst of the fighting and fought off the worst infections. None died; none returned home with debilitating ailments or injuries. Major Clement Kirk, my great-great-grandfather, was saved by his training at the illustrious Eclectic Medical Institute of Cincinnati, becoming a regimental surgeon for the Thirty-fifth Mississippi. My great-grandfather Sion Lawrence was saved by his youth, being a teenager who served out the war in the North Carolina Home Guard, while his older brother had died at Antietam. Sion became a doctor after the war and moved to Calhoun County, Mississippi, where he fathered seven children postwar, including a daughter named Clara. My great-great-grandfather Edley Wiggins of Alabama (Abner's brother) was saved by luck. He served in the Vicksburg Campaign, fighting in preliminary battles at Grand Gulf and Champion Hill but avoiding the trenches. Instead, he was assigned to the force—dubbed the Army of Relief—that was ordered by Confederate high command in Richmond to regroup in Vicksburg's hinterland and then to save the city by hurling itself headlong into the entrenched Yankees' rear, there, no doubt, to suffer catastrophic casualties. Except that the relief never came, the attackers never attacked. The army under Joseph Johnston dallied, dawdled, and did nothing. Vicksburg fell; Edley still stood, unscathed. After the war, he also decamped to Mississippi, taking his wife and six prewar children to settle one county south of Calhoun. There, his own doctor grandson would meet and marry the aforementioned daughter of Dr. Sion Lawrence. To this Dr. James Purvy Wiggins and that Clara Lawrence Wiggins, my father was born in 1910. Having passed through a keyhole fashioned out of minié balls and microbes, as "James Lawrence Wiggins," I am their grandson. In genes and in name, my entire existence is a random happenstance of that war.

For me, then, the meaning of the war is personal. The flag, when I was a boy, was sacred. To understand the war, though, I have to understand the Confederacy that waged it and the secession that began it all. And in fact, the reasons for it all are fairly straightforward. Despite the outcomes of public-opinion polls and balloting, and of childhood fantasies, virtually all scholars agree that the Southern states seceded and formed the Confederacy and fought the war to preserve and perpetuate white-supremacist slavery. Scholars prove this by citing the men who led the secession movement and created the Confederacy and led the war effort. Those men said so. Said so repeatedly and loudly, emphatically and proudly. Said so in speeches and documents explicitly intended to explain the Confederate cause to the public and to posterity. It is true that secessionists also affirmed "states' rights." But whenever that abstraction is invoked, we have to ask, The right of a state to do what? In answer, the southern states claimed their right to decide the fate of slavery for themselves and the right to secede if that right was violated. States' rights, in other words, were the means to the end of preserving slavery, not ends in themselves. This is not "the winners writing the history books" or political correctness running amok; it is the Confederates speaking for themselves. With "honor" originating from the same Latin root word as "honesty," in their honesty about this, if in nothing else, they were honorable. We descendants of Confederate veterans should listen to our elders when they speak to us. But if the Sons of Confederate Veterans insist on continuing to lie about their ancestors, I ask that they stop lying about mine. The men in gray spoke in plain terms of black and white.

And few spoke as plainly as Mississippians. The state's Secession Convention's Declaration of the Immediate Causes Which Induce and Justify Secession tells all. Here, in January 1861, the state could not have been more explicit. "Our position is thoroughly identified with the institution of slavery . . . the greatest material interest of the world," the document begins. To add specifics to that "material interest," in 1860, there were 4 million slaves in the southern states valued at $4 billion, worth more than all the lands and crops and railroads of the region. But the South's commitment to slavery was not exhausted by dollars and cents. Two years earlier, the state's pro-secession Governor John J. Pettus placed race in the forefront when he called on the legislature to be prepared to secede in defense of slavery and, in so doing, to unfurl "a banner inscribed 'Superiority and Supremacy of the White Race.'" It is crucial to know that racism was seen as an essential prop for slavery and that racial slavery was held to be necessary to the survival of white rule. As important as slaves were as investments and laborers, it was this role of slavery as a bulwark of white supremacy that drove southerners to frenzy. One of Mississippi's official "secession commissioners," Judge William Harris of its High Court of Errors and Appeals, was charged with the job of persuading Georgia to join Mississippi in secession. He gave a speech to that state's legislature in January 1861 in which he assured all that his home state "had rather see the last of her race—men, women and children—immolated in one common funeral pyre, than see them subjected to the degradation of civil, political and social equality with the negro race." Encyclopedic volumes could be filled with even more of these quotes from any and all of the seceding states, but the point has been made. This was the cause for which nineteen of my relatives served and eight of them died. What do I say to them when they peer through my eyes as I look in the mirror?

There can be no moral-salvage operation for the Confederacy as an institution. It was an abomination. Its heritage is an abomination. But what of the individual soldiers who fought for it? Most of them were not slave owners nor from slave-owning families. This is frequently cited as proof that a defense of slavery could not have been their motivation for fighting. But obviously, for most nonslaveholders, it was not the material interest of slavery that mattered but rather the racial interest. It was insisted that all whites benefited from slavery, not only the master class. Still, for some, slavery truly was not the only or even the most important reason for them to serve. As in all wars, those who manned the armies had an assortment of reasons for their enlistments. Let's remember that many did not volunteer but were conscripted. Of those who did volunteer, some joined merely for the adventure, some to impress a pretty girl. Some really did fight "those people" only because they were invaders. And for all, in the fire of battle, loyalty to "the cause" was often reduced to a fierce loyalty to one's frontline brothers-in-arms—may the politicians and generals be damned. After our national experience in Vietnam, surely, we know that we can condemn a war without condemning all those sent to fight it. We can remember and honor the valor and sacrifice of individual Confederate soldiers, but we must also remember the moral bankruptcy of the cause for which they fought.

But why must we remember? Why should we care more than 150 years later? This is a vital question, one with a vital answer. Racism in our history has extended from sea to sea, from our origins to our present, targeting Native Americans, Latinos, Asians, and others, as well as African Americans. I freely acknowledge the full color range of our nation's racial biases and the callousness and hypocrisy of them all. However, this book's overwhelming focus will be on only one of those colors, the one that led us to risk the very survival of our liberal democratic system, to endanger the nation itself. It was in our violent dispute over the racialized enslavement of Africans and their descendants—culminating in the Civil War—that we did precisely that. The Confederacy did not only fight to defend bondage, but it was also willing to destroy the United States of America to do so. Yale constitutional scholar Akhil Reed Amar puts it bluntly: "the Founders' Constitution failed in 1861–65. The system had almost died." Like a faulty heart, our government experienced its one and only near-death experience. Only the bloody, painful surgery of war saved its life. It was not redcoats or communists or Muslim jihadis that caused the malfunction. We did it to ourselves.

Therefore, even now in the twenty-first century, the reason for that life-threatening, nineteenth-century conflict should be seen as more than an obscure academic debate. Out of self-interest, I would think that those who love this country would demand to know the whole truth about what caused its almost fatal trauma. Out of self-interest, surely, we need to know if it could happen again. Knowledge of this dangerous episode in our country's history is as essential to its present-day health as an understanding of our personal medical history is to our present well-being. Under the circumstances, self-delusion about the ailment borders on the suicidal.

But we do appear to have a death wish. In large measure thanks to our refusal to face the legacies of the Civil War honestly, its most poisonous legacies have survived. Despite the Confederacy's failure to preserve slavery, the essence of its purpose did not fail. White supremacy and systemic racial repression not only lived on but thrived in the generations after abolition. And the banner of the Confederacy—the banner of racial prejudice, not only of slavery—was there to lead the charge as the violently white-supremacist Ku Klux Klan sensibly adopted the flag of the violently white-supremacist

Confederacy as its own. And once racial inequality was fully institutionalized with the establishment of Jim Crow, Mississippi marked the restoration by adding the Confederate battle banner to its official state flag in 1894. It was to be an omnipresent reminder for blacks, even with slavery abolished, to "stay in their place." But this was not just a regional triumph. Today, many nonsoutherners eloquently hold forth about "their" Confederate heritage to the great confusion of some. But that heritage had little to do with a defense of the South or southerners. It was a defense of white supremacy, a siren song even to natives of Queens, New York, and Oshkosh, Wisconsin. Or Nuremberg, Germany.

And yet when attempting to raise the issue of slavery and racism for general discussion, we are met with a flurry of complaints that we should move on, get over it, and let the past be the past, even as we are told how important it is to commemorate the Confederate heritage with flags, monuments, and even state holidays. The difficulty is that the defense of white-supremacist slavery, the thing we are told we must forget, was the very reason for the creation of the Confederacy, the heritage we are told we must remember. The pleas to move on are disingenuous, therefore. Their purpose is to perpetuate lies—the lies about the Confederacy's nature that have, somehow, prevailed deep into their second century.

We all know the drill. Before testifying in a court of law, a witness is sworn to "tell the truth, the whole truth, and nothing but the truth." To "tell the truth," in other words, the witness must not lie but, in addition, must not withhold information known to be true. The intent is to stress that telling only part of the truth is a way to avoid the greater truth. It is a way to deceive. For today's "neo-Confederates"—those dedicated to the glorification of the Confederacy itself as well as its common soldiers—this is their purpose. In their typical line of argument, they offer up cherry-picked partial truths rather than outright lies, ballyhooing the few facts that support their conclusion while omitting the more plentiful facts that demolish it.

For example, to vindicate the Confederacy, it is pointed out, breathlessly but accurately, that, in 1861, most white Southern households owned no slaves, and most Northerners were not abolitionists. And, accurately, that

Confederate icon Robert E. Lee called slavery "a moral and political evil," while Abraham Lincoln publicly endorsed racial discrimination. And, to excuse the South's system of slavery, neo-Confederates point out—just as breathlessly and just as accurately—that many nonslaves throughout history also suffered terrible exploitation; that antebellum southern slavery was just one among countless systems of slavery throughout history; that slavery existed within Africa long before the transatlantic slave trade began; that after 1500, African kings and merchants willingly engaged in that trade with Europeans. And accurately, that many of the United States' Founding Fathers were slave owners. These are all undeniable facts. Each taken alone would lead one to conclude that secession and the Civil War must not have been about slavery and that antebellum southern slavery, in comparative perspective, was not "all that bad." Taken alone, however, they mislead—as we will see in the following chapters.

Thanks to this feat of forgetful remembrance, entering June 2020, even after 126 years, there were no indications that the majority of the populace of Mississippi nor of their legislators were even slightly inclined to replace the Confederate-themed flag. In fact, only a few weeks earlier the governor had proclaimed Confederate Heritage Month in the state. And yet by the end of the month, the flag was gone. What in the name of Jubal Early had happened?

Over the course of late spring and early summer of 2020, there is no doubt that the rapid spread of both the coronavirus and the Black Lives Matter protests played a role in changing the mood of the country. But there were clearly other factors in play. The legislators bribed themselves into voting for a new flag with a requirement that the replacement flag's design must include the phrase "In God We Trust," providing a fig leaf of conservative piety behind which legislators could hide an unconservative vote for change. But the real impetus for a redesign came not from protest marches or clichéd religious slogans. It came like a thunderclap from *the* religion: football.

It is hard not to notice that after 126 years of unwavering devotion to the flag, the epochal vote to adopt a new symbol came a few days after the Southeastern Conference (SEC) and the National Collegiate Athletic Association (NCAA) levied sanctions on the state universities due to the flag and after football players began to threaten a boycott of the upcoming season and after dozens of athletic department officials from all the state's public universities descended on the capitol to plead for deliverance from flag-imposed recruiting purgatory. And as if in a miracle, those legislators who had been blind began to see. Guided by the spirits of Bruiser Kinard and Shorty McWilliams, and calls from well-heeled alumni, they realized that if designing a new flag would help Mississippi State and Ole Miss beat Alabama, they should grant Betsy Ross an endowed chair. In amazingly short order, a bill was submitted. The vote was taken. The deed was done.

However, what exactly did that "deed" involve? And what did we leave out . . . again?

No one can provide a better coda to this discussion than the late Eugene Genovese—without qualification one of the great historians of the South and slavery. In his final years, this longtime Marxist and his wife, Elizabeth Fox-Genovese—also a historian of the South—repudiated the Left, embraced Roman Catholicism, and took up the cause of traditionalist conservatism, particularly its southern variety. This was, though, a strand of cultural conservativism, as Genovese wrote in in the 1990s, which "remains alive, if at bay"—one quite different from, and even hostile to, the materialistic, corporate conservatism that has become dominant. It was a traditionalism deeply hostile to dogmatic communism but just as wary of the abstractions of free-market fundamentalism. It preferred the near over the remote, the rural over the urban, the agrarian over the industrial. It abhorred the Ayn Randian veneration of selfishness as well as droning lectures on dialectical materialism.

Though Genovese avowed that there were things to admire in the antebellum southern tradition, he asserted that slavery was not one of them. And neither was the Confederacy that was formed to further it, that fought a war to preserve it, that bequeathed its racism to the South. Due to that racism, local communities had failed to uphold minimal standards of simple morality, decency, and the rule of law. The good and wise and pious peoples of these communities had abdicated their responsibility repeatedly, ultimately requiring intervention by the "remote and abstract" federal government.

Therefore, in advocating for his newfound, old philosophy, Genovese included a stern warning based on this flawed past. In 1994, he wrote, "The realization of the finest values of the southern tradition requires a total break with its legacy of racism. . . . If [it] does not include blacks as well as whites— if it is not deeply committed to racial equity and justice—it will degenerate into barbarism as fast as we can swallow our spit." And if not? "No crystal ball is required to tell us that every racist cockroach in the woodwork will rush to join the ranks." Mercifully, Eugene Genovese died in 2012 and so was spared the sorry spectacle of the present. His dreaded Day of the Racist Cockroaches has arrived. His "traditional southern conservativism" is no longer "at bay"; it has been swallowed whole by the cult of a venal, hateful autocrat. It parades its piety while serving no god but greed. And it reeks of duplicity—as we have encountered, again, in the nonresolution resolution of our flag controversy.

Let me make clear again that I am glad the state's emblem was changed. But by modifying this symbol, we have to remember that we have made only a symbolic change. It is not that symbolic changes are pointless. As embodiments of a commitment to substantive change, they can inspire. But we have made no such commitment. Like a corporation sweeping inconvenient controversy off its agenda, we have reached a settlement without an admission of wrongdoing, much less responsibility. To this, the governor proposed, in effect, a nondisclosure agreement for our public schools. In the form of a Patriotic Education Fund, the state would offer bribes to any who agree to omit discussion of, among other things, the central role of slavery in our history. With the new flag displayed ostentatiously outside the window, inside the classrooms, students would not be taught about the origins of the old flag in an attempt by white-supremacist slave owners to destroy the nation. Therefore, instead of symbolizing a deeper change, the new flag becomes a photo-op behind which the ever-grinning cockroaches can continue to proliferate, their ugly prejudices laundered through loudly chanted prayers for biracial harmony.

It is worth noting that the old flag is not being discarded but is being officially "retired," apparently to bask, along with its manifold sins, in an honored repose. There, politely out of daily view, it will loom like a ghostly gray eminence—the state's distinguished Error Emeritus.

CHAPTER 3

Becoming Abraham Lincoln; Remaining Robert E. Lee

But didn't Robert E. Lee say that slavery was evil? And weren't Abraham Lincoln and most of his fellow Northerners racially prejudiced and not abolitionists?

In 2008, on the bicentennial of Abraham Lincoln's birth, my wife and I visited his home in Springfield, Illinois, now a historic site ably administered by the National Park Service. In my pocket, I brought a token of my esteem for Abe—a Ziplock bag of dirt that I had dug from my own back yard at home. I'm sure I violated a dozen or so federal regulations in doing so, but in a very short, very silent ceremony for this throng of two, I sprinkled my handful of southern earth over Lincoln's northern earth. It was my small way of saying "thank you" to the man who, more than any other single individual, was responsible for that Mississippi soil—and me—still being American in 2008. He had not saved me from foreign demons but from my own Confederate ancestors—all the more frightening because all the more familiar and familial. With my votive offering, my gratitude was acknowledged, symbolically at least.

The bit of dirt I brought was not, unfortunately, the rich and vital humus of pure cussedness distilled from the buckshot/gumbo of Longshot in the Delta. By 2008, I was long gone from there. Home was in the woods south of Natchez. But the perversely contradictory soil of my Delta upbringing would have been appropriate. In light of all that historians have discovered, it's still easy to grant Lincoln his due as savior of the Union, but in his singular role as the "Great Emancipator," inconsistencies abound.

A century and a half before our visit, Lincoln—"the black man's best friend"—said, "I am not, nor ever have been, in favor of bringing about in any way the social and political equality of the white and black races" or "of making voters or jurors of negroes, nor of qualifying them to hold office, nor to intermarry with white people." This quote is not the only example of Lincoln's bigotry. Some are shocked to learn about this side to the man that most scholars rate as the greatest president of all time. But there are no surprises here. Lincoln's opinions on race were certainly not a revelation to anyone in 1860 as he ran for president. The above remarks were made in his debates with Stephen Douglas during his campaign for the US Senate in Illinois. They were made to defend himself against the "slur" that he believed in racial equality. Lincoln was a practical politician. He wanted to win, and in his home state of Illinois, slavery may have been illegal, but discrimination against blacks was accepted, expected, and entirely legal. But to comprehend Lincoln's greatness, we have to confront, not ignore, this racism on which he had been weaned. As did Frederick Douglass (not to be confused with Stephen).

Douglass was a leading abolitionist and crusader for racial equality who was himself a self-emancipated slave. As such, he knew that "Father Abraham, the Great Emancipator" had not come to that role out of flaming passion, but only by pragmatic increments of policy. Lincoln, therefore, was no demigod to Douglass. In 1876, eleven years after his death, Douglass remarked candidly, "It must be admitted . . . Abraham Lincoln was not, in the fullest sense of the word either our [blacks'] man or our model. In his interests . . . and in his prejudices, he was a white man. He was preeminently the white man's President, entirely devoted to the welfare of white men. You [whites] are the children of Abraham Lincoln. We are at best only his stepchildren; children by adoption, children of forces of circumstances and necessity." And still, Douglass had come to admire Lincoln greatly. He gratefully acknowledged, "While Abraham Lincoln saved for you a country, he delivered us from a bondage." Douglass understood that there was no singular, static "Lincoln" to be judged good or ill. The bigot of 1858 had been transformed—to a degree—by 1865. How?

We have to understand that, though Lincoln originally shared the prevalent racial prejudices of his day, there had always been a vast difference between his views and those of his soon-to-be wartime foes. Vice President Alexander Stephens had boasted about his Confederacy's founding tenet that blacks were not only inferior but were "natural" slaves. Here, Lincoln disagreed vehemently. And did so long before he became president. However, in answer to the slave's challenge of "Am I not a man and a brother?" Lincoln answered, in effect, that he was "a man but not a brother." Lincoln insisted that, as a man, like all men (and women), his enslavement was immorally *unnatural.* In 1858, Lincoln did not think blacks should have government-granted political rights, like voting, but he emphatically believed they had the God-given "natural right" to life and, therefore, the right to own one's own body and to own the product of one's own labor. But when he talked of ending slavery, he talked of gradualist plans ending in an indeterminant future, including compensation for slave owners and colonization of the freed slaves outside the United States. Though he championed the natural rights of blacks, he said that the prevailing prejudices within the country—in the North as well as the South—would never allow the races to live together in that country as equals. So, yes, Lincoln shared the racial biases of his day, but for him, slavery was nevertheless an abomination. "If slavery is not wrong, nothing is wrong," he declared. It's not special pleading to say that in an era when racism was the nearly unquestioned standard, the Lincoln of 1858 was less racist than most. And that would provide an opening to further change.

In 1860, as he ran for president, he was not an advocate of immediate abolition but sincerely hoped the institution's expansion could be limited in the near term, with this being a means to its elimination in the longer term. He was, therefore, among the northern majority as a "Free-Soiler"—someone opposing the expansion of slavery into the territories of the West but accepting the institution in the South where it was already established. This was the unifying principle of the Republican party. The problem was that southerners were convinced that if slavery was to survive, it had to expand. To white southerners, therefore, if the demand "only" to limit slavery was accepted, it would destroy their investment in slaves and reduce them from racial supremacy to racial parity. Any party advocating Free-Soilism, as surely as any favoring abolitionism, was believed to be a mortal threat to slavery and the southern way of life. The divide between the Free-Soil doctrine and abolitionism, therefore, was a distinction without a difference as far as southerners were concerned. It's telling that Lincoln, the nonabolitionist Free-Soiler, was not even on the ballot in ten of the eleven states of the soon-to-be Confederacy, of which, after his election, seven would secede even before his inauguration.

Once in the presidency, consistent with all the points made above, Lincoln quickly declared that the war's purpose would be to save the Union, not to end slavery. It is, then, with Unionism foremost in mind that those legions of Northern nonabolitionists marched off to war in 1861. The following year, Lincoln famously said, "My paramount object in this struggle *is* to save the Union, and is *not* either to save or to destroy slavery. If I could save the Union without freeing any slave, I would do it; and if I could save it by freeing all the slaves, I would do it; and if I could save it by freeing some and leaving others alone, I would also do that."

This often cited and often misconstrued quote did not mean that Lincoln didn't care about slavery; on the contrary, it was an institution he sincerely hated. It is simply a statement of wartime priorities in these first years of the conflict. He still hoped for an eventual end to bondage in the United States, but he saw the salvation of the Union as an immediate necessity. In fact, it was the prerequisite for that eventual abolition. Again, it was plain that an independent Confederacy would never end slavery. So, to understand Abraham Lincoln's personal and presidential journey from Unionism to abolition and black rights, we have to begin at that "paramount object"—the Union. Why was its preservation so important to him, and what was the nature of the threat to its existence?

As president, he was sworn to "preserve, protect and defend the Constitution," and he was convinced that secession was unconstitutional. But more, it was, he said, "the essence of anarchy" and, therefore, was elementally antithetical to democracy. To allow secessionist majorities in states within one of a nation's regions to overrule the Unionist majority within the nation as a whole would be to make a mockery of majority rule. If the practice were tolerated once, it would be used again and again. The secessions of 1860–61 would be followed by more in the future. It would be proof that a democratic regime could not even ensure its own territorial integrity. To Lincoln, then, the preservation of the Union was synonymous with the preservation of democracy itself.

And in 1861, democracy was in retreat all around the world. In this world setting, the great republic of the United States, even with all of its flaws, was by any estimation the world's greatest remaining experiment in representative government. If democracy (majority rule) failed in this, its bastion, Lincoln feared it would fail once and for all. It is in this specific geopolitical context that he called the Constitutional Union "the last best hope of earth." Thus, if war against slave-owning secessionists was required to save it, thought Lincoln, then war it would be. But this is also why, from the beginning of the war, some wondered how a fight against disunion could be waged successfully without, at some point, eradicating the root cause of disunion—the institution of slavery. Frederick Douglass had already turned this insight into a slogan by 1861. "Down with treason [i.e., secession]," he proclaimed, "and down with slavery, the cause of treason!"

As compelling as the argument might have been, it would take time to convince the practical Lincoln of its political viability. And sure enough, most Northerners, still racists and nonabolitionists, would be even harder to persuade. But then, the war itself took care of the rest. All wars have unintended consequences. They seldom conform to the expectations of the people who make them. Often, therefore, war aims can and do change over the course of the fight. Speaking in his Russian context, Vladimir Lenin described war as "the midwife of revolution." By causing great societal strain, wars can radicalize both circumstances and people. Many things that seemed unthinkable when a war began can become thinkable by war's end. For Lincoln, as well as for Northern public opinion, the abolitionism that was far-fetched in 1861 would come to be seen as a useful tactic by 1863, a winning strategy by 1864, and an absolute necessity by 1865.

The Emancipation Proclamation is a case in point. It was clear by late 1862 that the war of armies on battlefields was nowhere near a resolution. Despite the naïve optimism abounding on both sides in 1861, neither was going to win quickly or easily. Lincoln needed to find a new line of attack on the Confederate armies, and he found it right before his eyes. As was patently obvious, the Confederacy had been founded to preserve slavery, and its economy as well as its armies depended upon it to an extraordinary degree. Quite simply, if the system of slavery was weakened, the slave society and its military would be weakened as well. Therefore, Lincoln did not proclaim emancipation as a moral imperative but as a war measure, a means to win the war and to save the Union. Not all, but most war-weary Unionists across the North saw the logic. With the Emancipation Proclamation of 1863, Confederates were deprived of slave labor—whether farming at home or digging trenches at the front—and the Union armies were bolstered with the wholesale recruitment of black men into new regiments. The document did not decree freedom for all slaves, but it was clear by 1863 that if the North won the war, not only would the Union be saved, but slavery would be finished.

Lincoln's path to emancipation had been circuitous, and his pace had been slow. But Frederick Douglass came to see the method to the president's maddeningly measured approach. "Viewed from the genuine abolition ground," he said, "Mr. Lincoln seemed tardy, cold, dull, and indifferent; but measuring him by the sentiment of his country, a sentiment he was bound as a stateman to consult, he was swift, zealous, radical, and determined."

By the end of the war, abolition was a given and, with it, a recognition of the former slaves' natural right to self-ownership, i.e., nonenslavement. And significantly, by 1864, Lincoln had abandoned all talk of colonization. But how, then, did he think that blacks and whites could live together after the end of slavery? Perhaps, as equals. Where Lincoln had previously seen "a man but not a brother" in a black man's face, he now was beginning to see a brother, a man on par with whites. The war—and blacks' role in winning it—had midwifed something of a revolution in his thinking about race. In April 1865, two days after Lee's surrender at Appomattox, Lincoln gave a speech in which he declared his support of voting rights for black men who were educated and for those who had "served our cause in the military." Lincoln held that men who had not only fought for their own freedom but had fought for the constitutional Union surely had earned political equality under that constitution—the very political equality he had opposed in 1858.

Lincoln had begun to rise above his racist inheritance, possessing the humility to admit his mistakes and to learn from them. He was beginning to see prejudice as a personal and societal failure rather than an accepted norm, a product of ignorance, not of insight. Vitally, for Lincoln, white-supremacist slavery was not a solution to a problem, but rather a problem in need of a solution. For all his limitations, he represented America's will to do better over time, to follow our "better angels," as he put it. The follow-through on that promise has sometimes been advanced forcefully; more often, it has moved at a glacial creep. But it has moved.

By contrast, for Jefferson Davis and Alexander Stephens, the matched set of racism and racially defined slavery was their new nation's entire reason for being, an ideal to be maintained and exalted, fixed in amber like an heirloom to be passed down to future generations. They embodied America's deeply flawed origins and, too, a blood vow to try *not* to be better, not to mend those flaws, a vow dogmatically kept.

Lincoln was no god nor saint, and we shouldn't remember him as such. But his complex humanness is precisely why he is so important to our history. In one of the finest tributes ever written on his achievement, W. E. B. Du Bois began by noting the inertia of his upbringing, that he had begun life as "a poor white, poorly educated." But, Du Bois continued, "I love him not because he was perfect but because he was not, and yet triumphed." And then in a ringing challenge to us all in 2022, "The world is full of folk whose taste was educated in the gutter. The world is full of people born hating and despising their fellows. To these I say: See this man. He was one of you, and yet he became Abraham Lincoln."

"I was in awe!" she fluttered breathlessly. "There before me were Gen'l Mahtin's epaulettes!" That outpouring of fervor came from the quivering lips of a true southern lady, a member of the Swiss guard of matriarchs who patrol the historical bastions of Natchez, Mississippi, the Vatican City of the Universal Church of the Lost Cause of the Old South, where the moonlight was softest and the magnolias were sweetest, where Confederate relics were holiest. And where proper ladies swooned before epaulettes. I was in awe of her awe and snickered accordingly, allowing myself that exquisite rush of faux superiority that comes from raising oneself up by pushing others down.

But maybe I was being too judgmental. The fine lady in awe of epaulettes was most interested in the man or, more exactly, the general under the epaulettes after all. These were not random military ornaments. They had once belonged to Major General William T. Martin of Natchez, the town's highest-ranking participant in the Confederate war effort. And it is in this capacity that he was held to be an object of such reverence. Was it wrong to respect the officer, the gentleman? The chivalrous southern gentleman? That is inarguably a worthy ideal, is it not? And that ideal is personified by Robert E. Lee.

Not only in the South, but in the North, Lee is still often held up to be the personification of those southern virtues that the entire nation admires. His character seems the standing rebuke to the identification of the Confederate cause with something so crass as human bondage. Surely, he had nobly led his outnumbered men in defense of the preference for quality over quantity, for community over bureaucracy, for farm over factory. And then, too, there are the "facts"—as trumpeted in one neo-Confederate polemic—that Lee "was not a slave owner," that he condemned slavery as "a moral and political evil," and that he "wished the quick abolition of slavery."

To whatever degree Lee was honorable, he is dishonored by such dishonesty. Let's take it from the top—Robert E. Lee did own slaves. Regardless of his legal ownership, though, he grew up in a slave-owning household, married into one with even more slaves, and never lived a day of his life outside of one until abolition. As the "master" of his slave-owning wife, he mastered her family's plantations and the two hundred slaves she had inherited, and he did not hesitate to wield the whip, dispatch slave catchers, and separate mothers from children as business considerations required.

However, in a letter to his wife, dated December 27, 1856, he really did say that "slavery as an institution is a moral and political evil." But the quote represents ten words cherry-picked out of a letter of 580 words. It is, in other words, a partial truth and, as is often the case, one wielded to deceive rather than inform. Lee, in fact, harshly criticized actual abolitionists, and Free-Soilers as well. As to how and when the "evil" of slavery would be ended, he judged that that must be left to "Merciful Providence . . . who Chooses to work by slow influences; and with whom two thousand years are but as a Single day." In other words, there was nothing that humans could or should do to tear down the institution of slavery, even though humans had erected it. Yet, while trusting "Merciful Providence," he did think humans can and should do all in their power to perpetuate it, as he himself did by lending his battlefield genius to the Confederate war effort.

It's important to note, too, that Lee's complacent tolerance of slavery was rooted in his presumption of blacks' gross inferiority. In his acclaimed "slavery-is-a-moral-and-political-evil" letter, he goes on to say that they were better off enslaved in America than free in Africa. After the war, he recommended an acceptance of Confederate defeat and vowed to stay out of politics, which, it is argued, is why he humbly refused to denounce the newly founded Ku Klux Klan's violence against blacks. That noble neutrality, though, was violated when he felt the need to denounce suffrage for blacks. In light of this, one has to wonder why he had called slavery evil in the first place. In the 1858 letter, he answered matter-of-factly, "I think it is a greater evil to the white than to the colored race."

Let's be plainspoken about General Robert E. Lee for once. In a few lines of stilted pomposity, he masqueraded as an opponent of slavery. In the real world, by word and deed, he supported it. He profited from it personally. He employed unadulterated savagery to enforce it. He damned any who dared criticize it. He waged war against those who would even try to limit its expansion. He was willing to destroy the United States to preserve it, which is why Ty Seidule—a retired brigadier general and former head of the History Department at West Point—bluntly calls him a "traitor." He was one more of those southerners who blathered about slavery's sinfulness but who had no intention of acting on their high-flown rhetoric. To apply the biting words of Tulane's Randy Sparks about southern evangelicals, they were mostly "content to decry slavery as an evil, wring their hands in despair over ever finding the proper time or method of abolishing it, and continue to buy, sell, and own slaves" in the meantime. Lee wanted to have the moralistic cake of antislavery rhetoric and to simultaneously eat the social and material benefits of the institution.

We misunderstand Lee's honorableness, though, primarily because we misunderstand the nature of honor in the slave society of the antebellum South. We should know that the honorific attributes we profess to admire were inextricably linked to slavery. They weren't distinctly southern; they were distinctly "masterly." Slave masterly. Harvard's Orlando Patterson says that the honorable gentleman's self-conscious pose of independence, command, courage, grace, and dignity is "the way in which *all* slave masters conceived of themselves . . . whether they were Toradja tribesmen in the central Celebes [in today's Indonesia], ancient Greek intellectuals, Islamic sultans" [emphasis mine]. Or, he might have added, julep-sipping southern planters. "What was universal in the master-slave relationship," he explains, "was the intense sense of honor the experience of mastership generated, and conversely, the dishonoring of the slave condition. . . . [W]herever slavery became important, the whole tone of the culture tended to be highly honorific." This needs to be stressed. Men like Lee were not honorable men otherwise guilty of a lapse in judgment over the institution of slavery. Honor was a function of slavery. "It was not in spite of," concludes Patterson, "but because of their slavedriving that they possessed these 'resplendent virtues.'"

Yes, Lee was the epitome of the southern gentleman, the southern slavedriving "gentleman." He memorized the script he was handed and performed his role with aplomb. But his moral vision at age sixty was exactly what it had been at fifteen. He was racist as a boy, as a man, as a mummified myth. In some ways, he personified the best of not only the South but of America, but in that, he personified the tragic and stubborn subservience of so many of our best to what was our worst. From birth until his dying day, he remained Robert E. Lee.

For a century and a half, we "decent" southerners have salved our consciences by making scapegoats of crudely racist plain folk, like Nathan Bedford Forrest, Theodore Bilbo, and George Wallace. And be assured, they do deserve our contempt. But they don't deserve all. We have reassured ourselves of our innate virtue as southerners by huddling under the umbrella provided by the impeccable character of those others, of our "best men" who lived their lives according to, we declared, a code of honor—men like Robert E. Lee. But when race was the issue, Lee was really just another chuckleheaded good ole boy. When the shit hit the punkah fan and their prerogatives were threatened, he and his august peers turned into whip-wielding vulgarians "as fast as we can swallow our spit." In his meditation on the Lost Cause, Du Bois notes that it is a "hard thing to live haunted by the ghost of an untrue dream, and many a man and city and people have found it an excuse for sulking, and brooding, and listless waiting." It is also a hard thing to live haunted by the ghosts of unworthy white-supremacist heroes, and many a people today find it an excuse for sulking and resentment and hate. I suggest we secede from our awe for these moral Neanderthals in epaulettes. Worthies, many without pretentious frippery, are available.

CHAPTER 4

The Riddle of the Confederate Sphinx

*Granted that the Confederacy fought to defend white-
supremacist slavery, but if monuments to Confederate leaders
must be removed—due to their defense of slavery—shouldn't
we also have to remove monuments to slaveholding Founding
Fathers, such as George Washington and Thomas Jefferson?*

Five blocks from my home in downtown Natchez, behind the apse of the
beautiful neo-Gothic St. Mary's Basilica, we find Memorial Park. It was the
town's original 1790s cemetery, though most graves were moved in the 1820s
to the more spacious and also beautiful City Cemetery on the north side
of town. But downtown, a few graves linger behind. It does, then, remain a
"memorial park." Which means that its purpose is memory, memory without
which we would be amnesiacs, at a loss as to who we are. It is not, therefore,
a place of judgment, neither a place of sanctification nor condemnation. A
place where all our good and bad can be buried, "memorialized," and so, not
forgotten. And it is there, facing Main Street, that we find a twenty-five-foot-
high column erected "in memory of the Confederate dead from Natchez
and Adams County, Mississippi." A large, ornate fountain bubbles in the
background, its tinkling music doing its best to drown out at least some of
the rumble of the Subarus and Dodge Rams that disturb the calm.

At the apex of the monument, there stands a statue of a disheartened
Confederate soldier leaning on his gun's stock, barrel to the ground in resig-
nation to fate. A wood henge of immense live oaks forms a circle around the

sacred site. Their limbs and evergreen branches twine around the soldier's head, as if nature has paradoxically fashioned a laurel wreath of victory to commemorate his defeat. A poem is chiseled into the column's base. It begins:

> Dear in the lifeless clay,
> Whether unknown or known to fame.
> Their cause and country still the same,
> they died—and wore the gray.

The lines are not quite Homeric, but the theme seems clear. This is to be a monument to the ordinary men and boys, many of them "unknown," who died in Confederate armies, however they may have understood—or misunderstood—their cause. That cause was an obscenity, but their personal motivations were many, and their suffering was real. It is right that we remember these Confederate soldiers. Though they died amid bloody havoc and controversy, may they rest in peace. Of my eight Confederate ancestors who died in the war, none of them were from Adams County. But I feel as if they, too, are represented here in this place, five blocks from my house, light years from the hellscapes where they bled and died. For that, I take some solace.

But from my perspective at ground level, something is awry. As seen from below, the soldier's face seems to bear a wound. The forlorn Confederate has no nose. It is apparent that he was sculpted with one but lost it at some point in the past. How? When? His exact identity masked by this absence, his noseless gaze is lent a sphinxlike air of mystery. And then I finish my reading of the commemorative verse. However the plain soldiers had interpreted their sacrifice at the moment of their deaths, their pain has here been turned into partisan propaganda.

> From each 'Lost Cause' of earth,
> Something precious springs to birth.
> Though lost it be to men,
> It lives with God again.

Then, on the front of the column, a picture has been carved into the monument—the second official flag of the Confederacy, which contains the Army of Northern Virginia's familiar battle emblem fills its upper left quadrant on a field of white. Here, it literally ascends through the clouds and on toward the stars. The caption reads, "The warrior's banner takes its flight / to greet the warrior's soul."

To summarize, the "Lost Cause," the Confederate cause—the cause that sought to destroy the United States of America for the purpose of preserving white-supremacist slavery—"lives with God." The banner invoked by Governor Pettus in his call for secession—the banner he wanted inscribed "Superiority and Supremacy of the White Race"—flies up to Heaven. The circle of branches above the soldier's head takes on a whole new meaning. It has been transformed from a laurel wreath into a crown of thorns. It does not represent a spiritual victory over death for the plain soldier but the righteous victimhood of the cause. The purpose of the monument is less to mourn those dead men and boys than to hallow the Confederacy for which they died.

In 2022, 156 years after the defeat of "the cause," should such pro-Confederate, proslavery columns be felled? Or moved? Or reinterpreted? Or left to be?

Jefferson Davis, the first and only president of the Confederacy, owned slaves. George Washington, the first president of the United States and "the father of our country," owned slaves. Thomas Jefferson, our third president and "the father of the Declaration of Independence," owned slaves. James Madison, our fourth president and "the Father of the Constitution," owned slaves. There you have it. All these men share a common failing. Thus, many are now asserting that they were morally equivalent to one another. Therefore, it is said, their historical reputations, as well as their monuments, should either stand or fall together. So, are the honorary bronzes of Jefferson and Davis honestly the same?

The noted leftist journalist I. F. Stone was a great admirer of Jefferson. He was once asked how a man of his views and background (the son of Russian Jewish immigrants) could hold an aristocratic slave owner in such high esteem. As historian Eugene Genovese recounts it, Stone answered, "Because history is tragedy, not melodrama." Point to the great Isadore Feinstein Stone.

This is not a world divided neatly between angels and demons. The Sage of Monticello wallowed in that middle ground with the rest of us. To study real history rather than feel-good antiquarianism is to watch in dismay as this great rational mind wrestled with his fatally compromised moral soul over slavery . . . and lost. Even the formidable Jefferson fell far short of purity, as did the tragic American experiment he helped to create. But if we only commemorate the perfect with statues, there will be no statues. And no heroes. But if we erect tributes to every "leader"—no matter how tarnished—then make room for monuments to corrupt rogues and murderous monsters, as well as humdrum mediocrities. To state the dilemma crudely, all our lives have debits as well as credits. The question is, Do our individual credits, in quantity and quality, outweigh the debits? Aye, there's the rub, the point of friction between competing Founding Fathers, between the United States of America and the Confederate States of America. Between statues, good and ill.

Let's not be naïve about slavery in the United States. Our celebrated founders from the South (Washington, Jefferson, Madison) had the spare time to found this "free" country thanks to the profits wrung from unfree labor. They all ruled with the whip when it was deemed appropriate and allowed their craven self-interests and prejudices to overrule their celebrated principles. They not only allowed the system of bondage to survive but allowed it to be codified (at least indirectly) into the Constitution and then to expand geographically. They failed grievously, each and every one. And our national incrimination in the sin of slavery goes far beyond the plantations of the Virginian dynasty. Every day, new historical research is revealing more about just how critical slavery (and its profits) were to the development of the economy of the entire country, not only the South.

And still, there is this huge caveat, as explained by none other than Confederate Vice President Alexander Stephens in his infamous "Cornerstone Speech" of 1861. He observed, "The prevailing ideas entertained by [Jefferson] and most of the leading statesmen at the time of the formation of the old [US] constitution, were that the enslavement of the African was in violation of the laws of nature; that it was wrong in principle, socially, morally, and politically. It was an evil they knew not well how to deal with, but the general opinion of the men of that day was that, somehow or other in the order of Providence, the institution would be evanescent and pass away."

Stephens is correct. Though they did not abolish slavery, the founders, from the beginning, expressed a desire to limit the institution, precisely so that it might be eliminated by future generations. Between 1777 and 1804, the northern states either abolished slavery outright or began a process of gradual emancipation. In 1784, the slaveholder Jefferson proposed keeping slavery out of the entirety of the trans-Appalachian West. That suggestion proved futile, but in 1787, slavery was in fact excluded from the vast Northwest Territory (today's Midwest). These half measures were cold comfort for those enslaved, but they do make plain that there was an awareness among many, if not most, that something was elementally wrong with the idea of a "slaveholding republic." Even our slaveholding founders saw the institution as a cancer to be cut out eventually, though they themselves recoiled before the pain of abolitionist surgery. Within the United States, even with all its flaws, there was still the possibility that slavery would be ended one day, as it was. That racial equality would advance one day, as it did. Racial slavery was America's sin from its founding, but its preservation was not its founding mission.

These antislavery inklings, though, said Stephens, "were fundamentally wrong. They rested upon the assumption of the equality of races. This was an error." And the Confederacy, he went on to explain in 1861, had just been created explicitly to correct that error. "Our new government [the Confederacy] is founded upon," he said, "the great truth that the negro is not equal to the white man; that slavery is his natural and normal condition. This, our new government, is the first, in the history of the world, based upon this great physical, philosophical, and moral truth." Slavery as an institution was not unique to, nor created in, the American South. Neither was racism. But Vice President Stephens here claims a different distinction for the Confederacy. Other countries had been founded under various circumstances and then, over time, had seen slavery and racial prejudice develop haphazardly. But the Confederacy was, he said, the first to make a system of slavery based on white supremacy its founding "truth," its defining principle, its literal reason for being. This, he proudly asserted, was unprecedented in the history of mankind. In this, the Confederacy was genuinely unique. In this, Stephens was, again, correct. There had never been anything like this in the annals of humankind. In light of this "great truth," the abolition of slavery and the recognition of racial equality were inconceivable in an independent Confederacy.

Therefore, when we build monuments to the slaveholders Washington, Jefferson, or Madison, we acknowledge men who created a nation that may have fallen far short of their ideals, but one with the built-in capacity to atone for their sins and in the future, live up to those ideals. For all their debits, there are credits to counter them. However, when we build a monument to the slaveholder Jefferson Davis or to the Confederacy's Lost Cause, we honor a man and a movement that were willing to destroy this nation expressly out of fear that it *would* live up to those promised ideals, a promise that some try to deny even today. We insult America's founders, even the slaveholders, when we honor Davis's Confederacy—which was a moral and intellectual fossil, a devolutionary ideal, and a cutting repudiation of the promise of America. While being fully cognizant of America's wrongs, there is no moral equivalency between President George Washington and President Davis, between the United States and the Confederate States.

But that does not mean we should destroy Jeff Davis's statues as part of a campaign to "cancel" the Confederacy. Just as the answer to lies should not be censorship but truth-telling, we should answer Confederate monuments with anti-Confederate monuments. Right across the street from Jeff, erect a statue of Frederick Douglass. Place the master and the self-emancipated slave eye to eye. Let them stare each other down. Counter monuments dedicated to Confederates with ones raised to the United States Colored Troops (USCT) who fought to save the *United* States as well as to exterminate slavery. As I write this, just such a monument is in the planning stages here in Natchez.

But to make the new tableaux complete, all monuments, wherever placed physically, should be placed historically into their proper context by adding truthful interpretive information. The Confederate memorial column in Natchez is a case in point. It should not be destroyed, and I don't think it should even be moved. It should be explained as a historical artifact of its own time. Not of the war years, though. It was erected decades after the war as Jim Crow era propaganda.

Ever since the mid-1600s, the key to wealth and political power in the agricultural South had been dominance over an adequate supply of cheap, unskilled labor. Over time, that labor might have been enslaved, indentured, or ensnared by crop liens, but the essential goal was always dependency. The raising of the "memorial" column in Natchez in 1890 was part of this ongoing process. After the end of chattel slavery, the need for labor had been satisfied by a system of sharecropping fueled by fraud and insured by violence. Mostly blacks, but also many whites, were its victims. But by 1890, there was talk of white and black sharecroppers joining forces against the rigged system. As a result, as had been done before and would be done after, racial hysterics were unleashed to forestall such stirrings. In Mississippi, a new constitution that disfranchised blacks (and many poor whites) was the spawn. Across the South over the next twenty years, Jim Crow emerged from its reptilian egg. Part of this endeavor was the redoubling of propaganda efforts to turn the white-supremacist slave-drivers' war of the previous generation into a God-blessed, heaven-sent Lost Cause. A proslavery lost cause, though, in which nonslaveholding men and boys of the South had done most of the dying, most of the losing. The goals in 1890 were to tell blacks freed from slavery that they were not actually free, that they should "stay in their place," and to guarantee that the poor white men and boys of the next generation would continue to enforce that racial status quo—to their detriment.

As we see, history really is tragedy, not melodrama. And in light of this, maybe the enigma of Johnny Reb atop the column in Natchez can be resolved after all. This, I now see, is the perfect monument to memorialize the plight of the war's Confederate dead. The downcast soldier personifies the self-destructive South of 1860 and of 1890 and, for that matter, the self-destructive America of 2022. The absence of the nose now seems to shout out in resounding tones. The soldier has finally seen that Truth. He has realized the error of his wayward ways, the cause of his political resentments and economic frustrations. The forlorn Confederate sees now that he has shot off his own nose to spite his white face.

CHAPTER 5

The Black Confederates Who Were, and Those Who Weren't

*If the Confederacy was so maniacally devoted to the
defense of white-supremacist slavery, how do we explain
the service of black men in its armies?*

Holt Collier was a black man, a slave, a bear-hunter extraordinaire, a cow-boy. And a Confederate soldier.

His parents were the house slaves of Howell Hinds of Jefferson County, Mississippi—one county north of Natchez—and as a child, he was assigned to be the body servant and constant companion of Hinds's son, Thomas. As a "house slave," he developed ties of friendship and loyalty with the Hindses over the years, such that he accompanied them to the front when war began in 1861. There, the teenaged bondsman "joined" the Confederate army, seeing action at Shiloh and eventually serving in the Ninth Texas Cavalry.

His is an interesting story, but all the more interesting because it was, by law, an oddity. State-level slave codes as well as wartime Confederate edict forbad the arming of slaves, for any purpose, at any time. Southerners' consuming obsession, after all, was not a hope that slaves would fight along-side them against Yankees, but a fear that they would fight against them in a Yankee-inspired slave rebellion. There were, as always, exceptions. The comparatively privileged Holt Collier was one. Out of four million slaves, there were few others.

Nevertheless, from such shiny, rare nuggets of fact, some have concocted a higher truth of fevered proportions—legions of black slaves fighting valiantly for the Confederacy, shoulder to shoulder with their masters. Some neo-Confederates claim that up to one hundred thousand served, which would be more than one-tenth of all Confederate forces, a percentage matching that of blacks in the Union army by 1865.

This is nonsense. There is nearly universal agreement among scholars that genuine "black Confederates" made up far less than 1 percent of the nearly 1 million men mustered into Confederate armies over the course of the war. The vast majority of these tens of thousands of "black Confederates" of legend were not Confederate soldiers; they were slaves of the Confederate army. Men and women coerced into serving as laborers, teamsters, cooks, or even personal servants taken to the front by their masters.

This last role was common enough to have become part of my family's lore. Growing up, I was often regaled with the story of my great-great-grand-father Samuel McNees who rode off "to fight with Nathan Bedford Forrest" with his black "manservant" in tow. "Lore," however, rarely comes with foot-notes. But only in fantasy could this man be considered a black Confederate. However, entirely by chance, I stumbled upon the 1917 Confederate pen-sion application of the "indigent" eighty-five-year-old W. M. Gaston who was "a servant of a soldier in the service of the Confederate States," spe-cifically, of my third-great-uncle Captain Hugh Gaston of the Forty-fourth Mississippi Regiment. He recounted on his application that he attended Captain Gaston "until the Siege of Atlanta, GA," stopping only because "my master was killed there" in the summer of 1864. Notably, his request for a pension was approved.

The neo-Confederate "interpretation" is not just an honest error, how-ever. Their elevation of the black Confederate molehill into a mountain is deliberate. The aim of their exaggeration is to burnish the Old South myth by implying that the masses of slaves were content with their enslavement and devoted to their masters. They were not. It is a classic example of the deliberate use of a partial truth to obscure the whole truth, to deceive rather than inform.

Still, in all the controversies about blacks in gray, one fact is too often over-looked. In the context of the global history of human bondage, there is noth-ing unusual about arming slaves during the crisis of wartime. Throughout human history, it has been common for masters to deploy their slaves not only as laborers but as frontline fighters. These soldiers sometimes remained slaves while being granted higher, even elite, status (the Janissaries of the Ottoman Empire being a prime example). Usually, though, the incentive for slaves to fight their masters' wars was a promise of personal freedom. Orlando Patterson notes, "Almost all societies that kept slaves used manumission at some time, both as a means of motivating slaves to help in defense of the master's territory or to invade the territory of others." For thousands of years, when faced with a choice between retaining ownership of a slave while being annihilated by invading hordes or freeing and arming the slave to prevent that annihilation, masters had always opted for emancipation. A one-time manumission to meet an emergency did not mean the end of slavery, after all. Once the war was won, more slaves could be captured or bought, and the system would survive. The reversal of conquest would not be so easily accomplished.

The Greeks employed slaves to fight the Persians in the early fifth century BCE and to fight one another in the Peloponnesian War of the late fifth century. Romans mobilized slaves to fight Hannibal and the Carthaginians in the second century BCE. A thousand years ago, an Old Norse law stated plainly, "when common danger calls all, free and slave, to arms in defense of the country, the slave who succeeds in slaying an enemy in battle is free." The Koreans mobilized slaves to fight Ogedei Khan and the Mongols in the thirteenth century. In colonial Brazil in the eighteenth century, masters offered some slaves freedom if they fought against other slaves who had run away to form formidably independent "maroon" communities in the back country. There are many other examples, but the lesson is plain. Slaves can make particularly good soldiers if, that is, their primary "combat pay" comes in the coinage of freedom. Historically, fighting in the master's war has proven to be a much more successful path out of slavery than slave rebellion—remarkably few of which have succeeded in the history of civilization. In a time of urgent need, spurning this pool of highly motivated warriors would seem to be suicidal.

But that is exactly what the Confederacy did. From a global, historical perspective, it is astonishing that the manpower-strapped Confederacy, one of the largest slave societies in world history, with millions of slaves within its territory, did not mobilize such armies. The crucial question is not why a tiny number of Holt Colliers may have "volunteered" for Confederate service; it is why, with its very existence at stake, the Confederacy didn't offer hundreds of thousands of Holt Colliers freedom in return for military service. And yes, someone did suggest just such an act at the time.

In January 1864, Confederate Major General Patrick Cleburne had few illusions. With its armies depleted, the Confederacy's hopes of victory were fading. However, with one reform, he believed, the cause could be revived. It was, though, not to be a change in battlefield tactics, but a reform in the nature of the very cause itself. Before an assembly of the officers of the Army of Tennessee, he proposed an emancipation of all slaves "who will remain true to the Confederacy in this war" from which would be drawn regiments of black soldiers. Although he wasn't explicit on this point, it was apparent to all that this would mean the end of slavery. In the high stakes poker game of moral high ground, Cleburne was proposing to see Lincoln's Emancipation Proclamation with an Emancipation Proclamation of Confederate vintage.

This was not idle rhetoric from an obscure officer. Cleburne had status. A nonslaveholder himself, he was an Irish-born veteran of the British military, who had immigrated to Helena, Arkansas—about eighty miles north of Longshot. At the outbreak of war, he had enlisted as a private and then had risen through the ranks to become, by consensus, one of the best division commanders in the entire Confederate army. He did understand that the forfeiture of slave property in the South would be a great economic loss for others. But looming defeat threatened far more, he said, "the loss of all we hold most sacred—personal property, lands, homesteads, liberty, justice, safety, pride, manhood." He challenged the South to stand on principle: "It is said that slavery is all we are fighting for, and if we give it up, we give up all. . . . [But] we assume that every patriot will freely give up the negro slave rather than be a slave [to Yankees] himself." "We" assumed far too much.

Though there was some support, the proposal was mostly met with outrage or stony silence. President Jefferson Davis had "Cleburne's Memorial" actively suppressed. He would be denied the promotion to lieutenant general that virtually all agreed he deserved. It was patently clear that the vast majority of Confederate leaders emphatically did believe that "if we give up [slavery], we give up all." It must be remembered that slaveholders were a minority in the Confederacy but a large majority within its political and military leadership circles, with planters being particularly prominent. Cleburne was asking this wealthy minority within a minority to sacrifice financially to ease the bodily sacrifices of the men in their beleaguered armies—manned primarily by the nonslaveholding majority. This the "slavocrats" refused to do. As a result, the black reinforcements did not come.

Over the remainder of the year of 1864, Atlanta and Mobile fell. Generals William Sherman and Philip Henry Sheridan gutted Georgia and the Shenandoah, respectively. Over the summer, Robert E. Lee and Ulysses S. Grant hammered each other relentlessly in Virginia through a series of battles until Lee's army limped into the trenches around Petersburg. But Grant could replace his losses; Lee could not. The greatest defeat, however, came far from the battlefields. The resolutely antisecession Lincoln was reelected in November. If needed to win the war and save the Union, there would be four more years of war. There would be no negotiated settlement, no relief for Confederate armies. There was now certainty as to the Confederacy's end. Entering 1865, its fate had been sealed.

Now with all hope lost—and not a moment sooner—ever-astute Confederate leaders, like Lee, began to reconsider Cleburne's year-old proposal. By this time, though, its author was dead. Major General Patrick Cleburne was killed a few weeks after Lincoln's decisive victory and after the outcome of the war had been foretold. He was cut down leading his men in a doomed charge in a doomed battle waged as part of a doomed campaign, all conjured from the worm-eaten mind of John Bell Hood, the murderously incompetent commanding general of the doomed Army of Tennessee. One could be crushed to death under the weight of such tragedy.

Even now, though, there was still opposition to mobilizing slave regiments. From some, vehement opposition. Robert Toombs of Georgia, the first Confederate secretary of state, bellowed, "In my opinion, the worst calamity that could befall us would be to gain our independence by the valor of our slaves, instead of our own. . . . The day that the army of Virginia allows a negro regiment to enter their lines as soldiers they will be degraded, ruined, and disgraced." His illustrious fellow Georgian, Howell Cobb agreed: "The day you make soldiers of [slaves] is the beginning of the end of the revolution. If slaves make good soldiers our whole theory of slavery is wrong." Biracial military service implied biracial equality. For some, therefore, it was flatly unacceptable on any terms.

However, in February 1865, Mississippi Governor Charles Clark (his home was about fifteen miles from Longshot in the Delta) was blessed with a startling revelation. Slaves, he assured, "can be made effective soldiers," but there was no need to emancipate them. "I do not favor the granting of freedom to slaves, or of offering it as a boon," he explained. "It is no boon to them. Few of them aspire to this or covet it. Steady, firm, but kind discipline, such as good masters enforce, is all that is required." Yes, he said, slaves as slaves would fight for their masters out of love for their masters and for their own enslavement. He made this observation on return from a conference in Augusta, Georgia, in which he was joined in this timely—and profoundly delusional—insight by the Confederate governors of Virginia, North Carolina, Georgia, and Alabama.

These were all intelligent men, but intelligent men who had truly become the characters they played in the daily make-believe of the master-slave relationship. Those relations were based on a mutually acted charade: the master's aura of airs, the slave's mask of humility. The slave knew the mask to be a mask, but the master puffed his intoxicant all too deeply. For the antebellum southern master class, the mirage on the horizon was taken to be reality. The toxic beauty of moonlight and magnolias—like Delta sunsets—became its classical ideal.

Nevertheless, the sheer force of this "argument" carried the day. On March 13, 1865, with their house in flames all around them, the conjurers of the Confederate Congress summoned phantasms to quench the fire. They asked masters to "loan" their slaves for military service while maintaining their ownership rights. To have slaves fight to avoid having the "boon" of freedom forced upon them. A week later, in an inexplicable fit of sanity, Jefferson Davis ordered emancipation for the enlistees in an executive decree, but the entire exercise had been nothing more than a deathbed farce. A few black Confederate units were formed in the next couple of weeks, and played tin soldier for a while in Richmond, but the war was over. Lee surrendered on April 9.

Fate had confronted the Confederacy with an unambiguous choice: "Your slavery or your life?" It had selected death. Uniquely in world history, it opted for obliteration with slavery intact rather than life without it. As it stood on its gallows to proclaim its last words, the Confederacy had rebel yelled the true nature of its sacred "cause." With deeds to match its words, it definitively confessed its mortal racist sin, though declared it to be its essential virtue. This is the real story of "black Confederates." It doesn't concern the insignificant few who were. It is the tale of the hundreds of thousands who might have been, but never were.

CHAPTER 6

The Sins of the Fourth-Great-Grandfathers

But isn't it true that, throughout history, many nonenslaved
laborers have also suffered terrible exploitation?
Why was "chattel slavery" different?

In 1825, James Greer died at the age of seventy-five in Clarke County, Georgia. Owning several tracts of land and over one hundred slaves, he had been a member of the planter class, though hardly one of the grandees. In his will, his "home place" and its twenty-one slaves were "loaned" to his wife for the duration of her life. Whatever social and familial relations existed among these people would be continued. The slaves included in the rest of Greer's estate were not so fortunate.

The remainder of his property, both human and nonhuman, was to be parceled out among his thirteen adult "beloved children" and/or their heirs (two children being deceased). Greer left each beneficiary a feather bed, a mare and saddle, a cow and calf. And also a slave boy for the males and a slave girl for the females. To his youngest and apparently favorite child, Delilah, he left the same assortment of furniture and livestock. But instead of one, he left two slave children, a boy named Isaac and a girl named Harriet. The remaining slaves were to be divided into batches, "as near equal [in monetary value] as possible," for which his heirs would then "draw for their lot." In other words, about sixty people in bondage on his plantations would be scattered among thirteen households. No more details are available, but it is all but certain that families were broken. On the dictate of Greer's will, sons and daughters were taken from their parents, spouses were separated. Some would never see their parents, children, wives, or husbands again. The doubly beloved Delilah, for example, would soon migrate with her husband to eastern Mississippi with her own children in her care, but with other mothers' children in servitude. With Isaac and Harriet in tears.

In his classic book on the internal slave trade, Joshua Rothman of the University of Alabama wonders at the "something inexpressible" that drove "the kind of men who sold other people's children for profit." And slave owners themselves made a vocation of vilifying professional slave traders (even as they cut deals with the very same flesh merchants as the need arose). Are we, though, to forgive the kind of men who bequeathed other people's children for the profit of their own heirs? Time and again, by the very act of inheritance that tore one family asunder, another family was bound together financially through succeeding generations.

Another family like mine.

James Greer was my fourth-great-grandfather. The fortunate heir, Delilah, who moved to Mississippi was my third-great-grandmother. Her son, Samuel McNees, born in 1820, was my great-great-grandfather. By 1860, Sam had built up his own estate, including forty-one slaves, with those bondsmen making up almost two-thirds of the value of his holdings. He had apparently purchased about half of these enslaved people, but the rest had been inherited from his parents or, through his wife, from his father-in-law. This productive/destructive process of family wealth building was a great part of Sam McNees's success, a part that he volunteered to defend in the Civil War.

And it was a part (of incalculable proportion) of my success. Going back five generations to about 1830, there are sixteen family lines feeding through my father to me. Of those sixteen, I have established that ten of them, at one time or another, included individuals who owned slaves. Of the sixteen lineages on my mother's side, the number is twelve. Each passed their human property to their heirs, and this wealth at least potentially produced more wealth for each succeeding generation, in turn transforming into land, homes, businesses, and education.

This is American chattel slavery. It was a system in which the enslaved were legally defined not simply as property but as "movable" property—literally equivalent to livestock or furniture and, therefore, unlike real estate. A person reduced to chattel could not only be exploited as a laborer and denied their freedom, they could be inherited, as we have just seen. And bought and sold, either as part of a set or separately. And rented out or used as collateral for a "slave mortgage" (and, therefore, occasionally foreclosed upon).

Which meant that, by definition, family ties among the enslaved had no legal standing. Slaves could and did form spousal bonds, and masters did often acknowledge them, but the marriages were no more secure than the master's current financial need or health or whim. Enslaved husbands and wives could be and were legally separated by their masters. Enslaved parents had no legal claim over their own children, who could be and were taken from them forcibly. In a society very much devoted to "family values," a slave's family had no moral value and so could be reduced to the monetary values assigned to each of its individuals. For the enslaved, it was the antithesis of familial paternalism. It was base capitalism in its most cold-blooded form. John Blassingame of Yale calls this breakup of families "the most brutal aspect of slavery."

Within the United States, how commonly were families broken through sale? Leaving aside the many intrastate transactions, there was the massive interstate slave trade that flourished between 1808 and 1860. In it, approximately 1 million bondsmen were moved, mostly through sale, from the slave-surplus upper South to the booming cotton lands of the lower South. This was a "trail of tears" almost twenty times the scale of that inflicted upon the Native American peoples of the American southeast in the 1830s. Blassingame examined records in Adams County, Mississippi (of which Natchez is the county seat and the location of the second largest slave market in the lower South). Relying on the papers of the Freedmen's Bureau, he found that 39 percent of the freedmen applying for marriage licenses after 1863 reported that a prior marriage had been ended by sale. More broadly, British historian Michael Tadman calculates that, in the internal slave trade, 50 percent of sales broke up nuclear families, ending marriages or taking children from one or both parents. He makes clear that, for the most part, these deals were transacted "simply for reasons of financial advantage."

Still, the evidence indicates that most masters in the United States did not split up members of nuclear families. That is, at least not through sale; the division of families to achieve an equitable division of an inherited estate (as we saw above) is another matter. Nonetheless, the "good" masters who refused to break up families seldom used their—supposedly—majority status to make such breakups illegal. And if they did, says Joshua Rothman, the laws were "widely ignored, poorly enforced, and filled with exceptions," thereby "exposing even the pretenses of protecting the interests of the trafficked as a sham." But there is a reason for this moral inertia. The legal option to sell slaves as individuals or as families helped to keep the market for slaves liquid and, in turn, helped to keep prices high. The fact is those who refrained from breaking up families nevertheless benefited financially from being part of a system that permitted the practice.

Quite simply, there has never been and cannot be a system of chattel slavery in which families were/are secure. J. W. C. Pennington was a self-emancipated slave who went on to become an abolitionist and Presbyterian pastor (ministering briefly in Natchez after the Civil War). Of the allegedly good masters of lore and legend, he admonished, the breakup of families "presents the legitimate working of the great chattel principle. It is no accidental result—it is the fruit of the tree. You cannot constitute slavery without the chattel principle—and with the chattel principle you cannot save it from these results. Talk not then about kind and Christian masters. They are not masters of the system. The system is master of them." As slaves well understood, some masters were unquestionably crueler than others, but none were kindly enough to mitigate the evils inherent to the system.

But the ever-present threat of family separation was more than just "the most brutal aspect of slavery," it was its prerequisite. Because unlike other chattel, human chattel was human, inconveniently so. Making a wagon or a cow do one's bidding is simple enough, but turning a person of whom one had legal ownership into an obedient slave was anything but simple. In the process of reducing humans to chattel, their humanity was nettlesome at best. It could never be obliterated, but it had to be diluted, degraded somehow.

As to how, with shackles and whips, surely. "There is no known slaveholding society where the whip was not considered an indispensable instrument," Orlando Patterson tells us. But in charting the human essence (that thing that must be degraded in slavery), Aristotle asserts that, "Man is by nature a social animal." By this, he doesn't mean only that humans like to socialize; he means that a large part of any human's identity and sense of self-worth comes from his/her social standing. Therefore, he says, one deprived of the "common life" necessarily becomes less human, more bestial. Which is the goal, of course, of enslavement. Thus, enslavement requires dehumanization, which requires desocialization—an alienation from all that was familiar and familial. It is no accident that, throughout history, the prototypical slave was the culturally adrift outsider, the foreigner. Masters have always known that an isolated individual will be far more obedient. Such "natal alienation" was as good or better than stripes on a back. It was a set of nearly unbreakable irons.

Patterson calls it "social death." In his global survey of slavery, he identifies this forcible separation of individuals from their homes, community, and families as the very essence of chattel slavery. It is what distinguishes it, he says, from other forms of coercive labor—serfdom, indentured servitude, debt bondage, and "wage slavery." Chattel slavery is far more, and far worse, than simply a life of poverty, confinement, and work-weary bones. "If you want to rule a person, steal the person," observes Edward Baptist. "Steal him from his people and steal him from . . . everything he has grown up knowing." In so doing, you steal the person's very humanity. But even within bondage, "Man is by nature a social animal." For the enslaved, therefore, slavery is a never-ending struggle to retain his or her humanity and thus to resist social death and to cling to family. And to resurrect themselves into social life, to recreate family if and when it was stolen away.

Abd-al Rahman Ibrahima ibn Sori was a prince of the Muslim kingdom of Futa Jalon in West Africa. His illustrious name gave proof of his illustrious standing in society—"servant of the most gracious (Allah), Abraham, son of King Sori." He had been educated in the madrassahs of Timbuktu and was fluent in Arabic as well as his native tongue of Fulani. But in 1787, he was captured in battle, sold to slave traders, and put on a ship bound for America. As such, he was stolen from his wife, his son, his parents, his siblings, and his home. In enduring the Middle Passage, he endured a social death. After passing through Dominica in the West Indies and New Orleans, he was finally sold to the owner of a small plantation near Natchez, then under Spanish rule. And there, he would be put to agricultural labor. Or not. He was a prince who loudly proclaimed his princely status, but his kingdom and family were lost across five thousand miles and an ocean of heartache. His royal status was mocked. His name was changed. His religion was banned. His warrior's long locks were shorn to a boy's crewcut. And he was put to "women's work"

in the fields. Not surprisingly, he refused. So, he was whipped. He refused again and was whipped again. And then he successfully escaped. He ran away.

He ran away from slavery and humiliation, but ran to . . . where? Alone in the deep woods of what would become Mississippi, where could he go for help, for shelter? He was truly a stranger in a strange land. He was physically alive, but he was socially dead. He had been a prince, highly educated. Now, he was alone, reduced to a beast. And so, he returned to the Big House and submitted. He had defied whips and chains, but he was subdued by his isolation.

But in this case, after a seemingly complete social death, there was a chance at resurrection. Natchez would pass to American control, and in the meantime, Ibrahima married and had children. But after nineteen years of enslavement and an extraordinary sequence of events, he was offered the hope of a return home to Futa Jalon. The campaign to gain his freedom would span twenty years and come to involve everyone from John Quincy Adams to Henry Clay to Francis Scott Key to the sultan of Morocco. But during this time, Ibrahima initially seemed unenthusiastic. No, he had not come to love his master, and no, he was not happy he was a slave. If he gained his freedom and returned to Africa, what and who would he find after two decades? And what of his new family in Mississippi? Would his freedom also yield freedom for his wife, children, and, eventually, grandchildren. He faced the prospect that his return to his original social life would require a second social death. So, yes, he hesitated.

After twenty more years, arrangements were made for his wife, some of his children, and their children. After forty years in America in bondage, he embarked for home by way of Liberia. Some others, though, stayed behind in slavery—again, not out of love of slavery but in order to stay with family. Ibrahima would never see them again, but then, he never reached Futa Jalon either. At the age of sixty-nine, he died not long after arriving on the continent.

In several of its books, the Bible tells of the Lord "visiting the iniquity of the fathers upon the children unto the third and fourth generation." So, am I responsible for the sins of my fourth-great-grandfather? Are the sins of the slaveholders—the owners of Isaac and Harriet and Ibrahima—to be assigned to their descendants who owned no slaves? No, they are not. With apologies to any who blindly cull their ethics from Deuteronomy, I feel no personal guilt over what we find in James Greer's will or the slave schedules for Sam McNees. I am not morally liable for any of their transgressions, and for that matter, I don't put faith in the common genealogical sorcery whereby I somehow deserve credit for their virtues.

But Horace, in his *Odes* (23–13 BCE), puts it more exactly, "For the sins of your fathers you, though guiltless, must suffer." However we allot the onus for the sin of slavery, we have all inherited its still tangible and intangible legacies. This is because we, of the succeeding generations, have committed our own sin. We most certainly have been dishonest about them or simply silent. And mute truth will lose every debate. For over a century and a half, we have lied—lied to the world and lied to ourselves. In 2022, we are reaping the whirlwind.

CHAPTER 7

Asset De-appreciation

Even if not paternalistic, wouldn't a rational slave owner take
good care of his enslaved assets out of self-interest?

On May 7, 1840, Natchez, Mississippi, was struck by one of the deadliest tornadoes in American history, with an official death toll of 317. But according to Federal Emergency Management Agency (FEMA) records, that total may be a woeful undercount. It seems that the 317 victims did not include any of the great many slaves who are known to have been killed in the storm.

The reason for the omission is simple and is inherent to the chattel principle that defines slavery on its most fundamental level. Slaves were valued, but as financial assets rather than as humans. In Natchez in 1840, they were not tallied among the people killed, but among the property destroyed, right alongside their masters' livestock, wagons, buildings, etc. The loss in monetary values was calculated. The loss in black lives was not. Black-skinned property "in bulk" mattered. Individual black lives did not. Quite the distinction.

To answer those who point out the brutalities inherent to a system that treated humans as property, it is frequently asserted that capitalist masters were bound to treat their slaves well precisely because they were property. The enslaved were commodities with a market value of their own, it is asserted, ones whose labor was essential to the production of still other valuable commodities. It is argued that rational self-interest dictated "kindliness." This thesis was advanced with great fanfare and quantitative analysis in 1974 by Robert William Fogel and Stanley L. Engerman in their book *Time on the Cross*. For the authors, capitalism inevitably equaled freedom, prosperity, and morality. In turn, they say, if American slavery was capitalist, efficient, and profitable (as it was), it could not have been harsh and could not have systematically wrecked slaves' families. Slaves' hard work, they declare, had to have been prompted by incentives rather than punishments. Their material well-being had to have been comparable to that of the era's free-wage factory workers in the North and in Europe.

It makes for a quaint picture. False, but quaint. As if human interests can be reduced to the sum total of material interests. As if the human mind can be reduced to its capacity for reason. As if a bright line can be drawn between a "rational" desire for private profit and a mania spurred by greed. As if rational judgment has ever stood a chance in the face of abject fear. As if enslavement was motivated only by material gain when it was always and everywhere also driven by the desire for status over others, by pride as well as greed, by the drive to dominate, by the lust for power whether expressed by means of whip or sex.

But even if raw material gain was the motive of the moment, historian Laird Bergad explains, "Mistreatment of slaves may appear to have been economically irrational. But if slaves were constantly available at reasonable prices, it may have been perversely logical from a strictly economic point of view for masters to literally work slaves to death because of the high short-term profit possibilities, and then to replace them with fresh imports." Pure sadism truly did make for bad business but using coercion to force the "asset" to labor harder and faster was, as the masters saw it, necessary to good business.

On this topic, Stanford's Gavin Wright makes an obvious but too-often ignored point: in slavery, a master was able to "extract much more labor from households than these households would voluntarily have supplied." He explains that relative to white southern farm families, slaves were compelled to work more hours per day and more days per year. And their households had a higher "labor participation rate." This involved the percentage of household members—of both genders, of all ages—who worked. In slave families, children went to work in the fields at an earlier age and the elderly stayed at work to a later age. Pregnant women stayed in the fields later into pregnancy and returned to the fields sooner after giving birth. Quite simply, slaves worked more and harder than nonslaves. And did so because they were forced to do so. And the force took the form of violence. On plantations, where most slaves lived and worked, they were organized into work gangs. Here, Edward Baptist of Cornell does not hedge his words. He calls the result "the pushing system" within a regimen of "military agriculture" centered in "labor camps" and relying on "innovations in violence." Each enslaved individual became part of a cotton-picking machine engineered from human hands and backbones.

The enslaved, we must remember, were worked physically but were also treated as financial assets with horrific consequences at times. Baptist offers an account of the, at times, surreal result. In 1827, a "bank" known as the Consolidated Association of the Planters of Louisiana (CAPL) was chartered. The plan was for individual member planters to use their slaves as collateral to secure loans of CAPL bank notes, with the loans to be repaid from future profits generated by those mortgaged slaves. To back its loans, CAPL itself took out a loan—it would sell ten-year bonds with a $500 face value paying 5 percent annual interest. In this way, as Baptist puts it, each bondholder would own "a completely commodified slave: not a particular individual who could die or run away, but a bond that was the right to a one-slave-sized slice of a pie made from the income of thousands of slaves." This was the "chattel principle" of slavery taken to its ultimate extreme.

More, the CAPL bonds came backed by the "full faith & credit" of the State of Louisiana, i.e., the taxpayers of Louisiana, most of whom owned no slaves, sold no slaves, rented no slaves, inherited no slaves, and mortgaged no slaves, but who now were legally responsible for the debt made up of slave owners' slave mortgages. Thus, the consolidated planters had managed to divert virtually all their risk to others while making their own individual gain all the more certain. They had achieved the crony-capitalist utopia—a system of privatized gains and socialized losses. With such a sterling guarantee, CAPL's broker, Baring Brothers of London, was able to sell $2.5 million in CAPL bonds on exchanges in New York, Boston, and Philadelphia, but also London, Paris, Amsterdam, Frankfurt, and Vienna. The entire Western world could now conveniently partake of the exploding profits of America's

Gulf South right alongside the sugar planters of Bayou Lafourche. Without seeing slaves' forced labor, without seeing slaves whipped, without seeing slaves mourn for lost relations, the fine and upright people of the North and Europe could still reap the benefits of the South's massive slave society.

Needless to say, other such "consolidated associations" were founded in Louisiana but also in Mississippi, Alabama, Arkansas, Tennessee, and Florida Territory, all for the purpose of issuing slave mortgage bonds. Often, also with state government safety nets. This debt, though, was an unstable pier of an already unstable pyramid of ever-expanding debt during the boom times of the 1830s. Collapse was inevitable. When commodity prices plummeted 1837, the entire edifice fell. Many lost their lands and their slaves. But in this tale of capitalism run amok, let's be completely clear about who bore the greatest risks—it was the enslaved. If the debt was not repaid, the slaves themselves, as the original collateral, would be the asset foreclosed upon. Which would almost certainly mean the breakup of families as creditors picked through the human "commodities" of their master's estate. Planters could lose their assets, but the human victims lost their spouses, their children, their parents, their siblings. Forever.

This loss, though, should not have been the cause of overmuch concern, at least according to mainstream medical opinion. Blacks were insensible to emotional pain. This was explained by the fact that they constituted a separate—and lesser—species from white humans. A prominent cheerleader for this line of reasoning was the New Yorker Dr. John van Evrie. In his pamphlet *Negroes and Negro "Slavery"* (1853), he argued that since blacks possessed a "feeble moral nature," the breakup of families that was an inevitable part of chattel slavery was not so traumatic for them. He explained, though "the negro mother . . . has boundless affection for her infant; it grows feebler as the capacities of the child are developed; at 12 to 15 she is relatively indifferent to it; at forty she scarcely recognizes it." The real victims of family separations in the slave quarters, therefore, were not the slaves themselves. "The happiness of the whites is more disturbed by [slave family separations] than the negroes themselves," he assured his readers. The slaves, however, were not heartless automatons. He pointed out that their emotional attachments simply were not primarily directed toward their own parents, spouses, children, or siblings. Instead, he explained, "The strongest affection the negro nature is capable of feeling is love of his master, his guide, protector, friend, and indeed Providence. . . . The affection for the Master [is] the sole enduring affection of the negro nature." Which explained why the slaves were happy.

All were happy, that is, except for those who weren't. Masters were vexed by the fact that many ran away from their unfree contentment and others were, at times, surly. How could they reconcile the objective reality of runaways and general disobedience with the romance of moonlight and magnolias? This great question became something of an obsession for Dr. Samuel Adolphus Cartwright, one of the most prominent physicians not only in the South but in America. Originally from Virginia, he spent over twenty years practicing medicine in Natchez before moving to New Orleans in 1848. He counted Jefferson Davis as a friend and patient and served as "surgeon general" of the Confederate army's Department of the West in 1863. His scholarly articles were published widely, and he lectured occasionally at the University of Louisiana (now Tulane). His "specialty," though, was "racial medicine," which concerned the study of the biological differences between the races, the differences in the afflictions endured, and the remedies to be applied. In this, it should be stressed, he was very much part of the medical establishment.

His best-known contribution to the field was, without a doubt, the series of articles he published between 1851 and 1853 under the title of "Diseases and Peculiarities of the Negro Race." The treatises had been commissioned by the Louisiana State Medical Society and were originally published in the *New Orleans Medical and Surgical Journal*. In the most cited findings, Cartwright set out to explain that vexing anomaly of happy slaves running away from their happy enslavement and of committing the lesser transgression of daily "rascality." It was a matter of mental health, he surmised. A happy and healthy slave quite simply could not run away, being "spellbound"—in other words, not bound by chains, but by the "spell" cast by his own natural childlike inferiority and the natural gravity of the master's paternal superiority. Therefore, the factor "that induces the negro to run away from service, is as much a disease of the mind as any other species of mental alienation." He dubbed the defect "drapetomania," a term he derived from the Greek word for runaway slave, "*drapeto*," and for crazy, "*mania*." Dr. Samuel Adolphus Cartwright had rendered his diagnosis. If you tried to escape from slavery, you were insane.

He attributed more general mischief making to another mental deficiency that he named "dysaesthesia aethiopica," which was "a disease peculiar to negroes" causing lethargy, leading inexorably to disobedience. Their rascality, he delineated, "is mostly owing to the stupidity of mind and insensibility of the nerves induced by the disease." Slaves afflicted with this disease destroyed the master's farm implements, mistreated the master's livestock, stole the master's property as a matter of course, and chopped down his cotton when hoeing it. A single cure, though, was available for both problems, he said. If the patient/slave was "dissatisfied," he prescribed a dosage of whipping—aka lithium-of-nine-tails. One problem, he noted, was that slaves suffering from these mental afflictions, particularly dysaesthesia aethiopica, were "insensible to pain." This time, physical pain. In which case, Dr. Cartwright recommended upping the dosage and "whipping the devil out of them." Again, the purpose being to restore the afflicted to health and happiness. We should recall that, in its most ancient formulation, the Hippocratic oath reads, in part: "I will abstain from all intentional wrong-doing and harm, especially from abusing the bodies of man or woman, bond or free." For emphasis, "bond or free."

It should be recalled that even Dr. van Evrie did allow that "the negro mother . . . has boundless affection for her infant," which undoubtedly drew the interest of the learned Thomas Affleck of Washington, Mississippi. The creator of a truly innovative accounting book for plantations, Affleck was particularly good at keeping accounts, at counting things so as to allow comparison with other counted things. Among the things he counted were child slaves, specifically their rate of mortality. And after his tabulations, he concluded, in 1851, "The mortality rate of negro children is as two to one when compared with the whites. Of those born, half die under one year; of the other half, one-tenth under five years." Scholars who have thoroughly researched the topic, such as Ohio State economist Richard H. Steckel, have corroborated Affleck's conclusions.

But something doesn't seem to jibe here. This indication of bad health comes strangely paired with a striking bit of evidence for the opposite: uniquely in world history and unlike circumstances in the contemporary Caribbean and Brazil, the enslaved population of the North American mainland expanded due to natural increase alone, i.e., its birth rate exceeded its death rate. Fewer than half a million Africans were brought to English-speaking North America during the centuries of the transatlantic slave trade. But by 1860, there were 4 million slaves in the southern United States—a remarkable tenfold increase. Surely, this is evidence of benevolence.

British historian Michael Tadman explains that it is not. Rather, it is evidence of the presence or absence of sugar cane. It has long been understood that sugarcane production places far greater physical demands on laborers than does cotton or tobacco. Demands that, alone, could and did reduce life expectancy. But due to the extreme exertions required, planters in the sugar-producing regions of northeastern Brazil, Jamaica, St. Domingue, and south Louisiana all preferred male over female slaves. All these regions, therefore, were characterized by pronounced gender imbalances in their enslaved populations—too many men and too few women to produce natural increase. By contrast, in the cotton- and tobacco-growing areas of the United States, with less onerous labor demands, the genders were more balanced. Most men could find mates. North American natural increase was the result of crop choice, not paternalistic care.

But to return to the original point, how can we reconcile such rapid population growth with such a devastating infant-mortality rate? Why was it that—as Harvard's Walter Johnson puts it—"motherhood and mourning were inseparable in this economy"? It's telling that Affleck, the unapologetic antebellum slaveholder, centered much of his explanation for the doubled death rates squarely on the institution of slavery itself, specifically on the problem of "the wearied mother," both before and after birth. Again, in slavery, pregnant women stayed in the fields later into pregnancy and returned to the fields sooner after giving birth. They were, therefore, more "wearied" than nonslave mothers. Pre- and postnativity, enslaved women were worn down and nutrition deprived. "Intra-uterine malnutrition" for their fetuses was the result.

For the enslaved, the upshot was predictable. Economic historian Richard H. Steckel reports that stillbirths were, therefore, more common. The infants who were born alive were smaller (averaging less than 5.5 pounds), weaker, more vulnerable to disease. And the problem of undernourishment persisted through early childhood. While new mothers in West Africa normally nursed their babies for two years, enslaved African mothers in the South were back at work full-time within about three months—again, working harder, for more hours, for more days—necessitating "supplementation" of breast milk in the infant's diet. Slave children in the United States were not only shockingly small (and unhealthy) when compared to nineteenth-century white Americans, says Steckel, but also when compared to the world's poorest populations in urban slums today.

In light of this, though, how to explain the population growth among slaves in the American South? Aside from the influence of types of labor and gender balance mentioned earlier, there is another factor: the fertility rate for enslaved women. The infant-death rate may have been double that for whites, but the rate at which women got pregnant was also considerably higher than that for whites. "Are [enslaved] Negro women as prolific as whites?" Affleck asked rhetorically. "Yes, more so," he answered. The higher pregnancy rate was not due to some miraculous fecundity peculiar to Africans, though. Rather, it was—again—a function of slavery. Neonatal breastfeeding—if done multiple times per day every day—acts as a natural form of birth control, inhibiting ovulation and reducing the likelihood of additional pregnancies. Therefore, the higher infant-mortality rates—by bringing breastfeeding to an early end—inevitably produced higher fertility rates. And even for those whose infants survived, more irregular breastfeeding—due to an early return to the fields—increased the chances of another pregnancy. This was well understood by rationally self-interested planters. Mothers with infants were sent back into the fields sooner rather than later not only for their labor in the cotton fields but in order to speed up their return to labor in the birth-ing bed—a point made by Jennifer Morgan in her strikingly entitled book *Laboring Women* (2004).

Tadman stingingly comments that the natural increase among American slaves was not due to masters' benevolence, but to a "Third Word population pattern" of high death rates combined with even higher birth rates, equat-ing to explosive population growth. The explanation is poor nutrition and the compromised immune systems that always partners with it. And the explanation for that is the "good business" of slavery. The fact is that—from the perspective of economic self-interest—the debit of an infant's death was more than compensated for by the credit of a mother's return to work and of another flip of the life-and-death coin in childbirth. Overall, in the big picture, enough babies were conceived and survived to expand the popula-tion, even as the cotton got picked, baled, and sold in the present. It's not that masters wanted slave children to die, but their profits were served either way. Walter Johnson notes, "cotton planters were both deeply interested in the reproduction of their labor force in the aggregate and astonishingly indifferent to the survival of any given (future) laborer." For any given mother, though—wearied in body and soul, trudging back to the fields, one child recently lost, another already conceived—the "aggregate" must have been a crushing weight. As it was, at times, even for those whose babies survived.

"1—6—F—M."

That's all we know. Such is the grand summation of a human life, specifically of the life of an enslaved human. These are the numbers and letters scratched onto a "slave schedule" amended to a census form in 1850, under the columns for "number," "age," "sex," and "color." This was, then, a single individual who was six years old, female, and a "mulatto," an offensive term for a person of mixed black and white ancestry. She personifies the "social death" of chattel slavery. Though born in the United States, she remained a stranger in a strange land, an outsider. Though not identified by name, her master was. He was my great-great-grandfather Thompson Lawrence, a forty-eight-year-old farmer in Moore County, North Carolina, in the south-central part of the state. Thompson was prosperous enough to own slaves but not nearly so prosperous as to be a planter. He owned four, including the biracial girl. Also listed on the census form for his household is a five-year-old girl identified as "black," as well as two twenty-one-year-old "blacks," a male and a female. Certitudes are again sparse, but questions abound. Were these elder two husband and wife (in the emotional sense even if not the legal)? Were the two girls the young woman's daughters? Probably. They would have been born in 1844 and 1845 respectively, when 1—21—F—B had been in her mid-teens. Was the black girl the daughter of the enslaved young man? Likely so. But what of the other enslaved girl, 1—6—F—M, the one identified as a "mulatto"? Given the nature of antebellum slavery, her mixed parentage almost certainly consisted of an enslaved black woman and a free white man. But who was the father?

The circumstance limits the possibilities. This was a small farm. There was no overseer. In 1844, there were no white males in the household over the age of five, except for the master and patriarch himself, Thompson Lawrence. Which means that he, my great-great-grandfather, is the likeliest candidate for fatherhood for the girl—the daughter who he would keep as a slave in his household for the next decade and more. Which would make 1—6—F—M the half-sister of my great-grandfather, Sion Lawrence, who became a doctor after the war, and bequeathed my middle name to me. She and Sion would have been "age twins"—born the same year, growing up together in the same household. This would also make her my great-great-aunt. Maybe, after emancipation, she went on to be the matriarch of her own family. One that would be my shadow family back in North Carolina. Maybe. However, for all that can't be known for certain, we can know definitively that there are no consensual relationships between middle-aged masters and fifteen-year-old enslaved girls. There is rape, or there are rapes. And there is the nausea that I am experiencing right now. The result was a crime, though one not illegal. One can't "vandalize" one's own property, after all—the property that the owner, we are told, was sure to treat with care and concern out of capitalist self-interest.

In cartoons, some claim the supernatural power to see through walls with X-ray vision, some the ability to communicate with the Great Beyond. In the real world, slavery and racism have imbued us with a different supernatural power: the astonishing capacity not to see wrongs committed in front of our own eyes. Not to hear pain screamed into our faces. And then to plead to a blissful ignorance.

Slave owners were most definitely capitalists, but that does not mean they were most definitely kind to those they held in bondage. A human asset reduced to a credit on a balance sheet can easily be reclassified as a debit. Credits and debits, benefits and costs, each being part of the price of doing business. And as they say, business is not concerned with morality, truth, or beauty. Business is business. Slave masters reduced humans to labor units to militarize and maximize hourly production, to financial instruments to maximize their access to capital, to cost-benefit ratios for comparing childhood mortalities to female fertilities. And into dehumanized assets segregated among their accountings of mules and faux mahogany tables. But then enslavement was never only about business. Slave masters objectified humans into "fancy girls" for their physical gratification, into a self-serving fantasy of "loyal darkies" for the gratification of their egos, into an alien species so as to rationalize violations of their sacred medical oaths. This much is clear. The abstraction of humans into anything less than human is not the path to benevolence.

PART 2

THE IMPORTANCE OF SLAVERY IN THE ANTEBELLUM SOUTH (AND BEYOND)

CHAPTER 8

The "Peculiar" Case of the Antebellum South

*Even if chattel slavery was worse than other forms of
exploitative labor, there have been countless systems of slavery
throughout history—including in Africa. Was the
American South any worse than any of these others?*

In my study of slavery in the antebellum South, I quickly noticed something: it is peculiar. Of course, antebellum southerners noticed the same thing. They insisted upon it, in fact. They set out to found a nation based on what they frequently called "our peculiar institution." They killed and were killed in its name. This cries out for some discussion.

In its origins, the word "peculiar" did not refer to a thing's oddness but simply designated the thing to be, according to the 2023 *Oxford English Dictionary*, "distinguished in nature, character, or attributes from others; unlike others, *sui generis*; special, remarkable; distinctive." And relatedly, then, something was peculiar in being characteristic of, unique to, essential to a person, group, or thing. It is in this sense that southerners called their system of chattel slavery—"our peculiar domestic institution." They held that it was different not only from systems of free labor but also from the other systems of bondage that had existed around the world throughout history. And they emphatically judged that "our peculiar institution" was characteristic of, and essential to, their place and time. It defined them.

Here, antebellum southerners were countering the arguments made by their own modern defenders. As is frequently pointed out, slavery is as old as civilization and—though now illegal everywhere—is still practiced to this day. And chattel slavery really has been found in many, many places all around the world. But its prevalence across time and space is often cited as a means to downplay the significance of slavery in any particular time and place, such as the antebellum South. Surely, when presented as just one more injustice among countless injustices in history, it is assumed, it fades in interest, to be reduced from a book to a chapter, from a chapter to a footnote. On the contrary, though, it is only by putting American slavery into global perspective that we can fully grasp its extraordinary scope and importance, can fully digest the "peculiar" comprehensiveness of the burdens it imposed. Comparisons are illuminating. They don't diminish the significance of antebellum slavery. They highlight it. To do so, we have to begin with the important distinction first made about fifty years ago by scholars of ancient slavery—particularly Moses Finley and Keith Hopkins of Cambridge—between "societies with slaves" and "slave societies." This point is essential to understanding the functioning of the institution in the real world.

In societies with slaves, those in bondage were fewer in number, no more than 10 to 20 percent of the total population in Hopkins's formulation. Of pivotal importance, though, was that collectively their labor was not central to the production of wealth within society. To the degree that they did any productive labor, they shared it with other "unfree" laborers. But then, in a society with slaves, the primary value of a slave was as likely to be the bestowal of status on the master rather than labor. Therefore, these slaves were not the primary source of the society's wealth and power but instead were a way for masters to show off their wealth and power, to raise their own social standing by degrading the standing of others. Crucially, slavery in such a society was not economically fundamental; it was incidental.

In slave societies, by contrast, the scale was greater, with slaves making up a quarter, a third, or sometimes even a majority of the population. Of greater importance than the numbers, though, was that their labor was economically vital, being the primary source of wealth, and therefore power, for their masters and for the entire society. Consequently, slavery was not incidental in such a place and time; it was fundamental. It has to be remembered, though, that even if its principal purpose was labor exploitation, it was—as always in a slave system—also a means to establish the master's status, his "honor."

For all the differences between these two cultures of bondage, it must be stressed that, on a fundamental level, some of the experiences of the individual slave were the same in both. In the chattel principle, people were treated as "moveable property" and so could be taken from their families and homes, could be subjected to "social death." And, in granting near-total power to one over another, slavery was, by definition, an invitation to abuses of power. These were ever-present realities of the condition.

Whatever the relative levels of injustice, however, there were far more societies with slaves than slave societies. Of course, there was no precise line separating the two categories of bondage. Inevitably, therefore, there is no scholarly consensus as to exactly how many true slave societies there have been. But the point is that, throughout history, there were comparatively few.

There were, though, five that undeniably rose to the rank of "great slave societies." Two were found in ancient times—classical Greece and classical Rome. And then in early modern times, there were Brazil and the Caribbean colonies of the Western European powers, particularly those of the British, the French, and the Dutch. And then there was the fifth—the antebellum American South. This system, then, was not simply one more place among the many with slavery down through time. This was no mere society with slaves. It was one of the few true slave societies to ever exist, the largest in modern times, and one matched in scale only by ancient Rome through the annals of human history. In its demarcation between slave and free, it was the most rigid of all time. It was, without a doubt, a singular institution— "distinguished in nature, character, or attributes from others; unlike others, *sui generis*; special, remarkable; distinctive." In a word, "peculiar."

In that, it was to a great degree unlike the societies with slaves that existed in the American North in colonial times and, in some cases, well up into the years of independence. And it was unlike the many societies with slaves that existed among Native Americans even before Columbus. It was unlike the slavery practiced in China and India for millennia but, there, never on the scale of a slave society. It was unlike that in ancient Egypt, where chattel bondage existed but slave labor had never become the basis of the economy— and had not built the pyramids.

And too, it was unlike the institution as practiced in Africa before 1500. On this issue, the scholarly debate is settled. Slavery within Africa did predate the establishment of the European colonies of the Americas that depended on enslaved African labor. Given that slavery was ancient in origin and nearly global in reach, its presence in sixteenth-century Africa was not in any way extraordinary; its absence, though, would have been. However, even though African slavery was hardly humane, it was undeniably less inhumane than that in the South. The root of the difference, though, was not some unique quality of Africa and Africans. The primary difference was that between societies with slaves and slave societies. In traditional Africa (areas beyond the influence of either the Islamic Middle East or Christian Europe), the former were common; the latter were rare, if they existed at all.

Accordingly, in Africa, slavery was practiced on a smaller scale. Though slaves might do some of the productive work, they were as likely as not to be household servants or concubines. Certainly, no African society up to the sixteenth to eighteenth centuries was dependent on the institution. Since the work was less essential, it was generally less strenuous. For Africans enslaved in Africa, there was no racial barrier between master and slave. People were enslaved over differences in culture and so were commonly assimilated over time into the enslavers' society and even, in a variation called "kinship slavery," into their extended families, thereby offering a built-in resurrection of a sort from "social death." Manumission (the freeing of individual slaves) was common. Slave status was usually not inherited.

By contrast, the antebellum South was a true slave society. Those enslaved were primarily employed in productive, wealth-producing labor, work that was generally harder and more unrelenting. In the South, the manumission rate was far lower; in fact, it was one of the lowest of all time. The rate of inheritance of slave status was far higher, one of the highest of all time. For Africans enslaved in America, there was little hope of full resurrection from social death.

On slavery in Africa, there is, though, an unfortunate addendum. It is obvious that the transatlantic slave trade—particularly after 1650 when it was simultaneously supplying three of the five true slave societies of all time—was the largest in world history. As a result, an equally massive infrastructure of slave capture developed inside the continent, with the capturing being handled primarily by the African states themselves. Of these African states that had never before depended on slave labor, some nonetheless became dependent on this massive slave trade. But when the British, the largest intercontinental slave traders by far, ended their participation in 1807, greatly reducing the demand across the Atlantic, the now well-greased gears of active enslavement continued to turn. The result was that, in the backwash of the abolition of slave societies in the United States, the Caribbean, and Brazil between 1833 and 1888, slave societies developed in Africa for the first time in its history.

In the 1880s, Europeans—made rich and powerful to a significant extent by the profits from their slave-labor American colonies but now self-righteously rid of the institution—were "shocked" to discover that their former business partners in Africa were practicing "barbaric" slavery on a large scale. Ridding the "benighted" continent of slavery became one of their justifications for the conquest and colonization of Africa. Thus, Western civilization would come to rule over Africa, wearing the mantle of high-toned morality.

There is another point of distinction between societies with slaves and slave societies that bears emphasis. But it also distinguishes among slave societies. In all preindustrial societies, an array of dependent, coercive, exploitative types of labor were employed. These ranks were reserved for the poor, but for those who were native born, those who shared the common tongue and religion—serfs, helots, indentures, debt bondsmen, etc. In other words, this group was made up of the poor who were cultural "insiders." And therefore, these people, however downtrodden, could not be reduced to the lowliest status of chattel slaves. That most extreme form of degradation was reserved for outsiders to the society—sometimes native-born outcasts (criminals, debtors) but far more often foreigners acquired through war or international purchase. That flow had to be continuously renewed since the foreign born tended to assimilate over time, thereby becoming less foreign and so less able to be enslaved. Sometimes, though, barriers to full assimilation were enforced. In these cases, slavery could become a multigenerational status extending from the first foreign-born prisoners to their stigmatized descendants. Even if native born, even if sharing in the common tongue and religion, the members of this group were still treated like outcasts, outsiders. The thoroughly racialized system that prevailed in the nineteenth century American South is the most obvious example.

It shouldn't need to be stressed that the members of these enslaved, outsider groups were not happy with their circumstances. They routinely assumed a mask of submission out of necessity, but it merely hid their seething discontent. Always, therefore, they represented some level of security threat. In societies with slaves, their numbers remained small, and as a result, the danger remained minimal. In slave societies, however, the numbers were large, at least a fifth, maybe a third, maybe more than half of the total population. The danger was imminent. But at the same time, the prospect for riches was immediate. The very group upon which the slave society depended for its wealth was the group that posed the primary threat to its security and to its members' safety. In a slave society, greed and fear mingled on a daily, hourly basis. They waged a constant battle for hearts and minds. In some circumstances more than others, though.

And in the American South, that struggle took place on a massive, very nearly unprecedented scale. Four million people were in bondage in the slave states of the American Union in 1860, making up about one-third of the South's population. That 4 million was about ten times as many as were enslaved in classical Greece. And it roughly matched the maximum numbers in Brazil and the Caribbean islands put together. Only the Roman Empire, which enslaved about 5 million during its Golden Age of the second century CE, can equal or exceed the absolute numbers in Dixie.

But absolute numbers don't tell the whole story. The slave population in Rome was spread over an empire twice as large in land area as the combined slave states of the South. In the entirety of the empire, slaves were only 8 percent of the total population. It was solely in the Italian peninsula and Sicily that the percentages and economic importance actually rose to the rank of a slave society. There, slaves were about one-third of the total population, similar to the proportion in the South. However, that percentage for the antebellum South was maintained over an area about six times as large as Italy and Sicily.

But within the South, naturally, there were great differences across regions. In the border states, the percentages of slaves in the total population were at or below 20 percent. Slave society percentages, though, were found in all the states farther south—from about a quarter in Arkansas and Tennessee to about a third in North Carolina, Virginia, and Texas to near majorities in Louisiana, Alabama, Georgia, and Florida. And there was a 57 percent majority in South Carolina, slightly surpassing Mississippi's 55 percent.

Within Mississippi, the percentages, of course, varied greatly from county to county, but remarkably, in all but two, the slave population exceeded the 20 percent slave-society threshold. It speaks volumes to note that one of those two lacking a slave-society percentage was Jones County in the Piney Woods of the southeast, the soon-to-be "Free State of Jones," which would "secede" from the proslavery Confederacy during the war. Here, slaves made up only 12 percent of the population, a percentage comparable to New York State at the time of the American Revolution.

At the opposite end of the spectrum, there was the plantation country. Here, in Adams County, slaves were 72 percent of the total population. They were 82 percent in Jefferson County and Wilkinson County, just to the north and south. Across the Mississippi River in Concordia Parish and Tensas Parish in Louisiana—largely composed of plantations owned by Natchezians—91 percent of the people were enslaved. Back in Mississippi, up in the Yazoo-Mississippi Delta, where my father and I grew up a generation apart, it had been 87 percent. Of the fifteen counties and parishes across the South in which 80 percent or more of the people lived in bondage, twelve were in the Lower Mississippi River Valley between New Orleans and Memphis. Even far to the east of the river, in the plantation county of Noxubee where my mother was from, 75 percent of the total population had lived and worked in bondage.

This focuses our attention on another factor that sets slave societies apart from societies with slaves. In a slave society, the extreme hierarchical values of slavery pervaded every aspect of the society in which, according to historian Ira Berlin, "the master-slave relationship provided the model for all social relations. . . . From the most intimate connections between men and women to the most public ones between ruler and ruled, all relationships mimicked slavery." Harvard sociologist Orlando Patterson, one of the leading scholars of world-comparative slavery, talks of the ways that slavery in such a system was intricately interwoven—"articulated"—into every aspect of life. In a slave society, slavery was not some inconvenient cyst that could be neatly excised with no disturbance to vital organs. In a slave society, slavery itself was one of the vital organs. In the American South, the most vital of them all. Vitally distinctive, defining, peculiar.

With this in mind, Patterson calls the antebellum South "the most perfectly articulated slave-society since Ancient Rome." As its own leaders frequently declared, it was a society openly, proudly defined by slavery. Secession, the founding of the Confederacy, and all that came in their wake emerged out of the dynamics of one of the largest slave societies of all time, one of the few racialized systems of slavery ever, and, of those few, the most rigidly racialized of all time. Slavery did not only "articulate" through this society. It metastasized. We as a nation almost died.

Alexander Stephens insisted that the Confederacy was the first society in the world founded on the "Great Truth" of white-supremacist slavery. And it would be the first in the history of the world to die for it. As C. Vann Woodward tells us, "Nowhere else did a slave society wage a life-and-death struggle for its existence with abolition at stake." He explained this both distinct and odd peculiarity by noting that "the end of slavery in the South can be described as the death of a society, though elsewhere it could more reasonably be characterized as the liquidation of an investment." Historian Peter Kolchin punctuates the point, saying, "the willingness of southern slaveholders to go to war for slavery, rather than yield as slaveholders did elsewhere (however reluctantly) to government-sponsored emancipation, points to their extraordinary commitment." A peculiar institution indeed.

CHAPTER 9

Slavery's Capitalism

So, slavery was capitalist, but was capitalism dependent on slavery?

The pilgrimage queen floats like a butterfly before her adoring subjects. As she waves her wand in delicate circles, she calls all in the throng to join figuratively into the ghost-dance soiree to summon up the halcyon days of gray-uniformed beaus and hoop-skirted belles, brought to life in the present by the king and court arrayed around her. This was the penultimate moment of the Confederate pageant. It was presented as an indispensable corollary to the tour of extraordinary antebellum mansions of the Natchez Pilgrimage, presented annually by the town's garden clubs for almost ninety years. And, of course, "pilgrimage" was the operative word. Those who witnessed this ritual were not properly tourists, but—according to the *Oxford English Dictionary*—those on "a journey made to a sacred place as an act of religious devotion."

In the instance of Natchez, the religious devotion was to be directed toward the Eden that was the antebellum South and so necessarily toward the Lost Cause of the Confederacy that fought to defend its God-ordained "way of life"—as one Confederate memorial puts it, "No nation ever rose so free from crime. Nor fell so free from stain." Few passages better express the mythology, the religious idolatry, of the Lost Cause. Here is proclaimed nothing less than the Virgin Birth and Crucifixion of the Confederacy.

And surely, the portal to that spiritual realm stood in Natchez. It was, as the town's slogan read until recently, "Where the Old South Still Lives"—conjured from the mists of immortal time for one enchanted month each spring. In this ahistorical Brigadoon, the Confederacy fought for freedom not slavery, though slavery was benevolent, and in fact, the slaves' work had made them free since they were much better off enslaved here than "free" in Africa. All of which meant that "slave" was not the proper word at all; rather "servant" was really more apropos, like in an idyllically hierarchical, benevolently paternalistic Medieval romance.

And the tourists came. And Natchez longed for their return. We are now hooked, economically but also psychologically. We need our annual fix of flattery. Truly, for nearly a century now, Natchez has depended on the kindness—and bankrolls—of strangers. Long after its cotton was sold around the world, Natchez found that a fantastical image of its cotton-growing way of life could be sold as a new commodity. Its annual renewal of the rituals of dominance and subservience proved to be highly marketable to northerners and southerners alike. And so, the town staked its economic future on a mythologized version of its actual past and earned its profits from pretense. Atop the grand white columned mansions in its midst, it built even grander white columned castles in its airs. Though the faery queen floats like gossamer personified, she is propelled by a profit motive as flinty eyed as the one that peddled slave-bound cotton bales to the world. And yet, with each fluttering pass of the faery queen and each waft of her wand, moral complications were waved away into the ether.

Except they weren't. As W. E. B. Du Bois asks of this sort of "entertainment," "Was not all this show and tinsel built upon a groan?" Amid the waltzing, was there not "blood on the piano keys"? Real blood for some, the figurative variety for others. Yes, the pilgrimage queen floated like a butterfly before her adoring subjects but, says James Baldwin, "People who imagine that history flatters them are impaled on their history like a butterfly on a pin." Thus, staked to their display, they then "become incapable of seeing or changing themselves, or the world."

It is said that, in the South, the past is not dead; it is not even past. It is a place said to be haunted by its past. I would add an amendment, though. We of the present also haunt the past. The shades don't refuse to let us rest; we refuse to let them rest. They speak plainly, regard us openly. We are the ones who avoid the truth and lurk in the shadows in disguise from where we insistently summon their spirits in ghost-dance pageants and reenactments. We exhume their remains for dismemberment and then refashion them into bizarre chimeras, like none who ever walked the earth. Maybe, if the past is not dead, it is because we keep it on life support in order to harvest its moldering organs, to pirate its heart and mind in order to fill the gaping void where our own should be. Maybe, just maybe, the dead really are just dead. We, the living, are the ghouls.

Southerners are not alone in this sort of witch doctoring, but we are among its most skilled practitioners. And I have had a front row seat in the operating theater. James Cobb calls the Yazoo-Mississippi Delta, the place of my birth and upbringing, "the most southern place on earth," but the writer Richard Grant has countered that Natchez, my hometown of forty years, is "the deepest South." However we judge this duel of southernness, there is a difference between the two to be emphasized. The Delta's southernness is unselfconscious, rooted in its still thoroughly agrarian socio-economic reality. But Natchez is self-consciously southern, entirely caught up in the need to show off, to act the part, to assume the role. In so doing, the role has consumed it. We all wear masks to greater or lesser degrees, but here, how to seem became more important than how to be. This does not necessarily mean that Cobb is right and Grant is wrong, however. In the South, even before the Civil War, consciously playacting the role of southernness was a vital part of being southern. Maybe, in the end, Natchez wins the prize for genuineness precisely because of its talent for artifice. Maybe clothes (i.e., costumes) really do make the southern man. But what exactly is the reality lurking beneath the cummerbunds and epaulettes? What are these selves unseen?

"Without slaves there could be no planters," observed Joseph Holt Ingraham of Natchez in 1835. "Without planters there could be no cotton; without cotton no wealth. Without [slaves] Mississippi would be a wilderness and revert to the aboriginal possessors. Annihilate them tomorrow, and this state and every southern state might be bought for a song." In 1861, as they took the first steps toward creating the independent Confederate States of America, the delegates to Mississippi's Secession Convention essentially agreed. In their Declaration of the Immediate Causes Which Induce and Justify the Secession of the State of Mississippi from the Federal Union, no words were wasted on romance in explaining their motivation: "Our position is thoroughly identified with the institution of slavery . . . the greatest material interest of the world." They added that "a blow at slavery" would not only endanger their wealth but also "civilization."

The antebellum South's planters, in other words, had no illusions. They were not extraordinary men who just happened to own slaves; they were ordinary men made extraordinarily wealthy by exploiting slaves' labor. Men who could then afford to buy the trappings of an extraordinary "culture." They were not an aristocracy ("rule by the best"), but a slavocracy (rule by slave drivers).

It needs to be stressed, though, that the slave-society's necessary role in the creation of the Cotton Kingdom does not mean that slavery was necessary to the simple cultivation of cotton. Varieties of cotton had been grown in countless places around the world for thousands of years, with and without coercion. We have to ask, therefore, why the early nineteenth-century cotton boom was centered in the Gulf South of the United States instead of one of the other more traditional areas of commercial cotton production. Why not India or Mesoamerica or East Africa or China or Central Asia? The primary reason is that these areas could not expand production fast enough. Being long-settled societies, with their land and labor resources already devoted to other uses, there weren't enough acres, nor enough hands, to meet the exploding demand from the new textile mills in England and New England.

However, in the South—as across the Americas—abundant new land and labor were available due to what Sven Beckert of Harvard calls "war capitalism," i.e., conquest, genocide, and enslavement, all carried out by or subsidized by European or Euro-American governments. Conquest of land and enslavement of people was hardly new, but seldom, if ever, had it occurred on such an epic scale. Hundreds of thousands of square miles of Native American land were not only annexed but were depopulated so that they could then be repopulated and made available for private, commercial exploitation. Simultaneously, millions of enslaved African laborers were brought to the Western hemisphere in chains to work that land. In the United States, forced "Indian removal" was thus paired with coerced "African retrieval" to generate astronomical wealth, not least in Natchez, Mississippi—said to be home to more millionaires per capita than any other city in the United States in 1860.

But many of the beneficiaries of this chain of events were found far beyond Natchez, far beyond the South. New England's prospering economy did not depend on slave labor, but it most certainly depended on trade with the slave labor economies of the West Indies, as well as on the trade in enslaved laborers. And more beneficiaries were found far beyond the Americas, in fact. UC Berkeley's Kenneth Pomeranz argues that Europeans' ability to exploit these non-European lands and labor—"ghost land" and "ghost labor" in his phrasing—largely explains that continent's economic takeoff into the Industrial Revolution in the eighteenth century. By no means is this a new idea. In 1847, Karl Marx alleged, "Without slavery you have no cotton; without cotton you have no modern industry." In 1935, Du Bois wrote, "Black labor became the foundation stone not only of the Southern social structure, but of Northern manufacture and commerce, of the English factory system, of European commerce." In 1944, Trinidadian historian Eric Williams had asserted that the stupendous profits from the transatlantic slave trade and slaves' sugar production in the West Indies had essentially financed the early phases of the Industrial Revolution in eighteenth-century Britain.

Today, scholarly debates continue over the cause-and-effect relationship between the "capital" generated by racialized slavery and modern capitalist development, but an entire school of historians has emerged to author a "new history of capitalism," which asserts the reliance of the former on the latter as a bedrock principle. Shaun Nichols observes, "the industrialization of the north and the proliferation of slavery in the south were not *rival* developments, but rather, transformations *deeply embedded* within one another" [emphasis original]. Edward Baptist adds specifics, calculating that if all aspects of the cotton business are included, "almost half of the economic activity in the US [i.e., GDP] in 1836 derived directly or indirectly from cotton produced by the million-odd slaves"—then only 6 percent of the national population. Sven Beckert compares the global importance of the cotton-sotted Lower Mississippi Valley in the antebellum decades to that of the oil-rich Persian Gulf states of more recent times. Walter Johnson expresses the realities of what he calls "racial capitalism" about as succinctly as possible: "Indeed, the history of capitalism makes no sense separate from the history of the slave trade and its aftermath. There was no such thing as capitalism without slavery: the history of Manchester never happened without the history of Mississippi." And so, we see, right in the center of this world-altering transformation was Natchez—Abu Dhabi on the bluffs.

I realize that this notion clashes with the doctrines spouted by capitalism's champions. Libertarian theorists frequently claim that capitalism and slavery were elementally incompatible, that free markets necessarily produce "free minds and free men." However, a growing corpus of evidence, as opposed to theory, indicates that in the circumstances of the eighteenth- and nineteenth-century global economy, capitalist development required unfreedom. Within this capitalist "world system," says Immanuel Wallerstein of Yale, a distinction must be made between the "core" and the "periphery." The core consisted of those areas that manufactured finished goods for export but imported raw materials. The periphery exported those needed raw materials (products of agriculture or mining), while importing the core's manufactured goods. In the commercial/industrial core—where most academic economists lived and spun their theories—free wage labor really was far more efficient, giving rise to the fairy tale that capitalism breeds freedom throughout society. But in the economy of the periphery—essential to the profits of the capitalist core, but far away and out of sight, unfree labor of some sort was not only viable but was preferred. In Europe, the rise of modern capitalism may well have nurtured the rise of liberal democracy, but elsewhere around the world, it was Moloch demanding imperialist conquest on a continental scale, enslavement of nonwhites on an historically unprecedented scale and, as a consequence, the rise of thoroughly modern racism.

And this was so most emphatically in the Cotton Kingdom of the American South. Though, let's be sure to pay homage to that royal realm's true sovereign. As Matthew Karp of Princeton puts it, for all his pomp and glory, "King Cotton" was mere vassal to "Emperor Slavery."

Cue the moonlight and the magnolias, and the faery queen . . .

I didn't grow up in Natchez, and so, I didn't grow up with the pilgrimage. But I have no illusions. If I had lived here as a child, I would have participated in the Confederate pageant through the years. My mother would have been a member of one of the garden clubs, and even if I had been hesitant, she (and my grandmothers) would have insisted on it. Dutifully, I would have complied. But in reality, if at the age of fifteen I had been asked to play the role of the "flag bearer"—the soldier who ran the Confederate banner into the auditorium at the beginning of the Civil War tableaux—I probably would have fallen flat on my face in ecstasy. Who knows, maybe I would have been a member of "the court" during my college years—if, that is, I had been asked. And if one of the duchesses had shown even the slightest interest, I would have blushed crimson and tracked the trail of her gin-scented breath like a goofy puppy. I also understand that, for many white Natchezians, the desire to continue the pageant has less to do with history and even tourism than it does with social status and multigenerational family tradition. After ninety years, there are pilgrimage dynasties, with queens begetting queens, and grandsons dancing the same steps trod by their grandfathers as boys fifty years before. And then too, it is, after all, a "pageant" complete with lots of pageantry and months of parties. There are good times. So, while admiring the gowns and downing the gimlets, what's the harm in participating in a little historical fib? Particularly if the queen, impaled but fluttering, bats her lashes as she looks your way.

What's the harm? It is that the faery queen is a femme fatale. It would help if we would amend our nostalgia by remembering something about the Old South "heritage" of which both neo-Confederates and pageant mavens are so enamored. The glorification of that Old South, which is the essence of the pilgrimage, was/is a very modern capitalist effort to market that image to tourists. But it is only a small part of a far larger, much more cynical ploy that began long before 1932. As C. Vann Woodward tells us in his seminal work, *The Origins of the New South* (1971), "One of the most significant inventions of the New South was the Old South." Louis Hartz elaborates, saying, "Southern thinkers invented a feudal past of honor and chivalry that never existed. . . . The sweat that had to go into making the South medieval was even greater than the sweat that had gone into making it modern." In other words, the leaders of the post-Reconstruction New South (many but not all of whom were antebellum leftovers) created the moonlit and magnolia-scented image of the old from whole cloth. They created it, nurtured it, propagated it, and swore belligerent fealty to it in order to obscure their ongoing efforts to sell out the South to Yankee industrialists.

Today, Natchez is a town amid an identity crisis. There is an ongoing multisided push and pull between the two garden clubs, individual home-owners, black-heritage groups, and the National Park Service over how we should present our historical face to the world. The town is not sure if it wants to be an "antebellum-world" amusement park designed to entertain and divert, with mansion tours, plantation weddings, hoop skirts, maypoles, loyal "servants," and—surely coming soon—an "old-Joe-got-snatched-up-by-the-cotton-gin" roller coaster. Or, say the very capable leaders of the Natchez National Historical Park, it should be a giant open-air historical museum designed to educate—paying proper homage to mansion tours, gardens, antique furnishings, and authentic period costumes but also to tours of the townhouse of William Johnson, the free black businessman and diarist, to tours of slave quarters, of the site of the second largest slave market in the lower South, and of sites important in the Reconstruction and the civil rights eras. To fit the pageant into this revised vision, in recent years, there have been good faith efforts at compromise and modifications. "Confederate" was dropped from its name, for example. But in this process, there have been ebbs and flows and disagreements between the two garden clubs and, too, within them. As I write, discussions continue.

But still . . . for years, to tell the history of Natchez, the pilgrimage (and pageant) told the stories of grand mansions and the grand lifestyles of the families they housed, with little or no mention of "servants." The reformers of recent years have tried to enhance this tale of mansions and pomp with selected stories of slaves and their sufferings. But both these approaches miss the point. The central plot of the history of Natchez and the antebellum South and its place in the national and global economies is defined by slaves and slavery. We must remind ourselves, "without slaves there could be no planters. Without planters there could be no cotton; without cotton no wealth," and "there was no such thing as capitalism without slavery: the history of Manchester never happened without the history of Mississippi." Within this story, the tour of homes can and should be included not as the central narrative but as a subplot to it. A home tour that omits this reality is not being "positive"; it is being dishonest.

Natchez was—and remains—a beautiful place, but it was never just another pretty face. Behind its parasol, it was economically dynamic and ruthless. How can and should this story be told in a way that is historically accurate, culturally sensitive, and tourist friendly? I readily admit that I don't have all the answers, and I am extremely glad that my friends at the National Park Service have this burden rather than me. But I cannot imagine how a costumed and cocktail-saturated musical extravaganza can be made compatible with its reality. In the end, for all the changes that have been made, the pageant remains a "pageant"—defined as "a brilliant and stately spectacle." Queens in gowns and kings in formal attire still promenade, attended by their courts, though now amid scattered tales of slaves, bowed but not broken. But if the kings and queens of the pilgrimage must reign, they are surely bound by that pretense to pay proper homage to their true liege lord. And that lord is not the fluffy King Cotton but the iron-willed Emperor Slavery.

A lord, we must recall, who was not an accomplished, wealthy man who happened to own slaves, but was an all-too-common man made rich by exploiting slaves. He was not an honorable man who lapsed into slave own-ership, but was a man who was addicted to the daily "fix" of others' submis-siveness that slavery commanded. He was not a kindly patriarch, but a chattel monger inflicting social death on splintered families, a financial predator who commodified and collateralized and securitized the living. And no graceful waves of a magical wand can make these realities disappear.

CHAPTER 10

Slavery's Freedom

How is that we hear the loudest yelps
for liberty from the drivers of Negroes?
—**Samuel Johnson,** "Taxation No Tyranny" (1775)

It was an age when every man could be a king or, at least, a president, an age when the chief executive of the United States had been hewn from a hickory knob. It was that era to which Andrew Jackson attached his name and for which his rough, born-in-a-log-cabin ways set the norm. After fifty years of governance by "gentlemen," the Common Man and his interests would be dominant. For the first time in American history, the adjective "democratic" could legitimately be added to "republic."

Mississippi epitomized this age of Jacksonian democracy, reports University of Alabama historian Joshua Rothman. In the state, these were the "flush times," says lawyer Joseph Baldwin, times of high prices for land and slaves, high profits and low morals for men on the make, times when everything "stood on its head with its heels in the air." A time in which "larceny grew not only respectable, but genteel, and ruffled it in all the pomp of purple and fine linen." The lands of the burgeoning cotton boom were, he says, a cauldron "of fussing, quarrelling, murdering"—sins of violence. But also, those of deceit—"violation of contracts, and the whole catalogue of *crimen falsi* [crimes of falsehood]." The entire state was in a frenzy of greed to borrow more money to import more slaves to grow more cotton to make more profits and simultaneously in a frenzy of fear over the exploding numbers of the enslaved—proclaimed to be happy, known not to be. This too was "freedom."

Mississippi's new constitution of 1832 was, says Rothman, "among the most democratic in the country." Given that the United States led the world in this reform, Mississippi's supreme law would have been among the most democratic and egalitarian in the world. In seven enumerated articles, the rights of citizens, the powers of government, and the whys and wherefores of its three branches were laid out. For the first time in the state's admittedly brief history, there would be no property qualification for suffrage. All significant offices were to be elective rather than appointive, even judgeships. There would also be no more imprisonment for debt. On the surface, Mississippi seemed to be the very model of a modern democracy.

However, these seven articles were followed by an unenumerated section. Outside of any assigned sequence, it was as if it was being sent to stand alone in the corner, the low-born, benighted bastard of the enlightened Higher Law. Clearly, it was seen that this section didn't fit in with its seven democratic brethren. It was segregated from them. Of course, it was labeled "Slaves," a vital inclusion given that, in the census of 1830, Mississippi, in its "flush times," had officially become a slave-majority state. Strikingly, at essentially the same time, Mississippi was becoming one of the most democratic states in the Union (and in the world) and one of the most thoroughgoing slave societies in all of human history.

Democratic freedoms and slavery. The terms grate against one another. We see them not just as opposites but as contradictions, as proof of hypocrisy. As with Samuel Johnson's scathing remark about the Washingtons and Jeffersons leading the American Revolution, "How is it that we hear the loudest yelps for liberty from the drivers of Negroes?" How could one society contain such antitheses? One way, perhaps, was to be a bifurcated society. In the 1960s, Belgian-American anthropologist Pierre van den Berghe recommended that societies such as the antebellum United States and apartheid South Africa should not be labeled "democracies" but rather "*herrenvolk* democracies," ones which are "democratic for the master race but tyrannical for the subordinate groups."

And the tyranny applied, to a lesser degree, to free blacks as well. In Mississippi, the law stated that every "person of color" within the state's boundaries was presumed to be a slave—unfree until proven free. The burden of proof was on the person of color. Therefore, free blacks had to go before a judge and acquire written certificates of registration ("freedom papers") proving their status, to be renewed every three years. If unable to produce those papers within short order on demand, any free person could be sold into slavery at public auction. Nonenslaved blacks couldn't vote, hold office, serve on juries, or testify against a white man in court. They were also limited to certain occupations. Within democratic Mississippi (and the rest of the South), while bondsmen lived in literal slavery, "free" blacks lived in a police state.

But the reality is this juxtaposition of freedom for some and despotism for others was not unusual in world historical terms. Freedom and specifically slave societies have often been linked, everywhere, for thousands of years. All the great despotisms of the world were societies with slaves, but it is hard not to notice that the world's few true slave societies tended to develop in the few places held up as shining beacons of freedom in world history. All were created by Europeans, the first two within the continent, the last three in their colonies in the Americas. The world's first slave society, the Greek city state of Athens, was also the world's first formal democracy, the two emerging together over the course of the sixth and fifth centuries BCE. According to the pioneering professor Moses Finley, "Bluntly put, the [Greek city states] in which individual freedom reached its highest expression—most obviously Athens—were cities in which chattel slavery flourished." The other ancient slave society was born in the days of Cicero and the Roman Republic, well before the era of the insanely despotic Nero and Caligula.

In the Caribbean, the pattern held true. John Locke's Britain, Benedict Spinoza's Netherlands, and Voltaire's France all created slave-society colonies in the West Indies. Regarding the first two, David Eltis of Emory notes that "of all European states, England and the Netherlands had the strongest conceptions of individual rights, had moved farthest down the road toward free labor, & had become the most secure havens for political refugees by 1700." However, he adds, "these northern European countries [created] the harshest and most closed systems of exploiting enslaved non-Europeans in the Americas. . . . [They] also gave the institution a new scale and intensity." But beyond golden-age Athens and golden-age Holland, Orlando Patterson notes that the juxtaposition of freedom and slavery "was to reach its zenith in the most democratic political constitution and social system ever achieved by a Western people—the experiment called the United States." And more, this modern democracy excelled the ancient civilizations in ruthlessness.

"In no ancient society," says the great Yale historian David B. Davis, "was the distinction between slave and freeman so sharply drawn as in America." One more example of "American exceptionalism."

By 1860, the United States could legitimately proclaim itself to be the world's greatest democratic republic. Simultaneously, though, we were also the nineteenth-century world's greatest slave society. The United States combined the most fluid class system in the world for some with the most inflexible barriers to upward assimilation for others. Unprecedented multigenerational opportunity was coupled with unprecedented multigenerational bondage. We had the largest enfranchised citizenry in the world and, at the same time, the largest enslaved underclass in the world. During the Jacksonian era and after, the freedoms of the free were being maximized over precisely the same decades in which the slavery of the unfree was becoming more intractable, more relentless, and more immense than ever.

From Athens to Rome to the British and Dutch empires to 1832 Mississippi—was this just a coincidence? No, says Finley; speaking of Greece, he notes, "One aspect of Greek history, in short, is the advance, hand in hand, of freedom *and* slavery." Speaking more generally, Patterson judges, "The joint rise of slavery and cultivation of freedom was no accident. It was . . . a sociohistorical necessity." The scholarly consensus is that this was not simply an odd juxtaposition of opposites. Freedom and slavery had an interdependent relationship. Slavery was not just a lapse from principle. It was not merely a cosmetic flaw in the otherwise flawless edifices of Athens and America. In 2006, Davis wrote, "We must face the ultimate contradiction that our free and democratic society was made possible by massive slave labor." Writing in 2016, Harvard's Sven Beckert and Brown's Seth Rockman told us that recent scholarship "has recognized slavery as the foundational American institution, organizing the nation's politics, legal structures, and cultural practices." To punctuate the point, it is not only our wealth but our freedom that rests on a foundation of slavery.

This is a profoundly disturbing notion. If true, it demolishes the pleasant myth of what has been called the "virgin-birth theory" of freedom. The one in which there was no cause for the outburst of the ideal of liberty, only an effect. We have been primed to believe that it sprung naturally from the hearts and minds of ancient Athenians like Athena birthed from the head of Zeus. But, says Patterson, "Our distress stems from a false premise. We assume that slavery should have nothing to do with freedom; that a man who holds freedom dearly should not hold slaves without discomfort; that a culture which invented democracy or produced a Jefferson should not be based on slavery. But such an assumption is unfounded." But even if the rise of freedom did not happen by spontaneous combustion, neither did the conjoined rise of slave societies and freedom. What was the cause that explains this unnerving effect? To say the least, it is a complex issue that begs for more discussion than can be allowed here. But a start must be made.

Patterson insists that we must reconcile ourselves to "the logic of contradictions," which reveals that "it is indeed reasonable that those who most denied freedom, as well as those to whom it was most denied, were the very persons most alive to it." He theorizes that the sheer number and public visibility of enslaved people in a massive slave society served to highlight the advantages of freedom—for both the unfree *and* for the free. The stark contrast was illuminating. Just as black is never so dark as when paired with white, freedom is never so dear as when compared with genuine slavery. The extreme of large-scale slavery, he asserts, fired the desire for personal freedom among the enslaved and the dread of losing it among nonslaves.

But Finley gives us a more nuts-and-bolts explanation, one that is considerably more unsettling. He begins with a simple premise—in preindustrial societies with limited ability to produce material wealth, elites existed only by means of the exploitation of a large underclass. In societies with slaves, foreigners who were imported as slaves were not numerous enough to fill that need, so native-born cultural insiders (who were, therefore, exempt from enslavement) were exploited to lesser degrees as serfs, helots, debt bondsmen, etc. Since their exploitation was still required, though, no ideology of equality developed, no notion of rights, no claims of "citizenship."

By contrast, those places where slave societies developed were, by definition, those where large numbers of foreigners were imported as laborers. As socially dead outsiders, they could be exploited to a much greater degree. Although this opened at least the possibility of raising the status of the native-born masses, another factor fueled the process as well. Bringing large numbers of brutally exploited outsiders into a society is an inherently dangerous venture. Correspondingly, all native-born insiders had to be recruited to help in the policing of the enslaved masses. Thus, the offer of "rights" and participation in governance. Thus, freedoms and democracy. Or at least, their forms.

Eltis doesn't delve into the origins of the ideal of personal liberty among Europeans but concerns himself with the practical consequence of its appearance on the world stage. Once those societies embraced radical individual freedom as an ideal, one to be mutually respected among all its cultural insiders, they unleashed creative energies of enormous potential in the areas of the arts and philosophy, as well as politics, business, and technology. Golden ages of genius, wealth, and power resulted. But that respect for freedom was not universalized—i.e., extended to cultural outsiders. It did not apply to all people, only to "our people." Those societies, then, from Athens to Amsterdam to London to America, also unleashed energies to exploit those outsiders on an unprecedented scale, to expropriate their property and their labor shamelessly—thereby explaining much of the wealth and power. Dark ages of oppression resulted, though to run concurrently with those golden ages of genius and to be born of the same minds. One's freedom was inextricably entwined with the other's bondage.

American slaveholders certainly understood, and endorsed, this dichotomy. As Louisiana State University's William J. Cooper Jr. puts it, "white southerners could not conceive of holding on to their own liberty except by keeping black southerners enslaved." Schooled in universalist rhetoric, we hear this as a rank contradiction, a hypocrisy. But it was only a contradiction if one accepted a universalist ethic. Nineteenth-century southerners did not. Inclusive rhetoric to the contrary, the distinction was the norm, not the exception. The same John Locke who wrote of the God-given rights of life, liberty, and property owned stock in the largest slave-trading company in the world. George Washington, Thomas Jefferson, and James Madison did him one better and owned slaves themselves. The lesson is plain and dreary. Absent a genuine commitment to and enforcement of universal rights, the maximization of individual freedom throughout human history has been both virtue and vice. Freedom's offspring was Mr. Hyde as surely as Dr. Jekyll.

So, was freedom a mere bribe for some to aid in the enslavement of others? Was universal suffrage for one group contingent on collusion in the oppression of another? We need to avoid reductionism here. Other factors could have contributed to the rise of free societies. There is still room for human genius to play its role. But at a minimum, from Athens to America, it seems that the development of a slave society acted as an accelerant for the fires of freedom, helping some societies reach critical mass while those that were not slave societies never did.

PART 3

HOW SLAVERY SHACKLED
THE WHITE SOUTH

CHAPTER 11

The Two Souths of Tom and Lewis, Sam and Elijah

*Even if we stipulate that slavery was horrific for the enslaved
since in the South it was a white-supremacist institution,
didn't it make all whites "supreme"?*

In June 1808, Samuel and Jane Davis's son Jefferson was born near Hopkinsville, Kentucky. Only eight months later, in February 1809, and about a hundred miles east near Hodgenville, Thomas and Nancy Lincoln's son Abraham was born. Both families were Baptists. Both fathers came from Revolutionary-era patriot stock. Both had been born in the South. Both possessed lands in the early nineteenth century because of the violent dispossession of Native Americans in the eighteenth century. Both were small farmers with ambitions. To an uncanny degree, their boys, Jeff and Abe, were twin strangers, even into adulthood when each would become a president. Even their terms of office almost exactly mirrored one another, beginning two weeks apart in early 1861 and ending a few days apart in April 1865. One in victory and glorious martyrdom, the other in defeat and ignominious flight. And each of those tenures would be completely consumed by war. Though, war against each other.

Because, of course, Tom's son Abraham became president of the United States; Sam's son Jefferson of the Disunited States, aka, the Confederacy. Abe in Washington, Jeff in Richmond—about a hundred miles apart. And these parallel, then later colliding life courses had been largely set by their fathers. Because the two similarly patriotic, Baptist, farmer patriarchs had profoundly dissimilar notions of what patriotism, Christianity, and economic opportunity meant.

Tom Lincoln was, as his son Abe would later put it, "naturally anti-slavery." In part, that was because he was a Baptist. Many seventeenth- and eighteenth-century evangelical Protestants—even those exploding in numbers across the South—had condemned slavery as fundamentally contrary to their ideal of Christian equality. Given this moral stance, the Baptist Sam Davis's pro-slavery convictions were "unnatural." His material ambitions depended upon cotton and slaves, so he had to give his old-time religion some modern modifications. Rather than embracing the faith of his fathers, he repudiated it. He moved his family to Mississippi, where evangelicals were undergoing a probondage reformation, where he could therefore enjoy modest, guilt-free success as a slaveholding planter. His sons, Joseph and Jefferson, though, would rise to be members of the slaveholding elite.

But Tom Lincoln's version of the American dream was quite different. Slavery, he thought, was not only unchristian but also an obstacle to, not a means to, economic success for the nonslaveholding white majority. He was convinced that most white men—honest, pious, and hard-working independent farmers like himself—would never be given a fair shake in a political and economic system inevitably rigged in favor of wealthy slaveholders. Believing the institution of slavery to be undemocratic and hostile to his own economic interests, he migrated north of the Ohio River where slavery had been banned by the Northwest Ordinance of 1787—a place that represented his freedom and opportunity just as it did for a runaway slave. Tom was not alone in this judgment. Even as slaves "self-liberated" themselves by fleeing north, white migration from slave to free states was three times higher than from free to slave. Over the same span, seven out of eight white Europeans who came to this country went to the North, not the South. The reason was the dead hand of slavery. A dead hand, that is, for those who owned no slaves; an enlivening hand, though, for those who did.

In the end, to make this familial, Tom Lincoln didn't want his son to become like my cousin Lewis Wiggins who was a poverty-stricken "turpentine laborer" in North Carolina. And Sam Davis very much did want his son to share the success of my third-great-grandfather Elijah Anderson, who was a well-to-do planter in Mississippi. As to the circumstances that had brought them to their divergent stations in life, we have to begin with whiteness.

In this land of upward mobility for white men, Lewis and Elijah represented families that for generations had embraced the promise of migration, the most common means of advancement for Americans from the seventeenth to nineteenth centuries. The reality was that if you were a hardworking but poor white man in Philadelphia or rural North Carolina in the nineteenth century, you were likely to stay poor if you stayed put. Upward mobility was usually achieved with a detour through horizontal mobility. You had to migrate to where new, cheap lands were "opening up." Of my Anderson ancestors, my fifth-great-grandfather had immigrated from Scotland in the mid-1700s to South Carolina. His descendants moved on to Tennessee and then to Alabama and finally to Mississippi in the 1840s. Of the Wigginses, my eight-great-grandfather arrived in Virginia from England in 1635. But by the end of the century, the family had moved farther south in the Commonwealth and then on into "poor Carolina," first the Tidewater, then the Piedmont. Part of the family (including Cousin Lewis) stayed there, but my direct line migrated to Georgia, then Alabama, and finally to Mississippi soon after the end of the Civil War.

But whatever their level of wealth, we must acknowledge that their opportunities came at others' expense. The Andersons' migration across four American states and territories was a migration through and to the lands of four Native American peoples—Catawba to Cherokee to Creek to Choctaw. In each, they claimed the land as their own before moving on. Likewise, the Wigginses' trek through five states and territories took them from Powhatan land to Chowanoke, Tuscarora land to Creek, and finally, to Choctaw lands a bit north of the Andersons in east Mississippi. In this system of "settler colonialism," the "opening up" of lands to white settlement began with the emptying out of those lands by means of the forced expulsion of their nonwhite inhabitants.

Though the process culminated in the 1830 Indian Removal Act during the presidency of Andrew Jackson, the clearing of native peoples had begun long before formal "removal." As is well known, Eastern Hemisphere pathogens had devastated the peoples across the Western Hemisphere after 1492. But as is less well known, scholars now agree that across what became the American South, the explosion of the trade in Native American slaves between 1650 and 1750 was also a major contributor to demographic and social collapse of Native American tribes, one that spanned a "shatter zone" from the Atlantic to the Mississippi River—stretching from my ancestors' points of disembarkation in Virginia and the Carolinas to their eventual homes in Mississippi. It was a commercial network established principally by the English but which eventually pulled the native peoples themselves into a cycle of mutual predation or, says Robbie Etheridge of Ole Miss, "an economic matrix of debt, slaving, militarization and warfare."

To be sure, slavery existed among Native American peoples, including those of today's American South, before contact with Europeans. And there is also no doubt that there was warfare among them. However, there is also no doubt, stresses Etheridge, "that the commercial trade in Indian slaves [established by Europeans] was not a continuation and adaptation of pre-existing trading patterns. It was a new kind of slaving." One which, when combined with war and disease, led to a more than 50 percent decline in the population of native peoples. This is the dystopian, apocalyptic backdrop against which both the Andersons and the Wigginses and almost all of my white forbears migrated across the South in search of their American dream. Some to prosper, but some—even with this race-based boon—to flounder. As it happens, access to cheap, stolen land alone did not guarantee great wealth. In this emerging slave society, success also depended upon the adept exploitation of stolen labor—i.e., enslaved Africans.

The Andersons of eighteenth- and nineteenth-century South Carolina, Tennessee, and Alabama never achieved the rank of planter, owning few or no slaves as they migrated, which explains their penchant for moving on. On his arrival in east central Mississippi around 1840, though, my third-great-grand-father Elijah Anderson changed that. In the wake of the Native American removal between 1831 and 1836, whites had acquired title to Choctaw lands, but in the wake of the twin financial panics of 1837 and 1839, a piecemeal "delinquent-white-debtor removal" followed. Elijah was there to scoop up the twice vacated lands at a discount. Having mastered the art of land acquisition on the cheap, he next mastered the science of exploiting forced labor. He would never approach the ranks of the Great Planters of fact and legend; Stephen Duncan of Natchez, for example, owned fourteen plantations in three states with over one thousand slaves allotted among them. But Elijah did quite nicely. By 1860, his one plantation in the Blackland Prairie, in east central Mississippi south of Columbus, covered 540 acres, and he owned forty-seven slaves. As to the true engine of his wealth, though, it is revealing that the enslaved humans, not the fertile land, made up the largest part of his estate of over $2 million (adjusted for inflation).

The Wigginses never matched Elijah's rise, but their pedigree in America was older and more historically impressive. The manifest of the ship bringing the twenty-year-old Thomas Wiggins to Jamestown in 1635 said that it carried "Persons of Quality, Religious Exiles; Political Rebels; Serving Men Sold for a Term of Years; Apprentices; Children Stolen; Maidens Pressed." We can say definitively that Thomas was neither a stolen child nor a pressed maiden, but otherwise, little can be known about his circumstances. The sketchiness of the details of Thomas's life, however, tell us that he was not likely among the "quality" but rather one of the quantity. The Wigginses may have been among the first English families in the colony in sequence, but they were not among the First Families of Virginia in prominence. But even if they began with disabilities, they improved their lot with effort and/or patronage, and by the second half of the 1600s, Thomas Jr. was a landowner in Surry County paying quitrents to the Crown. By the mid 1700s, "we" were slave owners. When my fourth-great-grandfather George Wiggins Jr. marched off to fight for his rights in the Revolutionary War, that included his right to own eight humans. Just in time for national independence, the Wigginses had established their own independence—by reducing others to dependence.

But the family was to be caught in a cycle of advance and retreat within white society in which each single step forward over the generations was frequently followed by one step back. Or two. As the nineteenth century unfolded and my Anderson ancestors ascended, the Wigginses were running as fast as they could just to stay in place, if that. Which meant that some of them, again, migrated. My third-great-grandfather, the son of a slave owner, moved on from North Carolina to Georgia in hopes of improving his station. There, he did farm his own small plot but owned no slaves—due to a decline in fortunes rather than a pang of conscience. His son Edley my second-great-grandfather, then moved to Alabama to acquire his scrap of land but could never afford slaves either. On the eve of the Civil War, each, though, still clung to the status of smallholding "yeomen." But other Wigginses had lost their lands as well as their bonded labor, thereby joining the South's rural lumpenproletariat of poorly paid wage workers.

In 1860, Abner Wiggins—Edley's brother and my third-great-uncle—was a thirty-year-old farm laborer in Alpharetta, Georgia, who owned no land or slaves and whose entire personal estate was valued at fifty dollars (about $1500 today). His cousin Lewis H. Wiggins was still back in eastern North Carolina working as a "turpentine laborer" who owned no real estate, though he did have a personal estate appraised at $118 ($3,700 in inflation adjusted 2018 dollars). At a time when the average enslaved field hand cost $800 (comparable to $23,000 today), he obviously owned no slaves. Lewis's impoverishment must have been all the more galling since, when he was ten years old, his father, Lewis Sr., had been a farmer who, according to the 1840 census, owned his own land and had four slaves. By 1850, though, he owned no slaves and no land, though he was still listed as a farmer—apparently, now reduced to tenancy on someone else's property. And then, ten years later, we find his "Tar Heel" son driven out of farming completely, an unskilled laborer toiling in the pine forests for low wages. Over the same decades during which the Andersons had clambered their way into the slavocracy, at least some of the Wigginses—scions of Jamestown settlers, slave masters, and Revolutionary War veterans—had joined the legions of "poor white trash."

There are many factors that might account for this discrepancy, but center stage must be given to the institution of slavery. A slave society such as this advantaged slave owners, with the greatest advantages accruing to those owning the greatest numbers. A slave society was, by definition, one distinguished by inequality.

In any discussion of wealth gaps in the South, one must begin with the gap between whites and blacks. About 95 percent of blacks in the region lived as slaves, who were, almost by definition, living in poverty. They made up one-third of the total population—40 percent in the soon-to-be seceding states and near or outright majorities in the Deep South.

But in the tales of Elijah and Lewis we see that there was also a great and widening chasm in wealth among whites. The fact is the forlorn tale of the Wigginses of the Piney Woods of Carolina—not of the Andersons of the Blackland Prairie—mirrored the regional trend throughout the decades before the Civil War. In a society in which the most valuable asset was not land or railroads or bank deposits but slaves, 75 percent of households did not own slaves. But even within the slaveholding minority, most owned five or fewer. Only a quarter of masters owned more than ten. Less than 1 percent of southern white men owned as many or more than Elijah Anderson. Slave owners had always been a minority in the South, but the percentages of both slave owners and landowners within the white population were in decline in the decades prior to the Civil War. Long before the post-Reconstruction era that we associate with sharecropping, one-third to one-half of southern white men were already landless by 1860, working as tenants or as itinerate, usually unskilled wage workers, like Lewis Wiggins. The 1850s were boom times, but the greater profits were flowing into fewer and fewer pockets. As the numbers of slaves increased, wealth inequality among whites increased too.

Historian Roger Ransom draws the obvious conclusion: among whites, "there were two 'Souths,' a slave South that experienced growth and expansion and a non-slave South that was far less prosperous." Yes, the white South in the antebellum period, with one-quarter of the nation's population, did have two-thirds of its wealthiest citizens, but it also had an alarmingly disproportionate share of its poorest. The reason, historians agree, was slavery. It's not simply that there were rich and poor. It's that the same system that made fortunes for a few stifled the economic prospects of the many. My fourth-great-grandfather didn't directly cause the hardship of my cousin. But the institution of slavery that raised my grandfather to wealth most certainly contributed to my cousin's poverty.

The reason is not complicated. Slave labor was the most profitable labor to employ. Again, it was the most exploitative—slaves could be forced to work harder, for more hours, for more days, with a higher labor-participation rate per household. Farmers with slaves, therefore, had a competitive advantage over those without. But this cheapest labor to use was the costliest to acquire, giving a competitive advantage to those who already had wealth or were skilled at rigging the system. Then, with slave labor, those that had got more. And, with that accumulated capital, they invested their profits in still more slaves, which of course only compounded the original inequality. For the slaveholders, this made good business sense. For the average white southerner—as well as those enslaved—it was disastrous. In a capitalist slave society, such as the antebellum South, wealth did not trickle down; it gushed upward. And stayed there. "If a master was very wealthy," remarks historian James Oakes, "the chances were that his parents had been as well."

It had been so from ancient to modern times. Throughout history, says Oakes, "as slave economies expanded, they tended to displace the [freeholding] peasantry." In ancient Rome, he adds, "as slavery expanded into the countryside, peasant farmers were steadily pushed off their lands." And then, Oakes continues, "Slavery's tendency to displace the peasantry reemerged in the New World some fifteen hundred years later. It was particularly relentless in the Caribbean." In Brazil, as well, "the steady expansion of slave plantations all but destroyed the small, independent farmers."

This is hardly a new insight. In 1922, in reference to colonial Virginia, Princeton professor Thomas Jefferson Wertenbaker wrote that slavery "practically destroyed the Virginian yeomanry, the class of small farmers who used neither negroes nor servants in the cultivation of their fields," thereby disfiguring Virginia "from a land of hardworking, independent peasants to a land of slaves and slave holders." So, the declining fortunes of the Wigginses were not unique, either in the American South or the world; they were typical of any and every slave society. Counterexamples like that of Elijah Anderson were real enough but were the exception, not the rule, more so the consequence of greater luck in timing than of greater business skill or harder work.

For white southern farmers displaced by the expanding slave society, there was another alternative, though. Wage work. But again, the same slaveholders who took their lands in the South worked to limit their opportunities in this field as well. For all their wealth, the slavocratic oligarchs did not act as the "job creators" of capitalist mythology. With few exceptions, they did not invest their vast monies in ways to develop the economy in a diversified way, but rather to expand their slave society. Gavin Wright of Stanford observes that they were "indifferent or hostile" to investments in industry, infrastructure, and education in the South. Quite simply, there weren't many wage-paying jobs in the region. And those that did exist paid less than comparable jobs in the North. Again, because of slavery. Whether for a skilled blacksmith or an unskilled laborer like Lewis, the ready alternative of enslaved workers depressed earning potential. W. E. B. Du Bois summarized it well: "slave labor in conjunction and competition with free labor tended to reduce all labor toward slavery."

The idea that poor southern whites suffered in a type of bondage as well was common in the antebellum decades. Hinton Helper, the antislavery North Carolinian, said that they endured a "second degree of slavery." Carl Schurz, from the slave state of Missouri, said, "By the necessities arising from their condition," ordinary whites were "the slaves of slavery." Frederick Douglass, the self-liberated slave and leading abolitionist, commented, "The difference between the white slave and the black slave was this: the latter belonged to one slaveholder, while the former belonged to the slaveholders collectively. The white slave had taken from him by indirection what the black slave had taken from him directly and without ceremony. Both were plundered, and by the same plunderers."

These are strong words, and the points are well taken, though they must be taken with a caution: no whites in the antebellum South, however lowly, were literally enslaved. Wherever and whenever, "wage slaves" were not enslaved. Crucially, though they may have been exploited, they were not "chattel." They could not be bought and sold or inherited. Their families were legally secure. They were never collateralized and securitized as investments. Their infant children's mortality rates were never the subject of cost-benefit analysis. They never suffered forcible "social death." They were better off than those who were actually enslaved. But they were surely oppressed by the South's slave society, and they knew it.

It should come as no surprise to learn that many poor-to-middling whites, in the North as well as the South, therefore despised slavery as an institution—even if they cared little about the fate of the enslaved. British historian Robin Blackburn calls this "egotistical anti-slavery" to distinguish it from the "altruistic anti-slavery" of the abolitionists. We shouldn't discount the moral fervor and importance of those abolitionists, but it is this self-interested opposition to slavery that came to prevail in the North. It is why most northerners wanted slavery kept out of the North but also out of the western territories where they, or their children, might move one day. And when southern slaveholders, like Sam Davis's son Jeff, insisted that slave owners, with their slaves in tow, had a constitutional right to move into the territories, these northern "Free-Soilers" refused to compromise. Ruinous war was the result.

Who "drove Old Dixie down"? Far more truly than the armies of the southern-born Abraham Lincoln, the slavocrats' system of slavery did. The same system that the Confederacy was created to preserve provided economic opportunity to a few, brutally exploited many, and denied economic opportunities for many more, like my cousin Lewis Wiggins. And yet he would die for the "cause."

He was conscripted into the Confederate army in July 1862 to serve in the Third North Carolina Regiment of the Army of Northern Virginia. We can guess that he didn't go enthusiastically. What would become of his wife and child, after all? But let's not pretend that we can know his mindset. Even if reluctant, he may have been willing to fight to preserve slavery. Though no slaveholder himself, he had grown up in a slaveholding household. Though dirt poor, he may have been all the more willing to fight for his only claim to status—white supremacy. Maybe not. Maybe he correctly identified the institution of slavery rather than the people enslaved as the barrier to his success. Maybe he opposed the proslavery Confederate cause and slogged off to war only out of sense of manly honor or peer pressure complete with threats of legal—or physical—retribution. Whatever his motivation may have been, he went, and tellingly, he did not desert. Over the next year, military records show that he suffered through several bouts of "rheumatismus"—no doubt a consequence of his turpentine laboring, exacerbated by his infantry marching. And yet, however psychologically conflicted and physically aching, he was there to charge up Culp's Hill at Gettysburg with the Third North Carolina in the summer of 1863. The charge was futile and fatal. Cousin Lewis—figuratively "enslaved" by the slavery he was fighting to defend—was killed on the July 2, four score and seven years to the day after the liberating words of the Declaration of Independence were actually made official.

CHAPTER 12

The One Percent

But in the age of universal-white-manhood suffrage,
weren't all white men equal politically?

My great-great-grandfather Samuel McNees—son of the doubly beloved Delilah Greer and the man who supposedly took his enslaved manservant off to war with him—was a fairly wealthy man in 1861, owner of prime cotton land and almost fifty slaves to work it outside of Shuqualak, Mississippi. When war broke out, he was determined to put that fortune to good use. Family lore says that he personally funded and organized a company of cavalry to fight for an independent Confederacy and so for the preservation of slavery—the system that had made him rich.

He naturally assumed he would serve as captain after his men performed the formality of electing him to that rank. Apparently, though, Sam's countenance was not so commanding as he thought, his charisma not so effervescent. In violation of all that he assumed was right and proper, another "lesser" man was chosen to be captain, and he was denied his preordained position of authority. In a fit of pique, the story goes, he stormed off to "ride with Nathan Bedford Forrest." And he did fight under the command of the future founder of the Ku Klux Klan at least once, at the Battle of Tupelo in 1864. But this captain wannabe spent the war as a private.

Some would say that this was democracy run amok—a mob overriding the wisdom of a "natural aristocrat." Harvard historian David Donald (Mississippi born and raised) famously argues that the Confederacy had "died of democracy"—the self-defeating insistence on electing its army officers being but one example. Without judging the accuracy of this interpretation, it's worth remembering that this was the immediate aftermath of the age of Jackson, of the achievement of universal-white-manhood suffrage. The common man did rule, did he not?

Appearances say, "yes." Reality says, "no." In the Confederate armies, popular sovereignty was allowed space for play, but not much. Only company-grade officers (such as lieutenants and captains) were elected. Field officers (majors, colonels) and general officers were not. Not only were they unelected, but they were also overwhelmingly members of the upper class, which, in the South, meant slaveholders from slaveholding families. In other words, the common man could assert his sovereignty within small units—and bust my great-great-grandfather from the pretense of captain to the reality of private—but was gruffly advised to leave high strategy to his "betters." This provides us with a microcosm of Southern politics because what was true of military affairs in 1861 had always been true of governance. Yes, both small-land holders and landless itinerants were legally entitled to vote and hold office (as discussed in chapter 11), but on the truly important issues, they were almost always goaded/cajoled/intimidated/panicked into deferring to the leadership of the master class—an elite that was getting ever smaller and ever richer as the decades passed. It was the needs of that planter elite that determined the terms of public debate and set the limits to personal liberties and to majority rule.

Somehow the contention that wealth accumulation in the hands of an ever-narrower minority undermines majority rule is controversial today. The idea may be debated among political hacks, but it is, from a historical viewpoint, not debatable. As Supreme Court Justice Louis Brandeis put it a hundred years ago, "We must make our choice. We may have democracy, or we may have wealth concentrated in the hands of a few, but we can't have both." The South chose wealth concentration over true popular sovereignty, though it always maintained—and for propaganda purposes, celebrated—the tour-de-force theatrical performances of mass politics. Smoke and mirrors, bottle rockets and corn liquor all made for a mighty fine diversion from the dreariness of everyday life, made all the drearier by the perpetuation of slavery, which was made all the more certain by the diversion.

Time and again, mass democracy yielded elitist policies. Mississippi's Constitution of 1832 is a perfect case in point. It was, let's remember "one of the most democratic in the country." One would think, then, that majority rule and the interests of the common man held sway here, if anywhere. But what if—noting the stultifying effects on the economic prospects of those common men—the majority had come to favor the abolition of slavery at some time in the future? One would think that the state legislature would then exercise its undeniable right to end the institution. Except that it wouldn't, couldn't. The constitution itself stated categorically that the majority, working through the state legislature, "shall have no power to pass laws for the emancipation of slaves without the consent of their owners." Let's understand that allowing states, acting through their own legislatures, to decide on the fate of slavery within each state was the essence of the whole states'-rights argument. But Mississippi's fundamental law was saying that neither the US Congress nor the state assembly could abolish slavery "without the consent of their owners." So, it would seem that the constitution was placing individual property rights—as God-given, "natural rights"—above the will of the majority, whether on the state or national level. Well and good. Except that individual slave owners could not manumit an individual slave without legislative approval, and that approval was extremely difficult to get, and even if gotten, the emancipator would then have to pay to get the freedman out of the state. Not only was the majority forbidden to mandate the emancipation of slaves, the individual slave owner was all but forbidden to grant freedom to his own slaves.

The central intent of the constitution was clear. The perpetuation of slavery for the minority was more important than majority rule, more vital than individual liberty. It cannot be restated often enough—this was not just a society in which slavery existed; it was one of the largest, most relentlessly profit-driven, most rigidly racial slave societies ever to exist. Slavery was the foundation; all else was superstructure. This was not a democracy nor a republic. It was an oligarchy, more precisely, a "slavocracy," a society ruled by and for its slaveholding elite.

In any system of popular government, no matter how the electorate is circumscribed, the principle of majority rule prevails. But such a system also requires the minority to be willing to abide by that majority's rule without resorting to violence, to intimidation, or to fraud. The electoral minority has to be willing to lose, in other words, to accept the consequences of minority status, just as surely as the majority has to be willing to respect the liberties of the losers. And here is the crux of the matter. Slaveholders, a permanent minority within the South and an even smaller minority within the nation, were not willing to submit to the majority on the issue of slavery. To protect it, they were willing to withhold their allegiance from any government, to rebel against any government, to violate individual liberties, to mock the rule of law, to lie, to cheat, to steal, to wage wars of horrific destruction. And to clothe it all in heart-palpitating ideals and the mists of mythology. It is a tradition older than the nation itself.

In the 1770s, southern slave owners considered supporting the cause of independence only after legal rulings in London made them suspicious of an increasingly assertive Parliament's intentions toward slavery. Simultaneously, though, they also made plain to their compatriots in the northern colonies that they would not support any war for independence without guarantees for slavery in a newly independent country. Candidly put by Thomas Lynch, delegate to the Second Continental Congress from South Carolina, "If it is debated whether the slaves are their [slave owners'] property, there is an end of the confederation." For "patriots" like Lynch, slavery's preservation was the sine qua non—the only question was whether it was safer inside or outside the British Empire.

In 1787, the circumstance was much the same. The slave-owning elite asserted that they would not ratify the Constitution without assurances that slavery would remain a local matter and completely insulated from interference from the new, stronger national government. David W. Blight of Yale reminds us, "the nature of federalism—the attempted balancing of state and federal power—at the heart of the Constitution is itself rooted in the protection of slavery." As we've already seen, ensuring the safety of slavery was always the ultimate aim of states'-rights ideologues. Slavery was more important than the Constitution as such, more important even than a united and independent America. Is it any wonder that slave owners would be willing to sacrifice the Union for slavery in 1861? In the meantime, though, they set out to dominate government at every level.

As to this elite, it needs to be repeated that in 1860, only 25 percent of white southern households owned slaves. But within that slaveholding minority, only 12 percent of the 25 percent were "planters" who owned more than twenty and one-tenth of 1 percent owned more than one hundred. But it was this small minority of planter slave owners who dominated not only the higher ranks of the officer corps of the Confederacy but also controlled southern state governments throughout the antebellum period. Says historian James Oakes, "virtually every southern governor was a slaveholder, as were nearly all the justices of the various state supreme courts. Wealthy slaveholders dominated the structures of the two major political parties throughout the antebellum years. In almost every southern state the slaveholders, especially the planters, filled the legislatures in numbers far beyond their proportion in the general population. Indeed, as the percentage of slaveholders in the South fell more rapidly than ever during the 1850's, their numbers in the legislatures rose all across the region."

But this planter-slaveholder dominance extended beyond the slaveholding states. "There is no question that the slaveholders exercised a degree of political power that far exceeded their proportion of the electorate, both nationally and regionally," continues Oakes. This was even more remarkable since, nationally, slaveholder households represented only 6 percent of all households. And within those households, there were only 385,000 individual slave owners out of a national population of 31 million. Antebellum America was in thrall to what was America's original, and nearly literal, One Percent. How had this been achieved?

Southern slaveholders had employed a variety of techniques to turn their minority status into preeminent power within the national government—not least, the famous/infamous Three-Fifths Compromise that enhanced their representation in the House of Representatives and, therefore, in the Electoral College. The additional electoral votes in presidential elections translated into more proslavery presidents. More proslavery presidents in turn yielded more proslavery Supreme Court justices and cabinet officials.

The numbers tell the tale. For forty-nine of the first seventy-two years of our constitutional system, 1789–1861, the president was a southern slaveholder, a member of the 1 percent. As for the other twenty-three years, an even somewhat antislavery president had occupied the White House for only eight—the single terms of the two Adamses, father and son. The others, to varying degrees, were "doughfaces," northern allies of the South's slavocrats who could be relied upon to support the institution almost as surely as any slave owner. The chief justice was a southern slaveholder for sixty of those initial seventy-two years of the constitutional system. Of the thirty-four men to serve on the court during those years, nineteen had been southern slaveholders. Essentially, two of the three branches of the national government were in thrall to a small minority from one section of the country.

So, they ruled, but ruled how? Wisely? Benevolently? Here, we need to remember one of the characteristics of all slave societies. As Ira Berlin puts it, in a slave society, "the master-slave relationship provided the model for all social relations. . . . From the most intimate connections between men and women to the most public ones between ruler and ruled, all relationships mimicked slavery." On the nature of the master-slave relationship that was mimicked and articulated throughout society, none other than Thomas Jefferson—who never spent a minute of his lifetime in a nonslaveholding household—provided these comments in *Notes on the State of Virginia* (1785), "There must doubtless be an unhappy influence on the manners of our people produced by the existence of slavery among us. The whole commerce between master and slave is a perpetual exercise of the most boisterous passions, the most unremitting despotism on the one part, and degrading submissions on the other. Our children see this and learn to imitate it." The children of the master class, said Jefferson, were "nursed, educated, and daily exercised in tyranny," and thus were "transformed into despots." As Americans, we are taught that, in Lord Acton's words, "power tends to corrupt, and absolute power corrupts absolutely." In theory, at least, what was slavery other than a daily exercise of absolute power of one over another? Are we supposed to be surprised to learn that the masters were corrupted by the experience as surely as the enslaved were degraded? And not only corrupted in their relations with their slaves but also with the white nonslaveholding majority. So, how did this self-corrupted "aristocracy" rule?

"Exercised in tyranny" and thus "transformed into despots," the slavocrats ran roughshod over the most basic liberties that Americans, supposedly, held dear. On the issue of slavery, the master class did not tolerate back talk from slave or free, black or white. Dissent on the topic was not healthy; it was heresy. Princeton's Eric Foner is emphatic: on the subject of slavery, a "veritable iron curtain" was drawn around the entire South, imposing "the most thorough-going repression of free thought, free speech and free press ever witnessed in an American community." Antislavery orators were physically threatened and sometimes murdered. Newspaper offices were burned; books were banned; college professors were fired. Private mail sent into the South from the North was routinely opened by postmasters and censored. But again, the despotism extended beyond the slaveholders' home region. In "Bleeding Kansas" in the 1850s, the proslavery minority in the territory—with the full-throated endorsement of the South's leaders—blatantly stole the election for delegates to the territory's constitutional convention. They then enacted a supreme law that barred opponents of slavery from public office, from speaking out on slavery, and from jury service. Those who gave aid to fugitive slaves were to be hanged. Anyone who criticized any of these laws was subject to two years in prison. To keep their slaves in shackles, the master class was more than willing to shackle white citizens as well, in the North as well as the South.

The slavocrats had widened their power beyond their region to the nation, and they then extended their power beyond the nation to the hemisphere. Princeton's Matthew Karp details their influence over American foreign policy. This was all the more vital since the abolitionist movement was becoming increasingly international. After the abolition of slavery in its Caribbean colonies in 1833, Britain was at least somewhat more active in suppressing the transatlantic slave trade and in supporting efforts to end slavery elsewhere in the Western Hemisphere, and a trend toward emancipation was apparent across the Americas. To slaveholders in the American South, though, this was anathema. With proslavery presidents, secretaries of state, and secretaries of war at the helm, Karp adds, the United States did all in its power to counter these efforts. The US Navy was ordered to help oceanic slavers—despite our own prohibitions dating back to 1808. The United States actively encouraged the maintenance of slavery in its remaining strongholds of Spanish Cuba and Brazil. In this cold war of the 1840s and '50s between the United States and the UK, therefore, the United States was the "evil empire," promoting literal, rather than figurative, slavery.

By 1861, then, it was increasingly apparent that slavery and its slavocratic overlords posed a threat to white men's liberties, even as they enslaved black men. This is what had roused the average white northerner to anger, what had fueled the rise of the Republican Party of Abraham Lincoln. Historian Leonard Richards puts a fine point on the resentment: "Men and women [in the North] could differ on scores of issues, hate blacks or like them, denounce slavery as a sin or guarantee its protection in the Deep South, and still denigrate the 'slavocracy.'" They may or may not have loved the slave, but they hated the slave masters—the 1 percent—"with a passion."

CHAPTER 13

The Miseducation of the South

*But with even basic literacy denied to the vast majority
of blacks, didn't all whites have access to education?*

Pap Finn's face was "white," though "not like another man's white." It was "a white
to make a body sick, a white to make a body's flesh crawl—a tree-toad white, a
fish-belly white." That's how Mark Twain introduces us to Huck's drunken and
abusive father in his novel, *The Adventures of Huckleberry Finn* (1884).

Soon enough, too, we learn that Pap, by his own admission, "knowed
nothing." Though, he did know that he despised a "free n----- p'fessor from
Ohio" whom he hated because he "could talk all kinds of languages, and
knowed everything." There was more—and worse: "They said he could vote,
when he was at home [in the North]." So, Pap raved about the "govment" that
allowed this abomination against the natural order of things, "They call that
a govment! A man can't get his rights in a govment like this." What rights
were threatened? None. All. None in fact, but all in the mind of a Pap Finn.
The "govment" was taking away his rights, he believed, by asserting rights
for others, taking away his rights by simply requiring him to abide by the
same laws as everyone else. Being so lowly, for Pap to be up, someone else
had to be down. An assertion of his rights, therefore, required not equality
with others but the systematic subordination of others. His primary right
was the "right" to be superior.

In the racialized slave society of the American South, the "others" had to
be black. For a black man to be educated, to vote, to hold office, or—in the

ultimate apocalyptic scenario—to be president of the United States would be for the heavens to fall. Pap Finn, then, might have "knowed nothing," but that didn't mean he was necessarily unintelligent. Rather, he was doggedly, fearfully self-satisfied. He recoiled before any notion that might unsettle his mental status quo, and he shielded himself from intellectual novelty with bluster. The height of his arrogance, therefore, was quite literally determined by the breadth of his ignorance. Which brings us back to his face. His striking combination of arrogance and ignorance is explained by that self-sickening whiteness. Pap's is the face of the South's hallowed creed of white supremacy.

Under this doctrine, a white man's superiority was vouchsafed by a cradle-to-grave welfare system of unearned, hereditary privilege, what was, in fact, America's first and longest maintained entitlement program. His supreme status required no moral uplift, no spiritual enlightenment, no hard work, and most certainly, no education. And while Pap Finn may be fictional, the very real Senator Jefferson Davis of Mississippi precisely made this point in opposing a system of public schools in the District of Columbia in 1860. Taxpayer-supported education for blacks was unimaginable, he asserted, but even for most whites, it was misdirected charity. Already possessing the "exact political equality of all white men," those white men could be content in their illiteracy. A well-tutored elite (to include Jeff himself) was enough. It seems that, in the slavocrats' Orwellian universe, all white men were to be equal, but some white men—like Napoleon the pig—were to be more equal than others.

That this commitment to miseducation came from a man from Mississippi, the heart of the Empire of Slavery, is not surprising. But historian John Majewski finds the same mindset to be dominant in the far less slavery-dependent but still slavocratic Kentucky. There, he says, "economic inequality tied to slavery discouraged investment in education. . . . The slaveholders who dominated Kentucky educational policy believed that 'reforming' education meant subsidizing elite institutions so that a relatively narrow group of men could provide the state with enlightened leadership." And the masses conceded the point, thereby conceding their own lack of schooling. "Bluegrass residents seemed to have embraced a slaveholder's vision of enlightenment that explicitly started at the top before trickling its way down to the general population."

Despite this elitist bias against widespread book learning, public education (for whites only) did make progress in the antebellum South. A number of towns, enclaves of the small commercial middle class's influence, acted on

their own. For example, the Natchez Institute—a fine school by all accounts—
was established in 1845. With North Carolina leading the way, the states
also began to authorize the creation of public schools. But in the places
where schools were founded, there was the issue of funding and affordability.
Nationwide, in this era, some public schools were free, indicating that local
property taxes and state appropriations were adequate to their maintenance.
But more often, local and state taxes were not adequate, and public schools
still had to charge tuition. The varying commitment to education, therefore,
can be gauged by a comparison of tax rates. Communities that placed a
higher priority on public schools levied higher taxes, thereby kept tuition low
or nonexistent, and ensured wider access. Low tax rates, however, were an
indication of a lower level of commitment to taxpayer-supported education.

Historian Johann Neem tells us that, in 1850, white northerners taxed
themselves three times more heavily than white southerners on a per capita
basis. And so, in the North, tax revenues covered 90 percent of the public-
school bill, making for nearly universal access. In the South, it was 46 percent,
and thus, access for white children was far more limited. In a South plagued
by ever-greater economic inequality—due to the dynamics of a slave society—parents often couldn't pay for their children to attend public school even
when one had been opened nearby. In 1840, the slave states had 40 percent
of the nation's white population but almost two-thirds of its white adult
illiterates. The discrepancy would be narrowed by 1860 but was still apparent.

But why were southerners so much more averse to self-taxation? No one
likes taxes, but most see them as a necessary sacrifice for projects contribut-
ing to community well-being. When taxes were to be put to a social purpose
that most identified as good, like education, most southerners were not averse
to higher taxes. The dominant slaveholding-planter minority, however, was.
They could afford to school their children privately. But more, an educated
white majority of nonslaveholders—again, whose interests were not served by
the slave society—would be more politically assertive. And possibly, assertive
against slavery. Hence, the problem.

Sarah Hyde's study of education in the antebellum South is revealing.
Following the lead of Natchez, the Mississippi legislature passed a bill autho-
rizing the creation of public schools across the state in 1846. But the levy of
local taxes to fund the schools required the written consent of a majority
of the heads of households in each county—a near impossible hurdle to
clear in a nineteenth-century rural state with poor roads and widespread

illiteracy. Additionally, each county could exempt itself from the "system." Says Hyde, these self-inflicted wounds left "the law inoperable in most of the state." The planters of Mississippi who, as we have seen, dominated state government forbad education for blacks but bequeathed "a broken system" of public education to white children.

Be assured, though, this was not a matter of governmental incompetence. The planter-controlled legislature knew exactly what it was doing. The deviousness of the scheme was seen at the time of its passage. Hyde notes that the bill was called "a law which is no law, for it contains within its own bosom the seeds of destruction. It is made a suicide, holding in its own hand the knife to cut its own throat." Mississippi was a democracy with universal-white-manhood suffrage, and the people were calling for action. So, to placate "the great unwashed," the lawmakers gave them the appearance of public education without its substance. Once created, the dysfunctional system would not only fail to educate the public, but its failure would also discredit the entire idea of trying to educate the public. It was a way to defy the public without enraging it, to insult the public while lulling it to sleep. Which is one way for a minority to reign supreme in a system of majority rule.

In Louisiana, the planters' intent was more honest. In 1845, the state had adopted a new and much more egalitarian constitution, and under its terms, in 1847, the legislature passed an act to create a statewide system of free public schools. Progress was uneven since implementation was left to individual parishes, but by 1849, 56 percent of school age children in the participating parishes were enrolled. It was a good beginning. However, says Hyde, "Alarmed by the impressive reforms realized through the 1845 document, wealthy planters sought to reassert their control." By 1852, their coup was completed with the adoption of a new constitution. Immediately, the legislature began to undo the changes of the previous seven years and, in the process, by slashing funding and state-level supervision, "did irreparable damage to public education in the state." Hyde says simply, "These bills served the planters at the expense of the plain folk." It needs to be emphasized that the elite's lack of interest in, and funding for, public education had nothing to do with fears of racial integration. These were all-white schools intentionally undermined by all-white state governments.

Hyde is at pains to stress that the South was not as uneducated as is sometimes alleged. There were successes. But wholly apart from the lack of any public education for blacks, in both absolute terms and in proportion to population, there were fewer schools for whites in the South than in the North. And those that did exist were more likely to be underfunded and inadequately staffed. The reason was not southerners' stupidity. It was slavery, and the benighted governance of the already well-educated One Percent.

The One Percent's opposition to mass education extended to higher education as well. Beginning in the late 1840s, it was proposed that the federal government should give land to the states for the creation of public "land-grant colleges." These would be institutions dedicated to the application of scientific scholarship to the fields of agriculture and the mechanical arts. They would teach the traditional liberal arts as well, but they would broaden the purpose of, and access to, higher education. A bill to that effect was passed by Congress in 1857. But at the insistence of the southern slaveholders' bloc, then-president James Buchanan, a proslavery dough-faced Pennsylvanian, vetoed it. Southerners insisted it would be unconstitutional in that such a role in education had not been granted to Congress in the supreme law. To educate or not to educate, southerners sniffed, was an exclusively state matter. Let it be understood that these were not to be federally financed or federally controlled colleges. They would be state schools operated by the states and created at the individual state's discretion. The federal-government grant of public lands would simply be a way to help the states get the project started, to help states help the majority of their own white people. Yet, said the South's elite, it was the principle of the thing. The issue was one of states' rights.

Except that it wasn't. Once again, as we have already seen, the issue was really slavery. The Constitution, in fact, had not explicitly given Congress powers in the field of education. Therefore, a federal move to encourage education could be justified only through the use of "implied powers" found in a "loose constructionist" reading of the Constitution justified in pursuit of the "general welfare." Southerners had long feared, though, that a federal assault on the states' systems of slavery could be mounted using precisely the same legalistic tools. Once again, in order to defend slavery, the South's slavocratic politicians blocked a policy that would enhance the economic opportunities of the majority of their white constituents. The farsighted Morrill Land Grant Act would finally become law only in 1862, in the first Congress to convene after Southern secession, after the secession of the One Percent.

PART 4

HOW THE WHITE SOUTH WAS PERSUADED TO SHACKLE ITSELF

CHAPTER 14

The Invention of the White "Race"

But even if racism was used to suppress not only blacks
but also at least some whites, isn't the problem unsolvable?
Because isn't racism natural?

In 1492, when Columbus set sail on his first transatlantic voyage, white people did not exist. They, dog haired or otherwise, were yet to be invented. George Fredrickson of Stanford, author of *Racism: A Short History* (2002), explains that while Europeans were "aware of their own light pigmentation . . . whiteness, as opposed to national and religious affiliations, was not a conscious identity or seen as a source of specific inherited traits." In other words, in their allegiance to "affiliations" based on cultural rather than physical traits, they embraced ethnocentric identities, not racial ones. In fact, he continues, "The notion that there was a single pan-European, or 'white' race was slow to develop and did not crystallize until the 18th century." And, therefore, "no concept truly equivalent to that of 'race' can be detected in the thought of the Greeks, Romans, and early Christians." He might have added that there was also no concept of "race" among Africans, Asians, or Native Americans. So, in 1492, there were no white people, but there weren't any black people either. And if there was no concept of race, no consciousness of being a member of one race defined by skin color as opposed to another, there could be no racism. Fredrickson concludes that there is "no evidence that dark skin color served as the basis of invidious distinctions anywhere in the ancient world." Or, he might have added, in the medieval world.

Frank Snowden of Howard University agrees, saying, "The ancients did accept the institution of slavery as a fact; they made ethnocentric judgments of other societies; they had narcissistic canons of physical beauty. Yet nothing comparable to the virulent color prejudice of modern times existed in the ancient world." Bernard Lewis of Oxford University adds, "Like every other society known to human history, the ancient Middle Eastern peoples harbored all kinds of prejudices and hostilities against those whom they regarded as 'other.' But the 'other' was primarily someone who spoke another language or professed another religion. . . . It would be easy to assemble a fine collection of ethnic slurs from Greek and Latin literature—but they were ethnic, not racial, slurs." Modify the statement slightly, and we also have the attitude of the ancient Egyptians, the Chinese, and the Aztecs toward outsiders—extremely chauvinistic about their "way of life," little concerned with the physical attributes of those who exemplified it.

In 1492, therefore, Europeans identified as, for example, Danes or Venetians, as Roman Catholics or Orthodox Christians, but not "whites"—ever. Likewise, sub-Saharan Africans did not identify themselves as "blacks" or, for that matter, as Africans. They identified themselves by language—Fulani, for example—and/or as descendants of a common ancestor. A shared culture created brotherhood, not a shared bodily trait. And too, not only did the native peoples of the Western Hemisphere not collectively call themselves "Indians" or "Native Americans," they did not identify themselves collectively as "reds" either. They identified as Haudenosaunee (more familiarly today, the Iroquois) or Dakota. For all of these people, a group identity based on skin color made no more sense than an identity based on hair color or an identity based on the tint of one's irises. The idea of a "race" of whites seemed as absurd as a "race" of brunettes or hazels.

It was, therefore, on an ethnocentric, not racial, basis that cultural insiders throughout history had felt justified in enslaving cultural outsiders, a situation that allowed those outsiders at least the chance to assimilate into the insiders' culture over time. Exploitation, and even bondage, within ethnic groups certainly occurred, but the usually more extreme degradation of enslavement was most often reserved for foreigners, a designation that, with rare exceptions, had absolutely nothing to do with skin color. So, when "white" Romans enslaved "white" Britons, they were not enslaving their brothers any more than "black" Ashanti who enslaved "black" Mandingos in Africa or "red" Mexica who enslaved "red" Tlascalans were doing so. Correspondingly,

Europeans didn't initially target Africans or Native Americans for enslavement because of skin color but simply because they were collections of peoples who were alien in culture.

The languages of Western Europe give us a striking example of this historical disconnect between slavery and color. In the slave society of ancient Rome, a person in chattel bondage was called, in Latin, a "*servus*," the root of both our words "serf" and "servant." But after the fall of Rome, over the course of medieval times, it became commonplace for West Europeans to enslave East Europeans. The church teaching that Christians should not enslave their fellow Christians (i.e., should broaden their sense of "insiderness" beyond language and nativity to include all who shared their religion) had not yet fully taken hold. The prohibition was rationalized away by declaring these non–Catholic Christians to be heterodox, if not heretical, and so not true Christians. Since most of these peoples were Slavs (speaking one of the Slavic languages), variations of the word "Slav" became synonymous with "a person in chattel bondage," replacing "*servus*" in virtually all West European languages: "*esclave*" in French, "*esclavo*" in Spanish, "*sklave*" in German, "*slaf*" in Dutch. And in English, "slave." The word originally referred to a white-skinned person enslaved by another white-skinned person. In distinguishing master from slave, skin color could not have been more irrelevant.

Another instructive example can be found in the Middle East and North Africa. During the Islamic Golden Age (roughly, 750 to 1250 CE), the Arabs, Persians, Turks, and Berbers who inhabited this crossroad between continents readily enslaved non-Muslim Europeans, Central Asians, and sub-Saharan Africans with equal fervor. They, therefore, enslaved peoples who had every shading of skin imaginable, including ones who shared their own pigmentation. All without qualm. The common characteristic among the enslaved was their status as religious infidels, not any bodily trait. Despite long-winded and longstanding denials, prejudice against black Africans was apparent, but "race" still never became the predominant factor that unified/divided people into insiders and outsiders. Religious identity remained supreme; slavery was never racialized. Across the region, there were black slaves and white slaves, both black and white slave owners. Free black men who were Muslim could and did own white slaves who were not. Whatever degree of color prejudice existed, it was never institutionalized into racist laws. Clearly, we make a profound mistake when we project our own era's obsession with "race," i.e., skin color or hair type, onto the distant past. Neither race consciousness nor racism are primordial or universal. But if not, where and when did they originate? George Fredrickson explains that biologically defined racial identities are modern and are "mainly, if not exclusively, a product of the West." By the "West," he means Western civilization, centered in Western Europe. But why? How?

Of all those historians who have argued that racial prejudice was a congenital condition—at least for Anglo-Americans, few if any have had the prestige of Winthrop Jordan. The longtime professor at the University of California, Berkeley (and later, the University of Mississippi) made his case in his classic work *White over Black: American Attitudes toward the Negro, 1550–1812* (1968). Since its publication, any who venture into this field of study have had to take account of its theses.

As Englishmen first came into contact with Africans in America, Jordan notes, they harbored all the usual biases that have been nearly universal in world history—religion, language, dress. But these cultural differences inevitably waned over time. Africans in North America, whether by choice or force, eventually learned English, adopted European dress, and were Christianized. Based on historical precedent, these prejudices should have gradually disappeared as Africans assimilated culturally. But of course, English prejudice did not wane over time. It intensified. For Jordan, this indicated that something else, something deeper, was involved.

For Englishmen, he says, long before the colonies of Plymouth or Jamestown or even Roanoke were even contemplated, "black was an emotionally partisan color . . . the handmaid and symbol of baseness and evil." Therefore, when an Englishman first saw a black African, he didn't only notice difference. He saw both inferiority and menace. It was a primal reaction to biological difference. And that biological difference was inalterable, insurmountable. All the rest, says Jordan, naturally followed. Africans were originally enslaved on the basis of their religion, he acknowledges, but "heathenism alone could never have led to permanent enslavement since conversion easily wiped out that failing. If his appearance, his racial characteristics, meant nothing to the English settlers, it is difficult to see how slavery based on race ever emerged, how the concept of complexion as the mark of slavery ever entered the colonists' minds." This trait of Englishness would then become a hallmark of Americanness.

He states that, in this process of asserting "white over black," the white American was driven by "his passion for domination, his sheer avarice, and his sexual desire." But he finds that the most profound of these "urges" was "his yearning to maintain the identity of his folk"—a folk that, even as blacks learned English and converted to Christianity, could not be based on these cultural factors but had to be centered on color. It was quite simple. The visceral reaction to a visually obvious physical difference was fundamental. This, more than anything else, concludes Jordan, "impelled him toward conceiving and treating the Negroes as inferior to himself, as an American leper."

Subsequently, other scholars have echoed Jordan's conclusions. But have others challenged the determinism of his account? They most certainly have. Trinidadian historian (and future prime minister) Eric Williams had plainly staked out the contrasting view in 1944 in his own classic, *Capitalism and Slavery*. "Slavery was not born of racism," he insists, "rather, racism was the consequence of slavery." In 2002, the equally eminent George Fredrickson took on Jordan's thesis even more directly and asserted that any negative associations presumed by the English about black skin in the sixteenth century were "casually held and somewhat fluid rather than an expression of a fixed and deeply rooted colorphobia." He also points out that the negative stereotypes of black Africans that did exist were "probably less derogatory and venomous than that applied at this time to the Irish, who were undeniably white."

But the fact remains that, in the end, Europeans enslaved millions of Africans and transshipped them to the Western Hemisphere. Thus was created a racial system of slavery. Surely, one would think, a preexisting racial prejudice was a prerequisite for such an outcome. It was not. Today's growing historical consensus is that this shift in sources for enslaved labor—this Africanization of slavery in the Americas—had little to do with race. It was simply a response to supply and demand. On the supply side, Europeans faced a series of labor shortfalls between 1450 and 1650, during the early centuries of their explorations and colonizations. By 1500, access to their traditional Slavic "slave coasts" along the Adriatic Sea and the Black Sea had been blocked by Ottoman Turkish conquests. But labor raiders had always been opportunistic, being drawn like swarms of locusts tracking drought to prey on peoples in any and every "shatter zone" crippled by the calamities of war and accompanying famine and pestilence, a circumstance that did not discriminate on the basis of race, creed, or color. In the first half of the 1600s, the British Isles themselves were in turmoil. Chronic war and the worst of the Little Ice Age produced hordes of captives, refugees, paupers, and orphans to be exiled to colonial plantation labor. As Christians, they were not enslaved, but since most would not survive their "indenture," the legal distinction made trivial difference. But later in the century, conditions improved, peace prevailed, meaning that far fewer ready victims were available. And then there were Native Americans. Two million had been enslaved, millions more reduced to peonage, but by this same period, those populations had been thrown into demographic collapse by the serial effects of mass enslavement, war, and disease.

By this time, therefore, just as Brazil, the Caribbean, and North America were emerging as true slave societies in need of far more labor, they were in need of a new "slave coast" along which to acquire new laborers to coerce. The solution lay across the Atlantic, in West Africa. Slavery had long existed there, and Europeans were already tapping the market, but in the seventeenth century, an increase in warfare and crop failures created the conditions for the "crisis slavery" that traders desired. Europeans did not start these conflagrations within Africa, but they intentionally poured gunpowder into the flames. Literally. After 1700, more than 20 million European firearms were traded into West Africa by those same merchants. Africans became easier and cheaper to enslave because war became easier to wage because guns became easier to acquire. Accordingly, just as the numbers of European and Native American laborers declined, African numbers exploded.

Market dynamics, not racism, sent the slave ships to Senegambia, the Bight of Biafra, and Congo in ever-greater numbers. As a result, the labor force in America grew ever-more African and, therefore, ever darker in complexion as well. Soon enough, a momentous transformation had occurred across the Americas. Almost uniquely in world history, in the three post-seventeenth-century slave societies of the Western Hemisphere—Brazil, the Caribbean, the southern United States—slave status came to be identified with color, not culture. Slavery in the Western Hemisphere had not only been Africanized, it had been "colorized." Though most peoples with light complexions were not masters, none were slaves; though not all peoples with dark complexions were slaves, all slaves had dark complexions. From this color-coded result, though, we have to ask, was the development of "race consciousness" and "racism" inevitable?

CHAPTER 15

"Racecraft"

Do humans make racism or does racism make us human?

"He don't like n-----s," said Jesse. "He sure don't," added his brother, James. They were discussing their dog, currently mid-snarl and -slobber as two black children walked down the gravel road in Longshot. They quickened their pace accordingly as Jesse and James chuckled. It was impossible to deny; the beast truly did seem to harbor a deep hostility to blacks, though not to whites. So, there you have it—a dog seemingly as naturally racist as Winthrop Jordan's sixteenth-century Englishmen who had molded their own deep-throated snarls into centuries of slavery and exploitation. We all agreed—how else to explain it? But it turns out that the education provided by the mean streets of Longshot had its limits. There is an alternative cause for the prejudicial effect.

"To form groups, drawing visceral comfort and pride from familiar fellow-ship, and to defend the group enthusiastically against rival groups—these are among the absolute universals of human nature and hence of culture." So says Edward O. Wilson, Harvard's famed professor of socio-biology (the study of the biological basis for much of our social behavior). He explains that social identity gives people "a name in addition to their own and social meaning in a chaotic world. It makes the environment less disorienting and dangerous."

As to this "visceral" drive, Wilson adds that it is the "psychological equivalent" of the tribal bonds of yesteryear. This "tribalism," he states as incontro-
vertible fact, "is a fundamental human trait. . . . People must have a tribe."
This does not mean, of course, that the extended kinship group (the basis
for traditional tribes) remains the most important unit of our economic,
political, and social lives. In that narrow sense, we, in the modern, bureaucratic, urbanized West, with our highly mobile lifestyles, are not at all tribal.
But in a more general sense, we are as ever tribal in our need for something
beyond material wealth, beyond the right of individual self-expression—in
our need for communal identity. We are tribal in that we—as surely as the
Pashtuns of Afghanistan or the Pawnees of the Great Plains—need a sense
of belonging to a group, of inclusion among "my people." Today, the old
tribal ties based on kinship may have been eroded, but in the increasingly
"chaotic," "disorienting," and "dangerous" modern world, the need for "visceral
comfort and pride from familiar fellowship" is arguably stronger than ever.
New tribes have therefore emerged, tribes that make the same conformist
demands on their members as did the old. Know that the tribal urge is not
tolerant of individualism. Know too that to group with some is to divide
from others—every "us" will have a "them."

Stanford neuroscientist Robert Sapolsky, in his 2017 summary of the state
of biochemical research in the field, follows the same thread, showing that
humans are instinctively prone to divide our worlds into "Us and Them,
in-group and out-group, 'the people' and the Others." He calls the impulse
"Us/Them-ing" and stresses that it is controlled by the deep-brain amygdala,
is linked to the fear response that feeds aggression, and therefore is not a
product of the frontal lobes of the cerebrum, the seat of our reason. In other
words, our brains are hardwired to identify with groups based on common
traits and to be wary of those who somehow don't fit in with those groups.
This is biochemistry, not social theory. The dictate of nature, not the preference of calm reflection.

"Hallelujah!" sings the chorus of today's white nationalists—a neurological justification for racism, as well as a doctor's prescription for its use
as a sedative in the globalizing and ever-more bewildering world in which
we live. No, not really. Among the crop of world leaders in 2022, few need
to be enlightened about the use and abuse of us/them demagoguery. It is
proliferating. But more to the point—and I'm certain to the great alarm of
those fearmongering politicians—the reality is that the same scientists who

confirm us/them-ing and tribalism as part of our nature ridicule the notion of race. To understand this last point, we need to define some terms. What exactly is "race"? And then, what is "racism"?

Pierre van den Berghe emphasizes two essential elements when he describes a "race" as a group with "innate and immutable physical characteristics," which "are believed to be intrinsically related to moral, intellectual, and other non-physical attributes or abilities." Since these race-defining traits are "innate and immutable," he says, they are permanent—either external, as with skin color in white-supremacist racism, or internal, as with allegedly tainted blood in anti-Semitic racism.

But notice that van den Berghe did not say that the physical characteristics and the nonphysical attributes of a "race" actually are intrinsically related, but rather "are believed to be intrinsically related." The common concept of a "race" does not simply recognize variations in physical appearances. Many really do share the gene for dark skin, but many also share the gene for red hair. And still, we do not declare them to be a red-headed race blessed/burdened with this or that moral quality. Van den Berghe concludes, then, "It is not the presence of objective physical differences between groups that creates races, but the social recognition of such differences as socially significant or relevant." Let me repeat this point for emphasis: biological differences do not define races; rather, they are defined by the "social recognition" of those differences as "socially significant or relevant." And therein lies the problem. With "race," in the last few centuries we have come to attach great significance to something that science tells us is of no significance. Modern scholars dismiss the notion of race as a fallacy.

Genetics can certainly explain the variations in skin color over a range of peoples, but as to the character traits supposedly linked to those shadings, it stands mute. British geneticist Adam Rutherford gets right to the point: "There are no essential genetic elements for any particular group of people who might be identified as a 'race'. . . . As far as genetics is concerned, race does not exist." Science "makes a mockery of race." And therefore, it makes a mockery of the supposed neurological grounds for racial prejudice.

But what of our primitive, fear-inducing amygdala reacting to difference? Doesn't that mean that we are primed to see race and thereby primed to be racists? No. Our brains are wired for xenophobia, the "fear of strangers" (or as many sociologists now prefer, heterophobia, "the fear of difference"). But says George Fredrickson, "xenophobia may be a starting point upon which racism can be constructed, but it is not the thing itself." And this can explain an initial color prejudice between people of different skin tones but can also explain bias against any and all physical or cultural novelty. But a racist doesn't only notice a difference in a stranger and react defensively; as highlighted by van den Berghe, he asserts a hereditary and indelible difference that goes far beyond mere physical appearance. The biases of a xenophobe lessen over time as the "stranger" grows more familiar. The biases of a racist do not.

It also bears repeating that racism—a bias based on physical and moral qualities that are alleged to be permanent—is not the same thing as ethnocentrism, a bias toward cultural or "ethnic" traits that are learned and therefore can be unlearned, amended, changed. Fredrickson makes the crucial distinction that "the religious bigot condemns and persecutes others for what they believe, not for what they intrinsically are." This is the difference between the literally genocidal racial/biological anti-Semitism of modern times and the still-terrible religious/ethnic anti-Semitism of the Middle Ages—which, though, was mitigated by the possibility of conversion.

Sapolsky—who emphasizes the concept of "Us/Them-ing"—also emphasizes that this inclination to divide ourselves into groups does not inevitably lead to either racial identity or race hate or any other form of group prejudice, either xenophobic or ethnocentric. He notes that "we all belong to multiple categories of Us, and their relative importance can rapidly change." Yes, we are tribal, but we all belong to multiple tribes. We group ourselves by kinship, gender, language, religion, territoriality (from locality to region to nation to civilization), shared ideals, economic class, and/or skin color. Our brains tell us to identify with groups, but we are not genetically programmed to identify with any particular one of these groups over any other. And the memberships of these multiple categories of "us" usually overlap. A person who is one of "us" in one category may be a "them" in another. Which takes priority? Does a religion shared with one person top a language shared with another? Or as Marx insisted, does class cut through all else—"workers of the world unite"? Or does skin color trump all others? Our social identities, therefore, are normally fluid, not fixed, and complex, not simple. Out of this muddle of multiple identities, after initial suspicion, people will often settle into a pragmatic, live-and-let-live tolerance if left to themselves, even amid human diversity—even amid an overabundance of separate groups.

It has been repeatedly observed that small children of different "races" do not recoil in horror when meeting for the first time but instead quickly begin to play with one another. But even for adults, Sapolsky also stresses that, no matter the numbers or boundaries of our social groupings, "cultural mechanisms can sharpen or soften the edges." In other words, given that we are *Homo sapiens* rather than muskrats, our cerebrums can override our amygdalae, our reason can rein in our instinct to fear and aggression. Through conscious, rational effort, we can ease any particular us/them friction.

But obviously, through conscious, rational effort we can also exaggerate those differences, thereby intensifying hostilities. And here is the crux of the matter. The desire for social solidarity—like fire—is natural and is not a human invention. But—like with fire—humans have invented methods for making it, tending it, spreading it but also for extinguishing it and preventing it. We can use it for good or for ill. The "fiery" leader may be an arsonist or he may be a forger of shelter from the storm. No primal urge determines our allegiance. We choose which one to follow. Throughout history, preeminent leaders have been those who have found a way to get people to place priority on one of these allegiances in preference to others—possibly to the exclusion of all others. For inspirers of mass movements, whether religious or political, creating a sense of "tribal" bonds has been key to their success. And too, it has been key for organizers of global conquests and epic slaughters. A degree of suspicion of all outsiders may be natural, but a long term, focused prejudice against outsiders based on one particular characteristic is not. Conscious effort is required. Now, though, we have left the turf of neuroscience and ventured onto the fields of history. And of great literature.

In the first pages of George Orwell's novel *1984* (1949), we are introduced to the Two Minutes Hate, during which Big Brother appeared on television sets across the country to whip the public into a frenzy of outrage. This literally, legally "must-see TV" was, says Orwell, "a hideous ecstasy of fear and vindictiveness," invoking "a desire to kill, to torture, to smash faces with a sledge hammer," with the fear and loathing seeming "to flow through the whole group of people like an electric current, turning one even against one's will into a grimacing, screaming lunatic."

The Hate was inevitably directed against the enemy of Big Brother who was, therefore, necessarily "the enemy of the people." But also, it was channeled toward one of the country's two foreign enemies, depending on which one was the bugaboo of the moment—Big Brother always being at war with one or the other. But this, of course, makes the crucial point. One must have enemies, but the identity of the enemy was far less important than that they were "them" and not "us." In the end, any of them would do. Orwell observes that "the rage that one felt was an abstract, undirected emotion which could be switched from one object to another like the flame of a blowlamp." And the switching—toward this demon, then that devil—was orchestrated by Big Brother.

The public's malice, then, could be turned on or off, this way or that, just as with that trained, snarling dog in Longshot. Or just as with trained, snarling people the world over. In Rwanda in East Africa, Tutsis and Hutus shared both language and religion but were traditionally separated by economic and political class, though they commonly intermarried, and there was frequent upward and downward mobility between the two groups. Beginning in the 1920s, though, their Belgian colonial rulers taught them that they constituted two separate "races." They were encouraged to despise one another due to, supposedly, immutable biological differences. After independence, the teachings continued. In the 1990s, Hutus murdered hundreds of thousands of Tutsis. In order for Germany to be unified in the nineteenth century, people who differed over religion were taught to value their common language above all else. Then, in the twentieth century, "Aryan" Germans were taught to hate native-born German-speaking Germans who, though, were of the "alien" Jewish "race." Millions died. In each instance, ordinary Hutus and Germans chose to listen to their demagogic Big Brothers and to weaponize their differences. This is how genocides are born. Black Africans mutilated black Africans, and white Europeans gassed white Europeans because of "racial" differences. Few things better illustrate the deranged black magic of "race." It is very much in the eye of the beholder because it is very much a figment of the mind's fantasies.

We moderns like to pose as people who have transcended the musty-headed mythic thinking of our ancient and medieval ancestors. But race is a myth and a very modern "tribal" myth at that, although one that seemed bizarre to those musty-headed ancestors. They had their myths of monstrous "others" on whom to project their darkest anxieties, but now we have ours. Both their fiends and ours are eons beyond the realm of objective reality, but that could not be more irrelevant. In relation to the ideals of empirical science, theirs were pretruth, ours are posttruth. Both, though, for that very reason, are capable of enormous destruction. The scholarly sister duo of Barbara Fields (historian) and Karen Fields (sociologist) weigh in on the subject in their book, *Racecraft*, published in 2012.

The Fieldses acknowledge the influence of British anthropologist Ashley Montagu, who in 1942 noted, "In earlier days we believed in magic, possession, and exorcism; in good and evil supernatural powers; and until recently we believed in witchcraft. Today many of us believe in race. Race is the witchcraft, the demonology of our time, the means by which we exorcise imagined demoniacal powers among us."

Witches, the Fieldses observe, were and are fictions. But witchcraft was and is fact. Which is to say that the supernatural powers that make a witch a witch do not exist, but people who believe in the reality of those powers and who practice the craft of wielding them most certainly do exist. And others believe in their reality and act on that belief, all facts to the contrary. The thousands of nonwitches executed in the hysteria of early modern times are testament to that. But how had this happened? How had so many people all over the world throughout history come to take the real-world existence of fictional witches for granted? The real-world practice of witchcraft had convinced them. That and our human weakness for conjuring "devils" on whom to cast our phobias and resentments, our responsibility for our own faults and failures. Witchcraft, then, created witches, not the other way around.

So, it is with the fiction of "race" and the fact of racism, say the Fieldses. The "fingerprints" of this process constitutes "racecraft." How have so many in modern times come to believe in "races"? In much the same way so many came to believe in witches; the practice of racism convinced them. The preaching and practice of racism created race, not the other way around.

And in America, that myth is the product of a four-hundred-year Hate. And it's still playing on television every night. For four centuries, every abstract rage and undirected anger has been diverted and projected, artfully adjusted and aimed, "like the flame of a blowlamp" at the racial other. History tells us that racial consciousness and racial animus were nonexistent in the premodern world. Neuroscience tells us that neither is imprinted in our DNA. A degree of xenophobia is natural to humans. Ethnocentrism has been very nearly universal in human cultures across time. Racism is neither. It is not natural to believe that people sharing a skin color—white, black, brown, red—therefore share a distinct social identity with unique character traits, much less traits that are superior or inferior to others. It has come to seem natural because the society that we have created has told us, and still tells us, that it is so from the moment of our birth. Eras and places of its greatest prevalence are evidence of its intentional mass production—and voluntary mass consumption. If racism has and does dominate the consciousness of this country, the fault is not in our stars, nor in our genes, but in our selves.

It's time to watch the craftsmen of racism in action.

CHAPTER 16

The First Families of Racism

*If the practice of racism created "race," what were
the mechanisms of that process?*

My ancient and early medieval Celtic and Anglo-Saxon ancestors were ugly, lazy, stupid, dishonest, thieving, and bestial. At least, those who were enslaved were, and I'm sure some were enslaved at one point or another. And at least, they were all these things according to their enslavers, whether ancient Romans, early medieval Vikings, or late medieval Normans; according to the Domesday Book of 1086, about 10 percent of the population in England were slaves. I can be sure of this because Yale's David B. Davis points out that, throughout history—allowing for some variation for time and place— masters routinely subjected their slaves "to certain common [negative] stereotypes regardless of race, ethnicity, or time period." And that list of insults included but was not exhausted by "ugly," "lazy," "stupid," "dishonest," "thieving," and "bestial." The ancient Romans enslaved peoples of every variety of color and ethnicity, but almost all—whether Greek, German, Ethiopian, or some primeval Wiggins—were stigmatized by their masters in remarkably similar language. But then, according to Orlando Patterson, the image of the "degraded man-child" was "an ideological imperative of all systems of slavery"; always and everywhere, it was routine to call a male slave "boy" even if he was an old man. Therefore, the same stereotypes wielded by the tenth-century Norse to dishonor my enslaved Celtic and Anglo-Saxon ancestors were then wielded by my nineteenth-century Celtic and Anglo-Saxon southern ancestors against their slaves of African ancestry.

Such systematic dishonoring, in other words, was an age-old feature of all slaveries throughout history. This wasn't some inexorable destiny at work, however. It was a well-honed propaganda tool as necessary to the assertion of dominance as was any whip or any chain, a form of psychological warfare waged in conjunction with the constant threats of physical violence. Its use was very much deliberate. Again, regardless of the pigmentation and ethnicity of masters and slaves.

But by the seventeenth century, this studied process of degradation was being carried out in an increasingly racialized system of enslavement in the Americas. As we've seen, that development had been primarily due to economic calculations rather than racial prejudice. But it soon became apparent to the master class that this older, well-practiced prejudice against any and all slaves could now be molded into color prejudice, all while relying on the tried-and-true stereotypes of millennia past. First would come the establishment of race consciousness. Over time in this racialized system, by the crude calculus of stereotyping, white came to equal free and free had always equaled superior; black came to equal slave and slave had always equaled inferior. The pretense of superiority once associated with all masters everywhere regardless of skin color, therefore, became identified with white skin, regardless of differences in language, religion, class, or status. Out of a crazy-quilt array of peoples, "whites" would be born. The stain of inferiority once associated with all slaves everywhere regardless of skin color became identified with black skin regardless of cultural differences. Out of a myriad of languages, religions, kinship groups, "blacks" were invented.

This deliberate deployment and exaggeration of color prejudice would then be one of the principal bulwarks of the maintenance, growth, and extraordinary profitability of all the slave societies of the Americas. British historian Robin Blackburn says that, due in large part to that racial element of the exploitation, "New World slavery developed a novel ferocity, scale and focus" as "enslavement intensified." He reminds us that, here, because of lower manumission rates, "slavery had a new permanence. The great majority were destined to die in slavery, as were their children. . . . The New World did not simply reproduce the features of slavery in [the Old World]. It brought about what might be termed a degradation of slavery, violating on a massive scale traditional notions of what slavery meant."

And for all the damage done by this "novel ferocity," it evoked a fierce counter. As has been seen, we humans have an elemental need for a social identity, a sense of belonging to a group. On the most basic level, that need is filled by family. And it is on that most basic level of identity that all systems of chattel slavery mounted their most corrosive attack on the souls of their victims. By its nature, chattel slavery destroyed families, a dynamic that fed the financial interests of the master but that also, by isolating the enslaved from their prime social support group, rendered them all the more vulnerable and, so, exploitable. But even as the kinship network of the enslaved was under unrelenting assault, the enslaved were trying all the harder to reestablish new social groups, new kin, even if "fictive kin." Few things illustrate this better than Patterson's insight that those who shipped together in the horrors of the transatlantic slave trade formed "familial" bonds of such closeness as to prohibit sexual relations among them as incestuous. Having lost families that were based on shared ancestry, they formed new ones based on the bonds of their harrowing shared experience—an experience they came to share not due to common language, religion, folkways, or literal kinship, but due to color. Having lost blood brothers and sisters, they found and identified with new "brothers" and "sisters." In the face of predatory whiteness, the once mutually hostile Yoruba and Fulani and Bambara embraced a "black" identity in self-defense. Very much as James Baldwin put it in the 1960s, "As long as you think you're white, I'm going to be forced to think I'm black."

And so, the racial identity that had been invented as an ideological cudgel to enable "superior" whites to exploit "inferiors" simultaneously became an ideological shield to enable blacks to resist the blows of that racism. Over multiple generations, as they became English-speaking Christians and yet were still denied assimilation, an ever-more distinctive culture would develop based on blackness. And develop, to a degree, as a self-conscious counterculture that proudly rejected the prevailing norms of the white society that rejected them. However, race didn't only serve to reinforce the shackles of the enslaved, it was also used to sabotage cooperation with their potential allies among the nonenslaved, the ones who suffered oppressions and slights of their own.

My English ancestors were "vicious," "dissolute," "miserable," "ignorant," "seditious" and were given to "laziness, drunkenness, debauches, and almost every kind of vice." At least, those who were poor were, and I'm sure some were poor at one point or another. And at least, they were all these things according to their English "betters" in the seventeenth century. As sunset follows sunrise, the High disparage the Low. As to these English wretches—designated with the label of "nauseous to the beholders" by an Act of Parliament—many were shipped off to the colonies as various sorts of bonded laborers, some to the Chesapeake, to the tobacco fields of Virginia and Maryland, but most to the West Indies. And there they were to be joined by many more thousands of, no doubt, equally nauseating Irishmen and Scotsmen. One of the latter was Duncan Bohannon, a Highlander and my eighth-great-grandfather. Native to the shores of Loch Lomond, he fought on the losing side of the Wars of the Three Kingdoms, was captured by Cromwell's New Model Army at the Battle of Worcester in 1651, and then was sentenced to seven-years exile in the Caribbean, to virtual slavery in the cane fields, likely death. There, he not only labored beside others from the British Isles whose "lives were forfeit," but also beside African slaves.

As already pointed out, originally, Europeans were willing to exploit any and all varieties of unfree labor of any and all colors and ethnicities in their colonial ventures. As Trinidadian historian Eric Williams emphasizes, the early plantation workforce in the Americas included Africans but, in its totality, was "brown, black, white and yellow; Catholic, Protestant and pagan." All treated brutally. Again, it needs to be emphasized that, at this time, the distinction between "slave" and all other categories of unfree laborers was still a cultural one, not a "racial" one. Africans were suitable for enslavement because they were non-Christian, not because they were black. Duncan Bohannon was judged unfit for such degradation because he was Christian, not because he was white.

Which meant that in the early to mid-1600s, black Africans could escape slavery and the stigma that accompanied it. The great majority remained in slavery, but if these non-Christian "outsiders" were baptized—thereby becoming religious "insiders" and changing "tribes," so to speak—they could sue for their freedom. And in many cases, it was granted. A black-skinned Christian freeman could hold a white-skinned Christian indentured servant as a bondsman. A free black man could vote, hold public office, testify in court against whites, legally defend himself against assault by a white man, own guns, and serve in the militia. To be sure, this was no multicultural utopia, but contrary to Winthrop Jordan's contention, poor whites and blacks were not instantly and relentlessly hostile toward one another. With no legal distinctions between white and black workers as such, racial identity was blurred at best. In seventeenth-century Virginia, skin color was still only one among the many "heterophobias"—biases against difference—out of which group loyalties have been formed throughout our species's existence. In fact, both servants and slaves were acutely aware of their common plight as exploited workers. As Yale's Edmund Morgan reports, among bondsmen of all sorts, "it was common for [white] servants and [black] slaves to run away together, steal hogs together, get drunk together . . . make love together."

But what if the nonplanter majority—black and white—had formed an "us" on the basis of economic and political self-interest in order to challenge "them," their aristocratic exploiters? What if, asks Morgan, "[white] freemen with disappointed hopes should make common cause with [black] slaves of desperate hope . . . ?" In other words, what if they had joined together to mount a biracial insurrection? This was the great fear of Virginia's governing elite by the late 1600s. What to do?

Says Morgan, for Virginia's planters, "the answer to the problem was racism." They set out "to separate dangerous non-slave whites from dangerous slave blacks by a screen of racial contempt. . . . By a series of acts, the [colonial] assembly deliberately did what it could to foster hatred of whites for blacks." The solution was the time-honored strategy of divide and conquer, divide and rule. In this case, destroy nascent class solidarity by dividing it along color lines.

The members of Virginia's House of Burgesses did so by requiring colonists to define themselves and others, primarily, in terms of color, thereby dividing people with white and black skin into separate legal identities, with separate sets of rights, privileges, and immunities. All were now, in effect, required to make "race" rather than religion, language, or class their principle social identity. People with light complexions became "whites," and people with dark complexions became "blacks." In that "series of acts" through the late 1600s and first decades of the 1700s, the Virginian House of Burgesses decreed that no black man—even if free and Christian—could hold a white man in service. No black man—free, servant, or slave—could vote or hold office, testify against whites, raise a hand against any white (even in self-defense), or serve in the militia.

More, the colonial assembly intentionally pitted the newly minted "races" against each other. The seizure and sale of black slaves' livestock was mandated, with the proceeds going to white servants—establishing financial incentives for racial hostility. Loving marriages between whites and blacks were banned, while a white master's rape of his female slave remained legal—thereby criminalizing interracial affection while legitimizing interracial sexual abuse. As they codified racial identity, they discredited the alternate idea of religious identity by stipulating that Christian baptism did not imply freedom for a black slave.

But surely many poor, illiterate whites remained unaware of, unheeding of these laws. The assembly was very much concerned about such a "pretense of ignorance." Therefore, says historian Theodore Allen, "the general public was regularly and systematically subjected to official white-supremacist agitation." It was to be drummed into the minds of the people: "The ruling class took special pains to be sure that the people they ruled were propagandized in the moral and legal ethos of white-supremacism." In the Act Concerning Servants and Slaves of 1705, it was required that once in the spring and once in the fall of each year, parish clerks read the new laws on race aloud, in full, to the assembled congregation of each church. Sheriffs were to do the same at the courthouse during the summer term of court. The effect of the message was plain: blacks' wealth was gained at the expense of whites; blacks' participation in governance would be detrimental to whites; blacks were unworthy of whites' love but deserving of rape by whites; blacks with weapons were not to be seen as fellow citizens able and willing to defend themselves but were to be feared as a danger to whites. It was, you might say, the Thrice a Year Hate.

Here, we are witnessing one of the historical contributions to the invention of racial identity and, therefore, of "identity politics." Today, many like to pretend this practice is a recent development and one pioneered by minority groups. But this country was founded on identity politics, and the first racial identity was white—not black or red or brown or yellow. And that whiteness was defined by its difference from menacing nonwhiteness, even as whites were appropriating land from and enslaving nonwhites by the millions.

For their own selfish reasons, then, the ruling class sought to propagate racial consciousness and resentment among the masses of whites. In the context of the legally mandated discrimination of the Jim Crow decades, C. Vann Woodward once spoke of the elite's granting of "permissions to hate." Here, the Virginian elite was doing more than granting permission; they were giving instructions to hate. To be sure, the masses obliged. They might have peered through the cynical ploy, but they didn't. They took the bait as a short-term reward and chose to ignore the long-term penalties—which were described in an earlier chapter.

But this ruse did more than keep blacks and poor-to-middling whites apart; it would serve to persuade those whites to help police the ever-growing numbers of slaves who were arriving by the late 1600s—to entrench and enforce the very system that would deny them opportunities in the future. Allen adds, "In time, this 'white race' social control system begun in Virginia would serve as the model of social order to each succeeding plantation region of settlement." Allowing for some variation from place to place, explicit "race laws" were passed and applied in Barbados, Dominica, Jamaica, and Guyana in the Caribbean. They were applied in the rest of the Chesapeake, the Carolinas, and Georgia on the continent, later to be spread into the cotton lands of the Gulf South. Thereby, working-class men and women of different "races" were not only split from each other but were pitted against one another. The labor lords benefitted. Those who labored did not. At least, not most.

Make no mistake, though, some of those nonelite whites did profit over the longer term in very tangible ways from the new racial dispensation. Among them was the aforementioned Duncan Bohannon, my eighth-great-grandfather. Remarkably, he managed to outlive his sentence on the sugar plantations of Barbados. Freed, he had married in 1658 and migrated to Maryland, then to Virginia where he was granted a small piece of land. His story is instructive. His own bondage, like that of African slaves, had been horrific. However, his hell had lasted seven years, while theirs would last a lifetime, however long or short it may have been. Duncan was then able to enter into a matrimony that was not only holy but legal. The marriages of enslaved Africans, no matter how loving, would never be lawful and could be broken on the whim of the master. The children born to Duncan's union would truly be his own and would be born into freedom. The children born to slaves were not actually theirs in a legal sense, and their enslavement would be passed on for generations. And Duncan was allowed to own land and to work it for his own benefit. Or to have others work it for his benefit. This once enchained, exploited prisoner of war was also granted a "headright"— the privilege to bring in his own enchained, exploited laborers, whether slaves or servants. And in turn, by the early 1700s, his son Duncan Jr.—my seventh-great-grandfather—was the proud owner of an estate with eighteen black slaves. Duncan and his heirs personified both the American dream and the American nightmare out of which the pleasant reverie was summoned.

It should be made clear that these legal steps to codify racial slavery in Virginia were among the first in a long, incremental process of creating race consciousness and racism. Columbia University's Barbara Fields, in her now-classic 1982 essay, "Ideology and Race in American History," places her emphasis on developments in a later period of time—at the height of Enlightenment-era revolutionary fervor. She asserts, "American racial ideology emerged at a specific historical moment as a way of legitimizing the enslavement of individuals of African descent at a time when traditional explanations were becoming untenable. . . . Those holding liberty to be inalienable and holding Afro-Americans as slaves were bound to end by holding race to be a self-evident truth." By boldly proclaiming "all men are created equal," our Founding Fathers made it necessary to dehumanize enslaved blacks—to remove them from the ranks of men—so as not to be exposed as hypocrites. One cannot help but be reminded of the quip of eighteenth-century French political philosopher the Baron de Montesquieu about European enslavers' other universalistic ethic: "It is impossible for us to believe these creatures to be men, because, allowing them to be men, a suspicion would follow that we are not Christians."

Prior to the promulgation of the Enlightenment and its universalist ideals, there had never been a need to justify slavery. The institution was ancient, widespread, traditional. Freedom for some and bondage for others was taken for granted within avowedly hierarchical societies. But in light of the Enlightenment, slavery's extreme denial of liberty became an oddity, a problem. For the first time in over five thousand years, slavery had to be justified. The cultural differences and correctible inferiorities of ethnocentrism couldn't fill the bill, but the racial notion of inborn, immutable difference and inferiority could and did, says Fields. George Fredrickson notes the same dynamic, saying, "What makes Western racism so autonomous and conspicuous in world history has been that it developed in a context that presumed human equality of some kind. . . . It is uniquely in the West that we find the dialectical interaction between a premise of equality and an intense prejudice toward certain groups that would seem to be a precondition for the full flowering of racism as an ideology or worldview." It seems that a slaveholding denizen of the nascent Land of Liberty was all but required to embrace racism himself. But too, to propagate it among his fellows.

According to historian Robert Parkinson, that propagation proved particularly useful when engaging in a War of Independence in the name of that liberty. As the Second Continental Congress convened in May 1775, its delegates—at least those who were coming to favor independence—faced a problem. The Battle of Lexington and that of Concord had already been fought, and issues such as taxation without representation really were points of serious contention, but outside of New England and parts of Virginia, the majority of colonists did not favor independence in mid-1775. They were united with the British by ancestry, language, religion, and a glorious common history—from Beowulf to Punch and Judy. They had fought together against a common foe in war as recently as 1754–63. And even with the Intolerable Acts, tea taxes, and the Boston Massacre, colonists were among the freest peoples on planet Earth. They were more likely to own land and bore a lower tax burden than the English themselves. Also, the colonies had little tradition of working together. Often, each of the thirteen had closer ties to Britain than to one another.

Thus, "patriots," like Thomas Jefferson, John Adams, and Benjamin Franklin, needed to find a way, in Parkinson's words, to "make the familiar alien." They needed to split the massive oak of common culture and tradition that represented their United Kingdom. For that task, they needed a wedge. Because with the right wedge, even a small one—if properly forged and shaped, placed and struck just so—the hardwood trunk of union could be reduced to splinters. That time-tested wedge turned out to be—as it has remained in American history—race. The Founding Fathers, says Parkinson, "weaponized" it.

It has always been possible to create a tribal sense of "us" by emphasizing shared values, but the quicker and simpler way to achieve that goal has often been to raise the specter of a common enemy, a convenient "them" for all of "us" to hate. And then, the quickest way to transform a member of the tribe into a pariah to be banished into oblivion has been to accuse them of a treacherous alliance with "them." Thus, the master plan of May 1775 to July 1776.

In essence, they would charge King George III with not only a violation of their rights as Englishmen but also with race treason. Of pitting non-white "savages" against colonial whites. Of inciting slave rebellions against colonial masters, and of stoking Indian attacks on colonial settlers along the frontier. Given the backdrop of a century and more of systematic demonization of nonwhites as savages, it was easy to enflame white paranoia. To be plain, though, during the fifteen months of fighting that had preceded the Declaration of Independence, Lord Dunmore, royalist governor of Virginia, actually had offered slaves freedom for running away from their masters and joining Britain's fight against the colonial rebels. And quite a few Native American tribes did ally with the British in the conflict.

However, the fevered demagoguery disseminated by the informal ministers of patriot propaganda—Jefferson, Adams, Franklin—greatly outran reality. Patriot-inclined newspapers up and down the Atlantic seaboard were fed a steady diet of news articles describing the depredations of blacks and reds against whites, all incited to their treachery by British agents. Of course, most of the "news" about slave insurrections and Native American uprisings was false, as the founders well knew. And even when attacks did occur, their consequences were greatly exaggerated. The frightful lies were reassuringly useful, though, in rallying the public to the cause of independence.

But propaganda consists of lies of omission as well as lies of commission. In a considered attempt to deceive, what is left out is often as important as what is included. The Patriot Press rarely mentioned the Native American tribes who allied with the patriots against the British. And also missing were stories of the blacks, free and enslaved, who served the patriot cause. David Waldstreicher tells us that George Washington's Continental Army was the most racially integrated military force in our history until the Vietnam War. Stirring tales of multiracial valor in service of liberty, however, would not stir the laggard "summer soldiers and the sunshine patriots" to action. Racial fear would. The contributions of nonwhites to the patriot cause were little mentioned in the patriot press. The space was filled instead with black and red terror—instigated by Britain.

The propaganda continued into the text of the Declaration of Independence itself. Not in the frequently cited opening flourishes, but in the long bill of twenty-seven indictments laid at the feet of King George III with which the document concludes. Parkinson argues that these allegations should be read as a building crescendo of fear, culminating in the charge that

George III "has excited domestic [slave] insurrections amongst us, and has endeavoured to bring on the inhabitants of our frontiers, the merciless Indian Savages, whose known rule of warfare, is an undistinguished destruction of all ages, sexes and conditions." Waldstreicher, noting that Jefferson's early draft of an antislavery clause for the Declaration had been cut completely, says of the final document that it "had turned from antislavery in draft to anti-antislavery (if not proslavery) in publication." Yes, the revolutionaries were unified in their desire for liberty, but, says Parkinson, "separation from Britain was as much, if not more, about racial fear and exclusion as it was about inalienable rights."

In *White over Black*, published in 1968, Winthrop Jordan asserts that the English must have arrived in America with a pronounced and deeply seated aversion to blackness already in place, that the African's color was the reason for permanent enslavement and, inevitably, for racial prejudice. Without that factor, he cannot see how slavery based on race "ever entered the colonists' minds." Without reference to any culturally inbred bias, however, we see now how it entered their minds. With malice aforethought, racism—the contempt of racial "inferiors" coupled with anxieties over racial menace—was placed there *after* the English arrived in America. For economic and political purposes, it was placed there with great care. Over and over again.

I'll let the more incisive James Baldwin sum up: "We have invented the n-----. I didn't invent him. White people invented him. I've always known . . . that what you were describing was not me and what you were afraid of was not me. . . . But if I am not the n-----, and if it's true that your invention reveals you, then who is the n-----? . . . Well, he's unnecessary to me, so he must be necessary to you. I'm going to give you your problem back: You're the n-----, baby, it isn't me."

CHAPTER 17

The Solidarity Myth

*Did whites receive anything from the otherwise
impoverishing system of white supremacy?*

If only my cousin, Lewis Wiggins—turpentine laborer, rheumatism sufferer,
conscripted infantryman in a North Carolina regiment of the Confederate
army—had enjoyed the tender mercies of a "steam doctor." These angels of
mercy retailed heat and humidity to North Carolinians and to Mississippians
rather than taking coals to Newcastle or selling ice to Eskimos, but their
marketing skills were comparable. Across the South and West, it is believed
that somewhere between one-third and one-half of the populace heeded their
gospel—the gospel that since cold is the essence of death, heat must be the
essence of good health. The logic was indisputable. The allure was irresistible.
How could anything so right be wrong? Particularly when one was suffering
a bout of severe arthritis, and the rival "regular physicians" offered a leech
in lieu of a steam bath.

More correctly, they were called "Thomsonians," named after their New
England founder of the early 1800s, Samuel Thomson, one of the many practitioners of alternative medicine in the era. To be sure, though, these "steamers" and their rivals, the "regulars," did share an unshakeable agreement on the
need to evacuate bad "humors" from the body. But they disagreed ferociously
over the means to achieve the flow and over the orifices through which to
achieve it. And, it turns out, the devil was truly within these details. Bleeding
and bowel purging—the latter induced by heavy doses of mercury-based

calomel—were among the mainstays of mainstream "heroic medicine" in the antebellum period. Thomsonians abhorred these methods, and their contempt was a kindness. As a substitute, they offered the "American system," thereby emphasizing their reliance on home grown botanical emetics in addition to steam. But also, they celebrated their rejection of any practice originating in the formal European academic tradition in which to have "studied in Paris" was the ultimate proof of expertise. The steam doctors most assuredly had not "studied in Paris;" they not only foreswore bleeding and intestinal purges but also were self-assertive amateurs at their craft, heaping scorn on all higher as well as lower academic degrees.

But their populist approach certainly fit the times. These were the days when the common man—the white common man, that is—was king. In addition, their practices, perhaps, did some good. They certainly did less harm than their learned competitors, and they charged considerably less for the privilege. And however nauseating their emetics may have been, their care always concluded with the signature cure-all of a good sweat to exorcise one's ill humors in an all-enveloping cloud of steam.

All that aside, though, the question is, Why were several of these steam doctors—every one of them white—among those hung as slave insurrectionists during a summertime hysteria in Mississippi in 1835? Historian Joshua Rothman explains that the answer was slavery, as it seemingly was with every question in this highly articulated slave society, but one, at that moment, caught in the grip of a frenzy of greed and a tumult of fear. Both summoning up fever dreams of colossal and deadly proportions.

In those fateful months, rumors were rampant in and around Livingston in Madison County, about halfway between Longshot and Natchez in western Mississippi. A slave insurrection was in the offing, but worse, one instigated by whites, but worse, one plotted by "mysterious banditti" known as the "Mystic Clan," a criminal syndicate of slave stealers and protoabolitionists, more than one thousand strong, but worst of all, brazenly led by the nefarious outlaw John Murrell. As the panic spread, a Committee of Safety was formed to root out the conspirators, and "vigilance committees" were formed in many other places, not least of all Natchez to the south.

Natchezians thought they had good reason for their vigilance. A "confession" wrung from a slave under torture had informed the Livingston committee that the insurrectionists' plan was to lay waste to roughhewn Madison County but then to head for grand Natchez—the very beating heart of the

Cotton Kingdom—to kill all the citizens, pillage the banks, and make their final stand in the Devil's Punchbowl, a natural depression wedged between the Mississippi River bluffs on three sides and the river itself on the fourth. The Devil's Punchbowl is a very real place just north of Natchez that for many generations genuinely had been a haven for river pirates and runaway slaves. But for that reason, it had become a mythic place of wildly exaggerated legend—a magnet, surely, for a Mystic Clan of banditti. And so, Natchez called out its militia. The town was ready for Armageddon on the bluffs.

As you may have already figured out, though, almost all of this was sheer fantasy. It was true that slaves were not happy, and a John Murrell did exist and was a bit shady. Otherwise, all was fiction. There was no conspiracy, no banditti, mysterious or not. But then, this was not, as the phrasing currently goes, "a reality-based community." We see again that in a slave society, the living of a lie, the daily acting of the stage role of see no evil, hear no evil, speak no evil, had, in reality, made men blind, deaf, and dumb to reality, whether good or evil. And this inevitably led not only to the erosion of fact but also to the substitution of hallucinations. The rot of systemic deceit sprouts conspiracy theories like fungi. Too, it certainly didn't help that 1835 Mississippi was in the midst of an epic cotton boom—of a massive expulsion of Native Americans and of an even more massive importation of black slaves from the upper South. As a result, profits—and debt—were exploding. It was, as Joseph Baldwin puts it, a time when everything "stood on its head with its heels in the air." The rush of blood to the head was disorienting, to say the least.

As it happened, the steam doctors had no cure for such fever dreams, the ones incubated in the swamp of human greed and fear, the dynamos of every slave society. The Livingston Committee of Safety judged the steamers to be unsafe and "proved" them to be members of Murrell's notorious Mystic Clan. Along with at least a dozen slaves (many more were interrogated, harassed, beaten), these white men were hanged as slave insurrectionists. But whatever the cause of the panic over the nonexistent plot, why exactly were these men suspected?

I can't help but observe that the chairman of the inquisitorial committee was one Marmaduke Mitchell, a planter/physician of the "regular" persuasion. He was educated domestically, but his illustrious name alone conferred all the prestige of having "studied in Paris." It oozed disdain for all things irregular. One has to wonder about his ulterior motives. But Rothman, the authority on the topic, puts his emphasis elsewhere. He points out the simple distinction that those executed were nonlocal white men who owned few if any slaves and that the executioners were local white planters who owned a great many slaves. If anything struck fear in the bowels of slave owners more so than slave insurrection, it was the danger of white nonslaveholders inciting slaves and joining slaves in insurrection.

As we have seen, a constant of all slave societies—from Greece to Rome to Brazil to Jamaica to Mississippi—was the harm they did in the long run, most certainly to the enslaved but also, to a lesser extent, to the nonslave-holding majority. However, another constant was the absolute necessity for slaveholders to gain the support of those nonslaveholders in maintaining control over the very large numbers of the enslaved. To the degree that racial consciousness and racial prejudice were manmade in the Americas—and I assert that, for the most part, they were—it was done for this purpose. Bloody slave rebellions were feared, but slavocrats were confident in their ultimate suppression. The system would survive precisely because of the support, in the form of posses or full militias, of the white nonslaveholding majority. However, they knew that whites joining in, even leading, a slave rebellion could sound the slave society's death knell. If they, as a class, turned against the institution, it would be finished. Their support was essential to the institution's survival and, so, to the extraordinary profits, power, and status it conveyed. Not just the slave owners themselves, therefore, but all whites had to remain united. Hence, "race traitors," as one Mississippian put it during the insurrection scare of 1835, stood condemned as "fiends, for men they can hardly be called." And with such fiends, it was considered best to hang first and ask questions later, lest they reveal the dirty little secret of the "white-supremacist" slave society: that those who enforced it were actually harmed by it. Thus, the eternal dilemma of the masters in a slave society: how to enlist the majority's support for a system of oppression that undermined that majority's economic and political interests.

The answer is the third constant of all slave societies—from Rome to the Dutch Empire to Mississippi: in lieu of the wealth and power stolen away, elite slaveholders conferred political rights (if not real power) and social status upon nonslaveholders. The theft of that wealth was very real, but we must avoid the mistake of dismissing the value of the status gained in its stead. Too often in political discussions, it is assumed that economic self-interest is the only self-interest. It is not. Full citizen status—social honor—matters. Slaves, it will be remembered, were almost always societal outsiders, literally foreigners or their native-born offspring who were denied full assimilation. In slave societies, it was stressed that nonslaveholders were privileged simply in being nonslaves, which meant being included among societal insiders right alongside the slave masters—to be included in the rituals of status and perhaps also in the exercise of political rights. But in the three slave societies of the Americas, that nonslave status became thoroughly identified with race. In the southern United States—the largest slave society since ancient Rome, with four million slaves making up one-third of the total population—the cultivation of an ideology of solidarity among all nonslaves was all the more vital. The consolation of status was offered to ease the loss of economic opportunity. W. E. B. Du Bois called it the "psychological wage."

For this shell game to work, however, the upper-class propagandists of whiteness had to obscure the concrete characteristic that united poor non-slaveholders and slaves—the age-old plight of exploited workers—and substitute the abstract trait that united nonslaveholder and slaveholder—the modern identity of "whiteness." With this color solidarity, even the lowliest white man was assured of legal and social advantages over any and every black man, enslaved or free. He was entitled to a cradle-to-grave welfare system of higher—if not high—status, a safety net of social stature. It was an entitlement program based on birth, not merit; it was bestowed, not earned. On a daily basis, the poorest white man could improve his self-esteem by acting out the rituals of honoring/dishonoring, inclusion/exclusion. All without enduring the tedium of actual self-improvement. He could raise himself up simply by pushing another down. But historian William McKee Evans calls the idea of white unity the "solidarity myth." And he did so for good reason.

The short-term material gains of the white majority were dwarfed by lost opportunities for even more gains over the longer term. And so, whatever the short-term rise in status for individuals, the South, as a whole, paid a crushing price over the decades. Due to the trickle-up dynamics of a slave society, slavery and its accompanying white supremacy meant wealth for the few and comparative poverty for the many, of both races. Thanks to the slave society that they supported in the name of racial dominance, as we have seen, most whites were less likely to own property, less likely to have access to well-paying jobs, less likely to have access to good education.

And some, sometimes, took note. There was always a sense that the master class was pulling a fast one. Dreading the consequences of being found out, though, the slave owners, like all con men, knew to keep talking, keep walking, keep selling. To never let the target audience escape from their relentless marketing campaign for white supremacy. It was remarkably successful. As Eugene Genovese definitively puts it, the American South saw "the triumph of a racism more insidious than any other in the New World." And, it will be remembered, it was in the modern New World that racism had first emerged.

In this endeavor, Georgia Governor Joseph Brown excelled in pandering to white vanity. Speaking to whites who had lost their lands and self-determination and lapsed into tenancy or wage work, he assured them, "Here [in the South] the poor white laborer is respected as an equal. His family are treated with kindness, consideration and respect. He does not belong to the menial class. The negro is in no sense of the term his equal. He feels and knows this. He belongs to the only true aristocracy, the race of white men." But to such carefully crafted appeals to pride in whiteness, the master class also stoked fears of blackness. Mississippi Senator Albert Gallatin Brown warned that if abolition should become reality, "millions of Negroes [will be] set at liberty to maraud, and plunder, and steal," ending in "a war of the races." The wealthy slaveholders, he assured his audience, had the resources to leave the South; the poor, though, would be left behind to face the anarchic violence alone. Therefore, he said, they had more reason to support slavery than did the slaveholders themselves. And of course, the propagandists of white supremacy knew that the racial biases and terrors thus stoked could be used to redirect common whites' justifiable class resentments into racial resentments, to divert them downward and "blackward," rather than upward and "whiteward."

And we return to my cousin Lewis Wiggins—turpentine laborer, rheumatism sufferer, Confederate draftee—plodding up the slope of Culp's Hill at

Gettysburg on July 2, 1863. I desperately want to think well of him, but most likely, to secure his position on the second lowest rung on society's hundred-rung ladder, he found relief in the high provided by his little "white" pill. If we take the famous quote from Marx, southern fry it and revise it, we find that racism, not religion, is "the sigh of the oppressed creature, the heart of a heartless world, and the soul of soulless conditions. It is the opium of the people." As Lewis climbed the hill on aching joints only to be mortally wounded, as he then lay dying on the summer slope, it numbed his senses, both physical and moral. He died like so many others, bedraggled but peon proud—another Great Pretender, King at the Bottom of the Heap. All while the specter of the white-solidarity myth circled up above, waiting to pick through his pockets and his dead eye sockets, like a carrion crow.

PART 5

CONSTITUTIONAL CONSTRUCTIONS, RECONSTRUCTIONS, AND DECONSTRUCTIONS

CHAPTER 18

Diogenes Finds His
Honorably Honest Southern Man

Who won the Civil War?

So, who did win the Civil War—the North or the South? Respond offhand-edly at your peril. The issue is more complex than you think. Some insights, though, can be found within a few miles of where I once lived.

Before moving into downtown Natchez, my wife and I had lived, for nine-teen years, out in the country, eight miles south of town, between Second Creek on the east and the Mississippi River on the west. This means that we lived on land that was once part of a plantation because all the country-side around Natchez was once part of a plantation. In this case, Anchorage Plantation. The site of the Big House—still exuding its romantic aura under the shade of a dozen huge moss-hung, live oaks—was about a quarter mile down the road from our house. Other than the oaks, though, every trace of the master's house is gone, as is the cropland that has long since reverted to dense oak and hickory woods and is now heavily eroded into deep, pre-cipitous ravines.

Of course, as Edward Baptist reminds us, "plantation" is a euphemism for "slave labor camp," a designation which has a way of sapping the romance right out of things, moss hung or not. When the war began, Anchorage was home to and worked by eighty-four slaves; it was the place where they laughed and sang, suffered under the lash, cried over lost kin, died, and were buried. But like the evidence of the master and the fields, the slaves' footprints are also gone. In the 1970s, the land had been subdivided, sold off, and bulldozed to create an artificial lake and to make way for nice middle-class homes—ranch-style bricks or colonial cottages, like the one we bought in 1991. Still, one didn't have to contemplate for long to realize that the roots of our eighteen acres of wilderness clutched secrets. The comment of Isaiah Montgomery about the Delta applies as well to every square foot of land in the countryside of Adams County: "every acre represents a grave and every furrow a tear." But on other plantations south of Natchez and closer to Second Creek—such as Cherry Grove, Beau Prés, Palatine, Waverly, and Brighton—there were even more secrets and tears waiting to be revealed. Particularly on Brighton, a trek of a mile or so from Anchorage through the cotton fields now hidden under woods. And home to Orange Mosby.

Orange Mosby was one of dozens of slaves caught up in the Second Creek conspiracy that unfolded over the late spring and summer of 1861. Here, in the first months of the war, with so many of the young white men mobilizing to go to the battle fronts, a fear arose that a slave insurrection was imminent. On these plantations, many dozens of slaves were tortured to elicit confessions and also information on the plan and on the identity of coconspirators. Whatever accurate information was garnered, it came as a few choice nuggets of truth among an avalanche of false confessions and fictions—as always happens under torture. The victims told the questioners what they thought they wanted to hear, and they wanted to hear more names, names attached to more bodies to whip and interrogate, yielding more names. That summer, forty "conspirators" were hanged. But the mania didn't abate. Historian Justin Behrend of SUNY Geneseo says that, over the next two years, perhaps as many as 150 were killed. But there is no way to be certain. The "reign of terror"—as it was called by a contemporary—ended only with the Union army's occupation of Natchez in August 1863.

As it was unfolding, it was obviously a matter of intense concern for both whites and blacks in Adams County. But in its aftermath, it was suffocated under a blanket of silence. Whites didn't talk about it or write about it. By the next generation, it was barely remembered. By the next, it was essentially forgotten. The slave society of the American South was built on a lie, which meant that many inconvenient truths had to be denied but also systematically deleted from memory. We have already seen that slavery created unpersons. It seems it also created unevents. Winthrop Jordan, author of *White over Black*, won a Pulitzer Prize for his *Tumult and Silence at Second Creek* (1993) in which he drew back the curtain on this long-overlooked episode.

With the carnage, however, the question has to be asked, Was there an actual conspiracy? And the answer has to be we can't know for sure. The "Vigilance Committee" of inquiry at the time was not exactly objective and deliberate in the gathering of evidence. But the answer really depends on what is meant by "conspiracy." The situation was certainly far more complicated than that of the groundless hysteria and judicial murders in Madison County in 1835. Slaves everywhere and always hated slavery, but Orange and others on the Brighton Plantation, like his brother Nelson, had personal reasons for resentment toward their owner, John Mosby. They were angry over whippings and, particularly, over the sale of family members, both past and pending. Still, it is unlikely that a rebellion, originating with Mosby or anyone else, was imminent in Adams County in the summer of 1861.

But the date must be taken into account: May 1861. This was six months after the election of the Free-Soiler Abraham Lincoln to the presidency and four months after the formation of the Confederacy and one month after the shelling of Fort Sumter and Lincoln's call for volunteers to suppress the secessionists' rebellion. Slave insurrection may not have been imminent, but war surely was. The First Battle of Bull Run was still two months in the future, but the Mississippi River—the spectacular north-south transportation artery and natural path of Yankee invasion—bordered Adams County to the west. Clearly, Northern gunboats and bluecoats could be arriving in Natchez sooner rather than later.

In this context, in May 1861, slaves were sure that Abraham Lincoln and the "black Republicans" intended to end slavery and that their armies were marching and river barging south to do so. They knew this because their masters said so, loudly, publicly, repeatedly. They had said so in, among many other documents, Mississippi's Declaration of the Immediate Causes Which Induce and Justify the Secession of January 1861, which put it starkly: the Lincoln Administration "promotes [slave] insurrection and incendiarism in our midst." The slavocrats' own words explained their secession and the war it spawned in terms of the threat of abolition; to grasp the elemental nature of the war, their slaves simply had to listen to those in authority. They did exactly that. But by faithfully repeating what their masters were saying to one another, they "conspired" with one another and put nooses around their own necks.

"From this perspective," concludes Behrend, "slaves' hopes for freedom were turned into a rebellious act. Wishing that the North would be victorious became a treasonous offense. Wanting to join up with the Union army was deemed revolutionary." Was this, then, a slave rebellion in the making? Jordan reminds us that the mere utterance of such words was literally a "capital felony" according to Mississippi's Act in Relation to Slaves, Free Negroes and Mulattoes of 1857. Deeds weren't necessary and neither were actual plans to carry out deeds. Under Mississippi law (and that of every other southern state), talk equaled conspiracy, and conspiracy was an offense punishable by hanging.

Of course, all of this was news to the Lincoln administration in Washington. In 1861, the Emancipation Proclamation was still a very long, tortured, bloody year and a half away. The not-yet Great Emancipator was doggedly maintaining his intention merely to stop the expansion of slavery and to wage war only to block unconstitutional secession, not to end slavery. But the logic that abolition must be a war aim was already apparent to some. Secession was in service to slavery; it, not secession, was the root of the problem. In May 1861, here was the obscure slave Orange Mosby of the Brighton Plantation making that precise connection between the antisecession war and its potential antislavery outcome. He talked of joining the fight "when the abolitionists come." As to how soon he thought the "abolitionists" might arrive, there's no way to know. But the point is that the insurrection "plans," such as they were, were linked to the advance of Union armies.

Therefore, the slaves' "mere" talk mirrored the larger revolutionary events that were unfolding across the country, demonstrating that the enslaved people of the area were aware of them, of their significance, and of ways in which they themselves could, in time, contribute to their realization. Behrend makes the point that, whatever physical acts of resistance might take place, the enslaved were "developing a political consciousness." They saw that their small lives were part of much larger currents of societal change.

In this way, this "battle" of Second Creek in Adams County, Mississippi— begun a mile or so through the cotton fields–cum–wilderness from my home for nineteen years—produced some of the first bloodshed of the Civil War. And probably the first in which the stakes were quite explicitly understood to be the survival of the slave society of the American South. The slaves of the

Brighton slave-labor camp, and other such camps nearby, knew the war was about emancipation even before Abraham Lincoln did. They were certainly making their own proclamations to this effect long before Abe issued his.

But what Orange Mosby had assumed in 1861 did begin to become explicit Union policy in 1863. The Union cause was becoming the slaves' cause. As Lincoln himself freely admitted, they would contribute mightily to the ulti-mate Union victory. Three-fifths of the five-thousand-man Union occupation force at Fort McPherson in Natchez from 1863 to 1865 were black members of the United States Colored Troops (USCT), the vast majority of whom were "self-emancipated" from slavery in the Natchez area. In the Union army, they were segregated, always served under white officers, and were discriminated against in countless ways, but they were no longer slaves; they were new men.

One episode in Natchez embodies this transformation. In January 1864, the Union commander ordered that companies of the USCT be stationed at various points along the roads leading into the town in order to defend against Confederate raiders. One unit was sent to the Forks of the Road, the second biggest slave market in the lower South and a site through which many of these men had passed in the years before the war. Through which they had passed as slaves in chains. In which they had been sold and had mourned the loss of wives and children, parents, siblings, and friends. But now, to which they were returning as free men, as soldiers of the United States of America, in uniforms and armed with guns, with authority over their former masters. Their officer described what happened next in a letter to the *Milwaukee Sentinel*: "Our first quarters were in a long range of [buildings] used for a number of years as slave pens. . . . [W]e were ordered to construct barracks within the fortifications and to tear down these slave pens to obtain lumber to build them. This order was received just at evening and was hailed with the wildest enthusiasm by these men."

I put the question again, Who won and who lost the Civil War? These enthu-siastic black soldiers were southerners, and they categorically did not lose the Civil War. Slaves composed 55 percent of Mississippi's population. Almost all of them had been born and raised in the South, had poured more of their blood, sweat, and tears into its soil than had the typical white, and they certainly didn't lose the Civil War. They won. Demographically speaking, then, Mississippi wasn't on the losing side of the Civil War after all. In toto, over the last two years of the war, one-tenth of the "Northern" army and navy—almost two hundred thousand men—was made up of blacks, over half of whom were self-emancipated slaves from the South, particularly the Lower Mississippi River Valley. But then, another 175,000 men in the "Northern" army were white southerners from the border slave states that did not secede—Maryland, Delaware, Kentucky, Missouri, along with West Virginia, which seceded from Virginia at the beginning of the war and achieved Union statehood in 1863. And another one hundred thousand men in the "Northern" army were whites from the southern states that did secede from the Confederacy, mostly from Tennessee, Virginia, and North Carolina. All told, about a quarter of the "Yankee invaders" were southerners.

By contrast, it's revealing that extraordinarily few northerners served in the Confederate armies, though there were more than a few "Copperheads" in the North who sympathized with their proslavery cause. And it should be added that, by the last year of the war, up to one-third of Confederate soldiers were coerced conscripts of dubious devotion to "their" cause. In sum, though virtually all Confederates were southerners, by no means were all southerners Confederates. A salient point, therefore, is that, between 1861 and 1865, the South and the Confederacy were not synonymous. The cause of the Confederacy was not the cause of the South as a region but rather the cause of the white-supremacist slavocrats of the South as a class. The Confederate battle flag was not the flag of the South, but the flag of that white-supremacist slavocracy. That, not "southern pride," is what stained the Mississippi state flag until 2020. That, not southern heritage, is what is celebrated during official "Confederate Heritage Month" in Mississippi. Therefore, who lost the war? The Confederacy—not the South—lost the Civil War.

And also we see that, by fighting *against* the Confederacy, the southern men of the USCT were fighting *for* the South. In doing so, they risked their lives for the greater good of a region and a nation that had treated them with contempt. Illiterate, penniless, powerless, ragged, downtrodden, abused, insulted even by their northern allies, they rose above the petty prejudices imposed upon them. They endured and, in the end, triumphed. If this is not nobility, the word has no meaning. The contrast with that supposed exemplar of southern gentlemanliness, Robert E. Lee, could not be starker. Lee was highly educated, rich, powerful, impeccably tailored, exalted, coddled, and lauded even by his Northern enemies. And still, he refused to rise above the morass of his inherited prejudices from which he benefited. He endured but, in the end, lost. If this is nobility, the word loses all meaning. At last, we have found the model for the honorable southern gentleman. It is not Marse Robert; it is the average foot soldier of the USCT.

As a white Mississippian descended from countless slave owners and a score of Confederates, I say that it is because I love the South that I condemn the proslavery, white-supremacist Confederacy. And it is why I mourn the tragedy of Reconstruction, during which the South that had won the war would lose the peace, and the Confederacy—raised from the dead by the Lost Cause myth—would win it.

CHAPTER 19

Constitutional Construction and the Reconstruction of American Democracy

Even if we stipulate that the South was in the wrong regarding slavery, secession, and the Civil War, wasn't northern-imposed Reconstruction a catastrophe for the South?

John Roy Lynch was born in 1847 across the river from Natchez, on a plantation in Concordia Parish, Louisiana. The son of a white father and an enslaved black mother, he was, by law, along with his two brothers, a slave himself. His parents' relationship, though, was a loving one. But one infinitely complicated by the realities of a racist slave society. His father purchased his mother and their three sons so he could free them but was thwarted by the loss of his overseer's job, making it impossible for him to post the $1000 bond that the state of Louisiana required for each freed slave. This reflected the antebellum trend across the South of state governments making it harder and harder for individual masters to manumit slaves. But whether John's mother had been freed or not, his parents were, again by law, forbidden to marry. His father would die in 1849, still the legal owner and master, but not the legal husband, of the woman he loved. And still master and legal owner of his own enslaved sons.

John would gain freedom only in 1863, when he was sixteen years old. In that year, Union forces occupied the Natchez region and thereby brought the edict of the Emancipation Proclamation into the town. Over the next few years, he acquired some education, worked several jobs, and won a reputation for intelligence and responsibility. During postwar Reconstruction, in 1869, at the age of twenty-two, he was appointed justice of the peace and was then elected to the state House of Representatives. By the age of twenty-five, he had been elected speaker of the House. By twenty-six, in 1873, he had been elected to the US House of Representatives. He had ascended from chattel slavery to the halls of national power in ten years. A remarkable story.

But this story is all the more remarkable if we put it into broader perspective. Chattel slavery had been an accepted institution in countless societies around the world for over five thousand years. From the very origin of written law codes, it had been a legal institution. Across the world, across time, and across the world's great religious and moral traditions, well into modern times, its existence had rarely been questioned, much less condemned. There have been rebellions of slaves attempting to free themselves, but freed slaves often then looked to enslave others—as did the Hebrews in Exodus. Everyone agreed that they didn't want to be enslaved themselves, but virtually no one judged that there was anything wrong with slavery as an institution. There had never been a movement to abolish it. Until the eighteenth century.

The period of world history from 1778 to 1888 has been called the Age of Emancipation. In a little more than a hundred years, this practice of literally prehistoric origin was ended across the entirety of the Western Hemisphere—the site, let's remember, of three of the five universally agreed upon slave societies in world history. For good measure, serfdom was simultaneously being ended in Eastern Europe and Russia. To say this was unprecedented does not do it justice. Our enthusiasm does need to be qualified, however. This was not the end of chattel slavery everywhere on earth. Societies with slaves—as opposed to slave societies—continued to exist legally in many areas of Asia and Africa and did so well into the twentieth century, the final, formal abolition coming only in 1976. Also, we must be aware that a legal ban equals an actual ban only if laws are enforced. When and where the will to do so is lacking, slavery still exists to this day—again on the scale of societies with slaves, not slave societies. In addition, the end of slavery was not the end of all forms of coercive and exploitative labor—Asian "coolies" were brought in to replace slaves in many parts of the Americas, for example. But again, though they were treated brutally, they were not chattel. By any measure, the abolition of slavery in the West was one of the most astonishing transformations in the history of humankind.

But in every place that emancipation was enacted, pressing questions arose. What was to be the political status of those emancipated? Would they become full citizens, at least gradually? Or would they be transitioned into another sort of subordinate status? In other words, would the freedmen be free only in the sense of being nonslaves? Or would they be free in the sense of full and equal participation in the civil and political life of their home societies? They would have the "inalienable," natural right not to be enslaved, but what of the civil right of owning property in their own names? Of legally recognized marriage? What of the political "privilege" of voting? Of the social right of access to education? From Russian Smolensk to Brazilian Rio to British Jamaica and virtually all points in between, the answer was "no," they would not be "free" in any of these ways. Almost universally, the explanation was given that while the indignities of slavery and serfdom might be unfit for humans, these former bondsmen were necessarily unfit for the dignity of full citizenship. They would remain an underclass and, therefore, were relegated to one of the other subordinate categories of labor that still existed. Emancipation had its limits, sometimes severe.

There is one and only one exception to this rule, though. In one place, for one fleeting span of eight years. In that place and time, chattel slaves were granted the rights of full citizenship within a few years of their liberation. That was the post–Civil War United States of America, during the era known as Radical Reconstruction. It was, says the preeminent Columbia University historian Eric Foner, "a stunning experiment . . . to fashion an interracial democracy from the ashes of slavery." It was an emphatic vote for the capacity of ordinary people to be "wise in time," to harbor a deep wisdom drawn from experience even if denied the knowledge found in books, and to possess the capacity to govern themselves. And, in spite of enormous odds and inevitable mistakes, into the mid-1870s, this "stunning experiment" in postslavery interracial democracy was working. This must be shouted from the rooftops: it was working.

This still comes as a surprise to quite a few people, but the last sixty years of scholarship has shown that these Reconstruction governments—with variation from state to state—were effective. Compared to perfection, of course, they fell short. There was corruption. Some of their policies were wrongheaded. Several needed reforms were neglected. Which is to say that they were like all human-made governments. But compared to that reality, they were generally competent and honest—notably more honest than the

lily-white regimes that had used fraud and intimidation to win the secession vote before the war and those that would enshrine the same tactics
after Reconstruction.

These postwar governments sought to do the things that all-white antebellum governments had refused to do. Since do-nothing governments had been
replaced with do-something governments, taxes did go up, though not to the
crippling degree that has been alleged. They established statewide systems of
fully taxpayer-supported, free public schools for children of both races—the
first time most whites, much less blacks, had had this opportunity. But they
spent even more money on subsidizing business—promoting transportation
infrastructure projects to stimulate commerce, encouraging industrialization
and economic diversification to break the South's dependency on agriculture.
If anything, given the results, they went too far in this regard. But still, into the
early 1870s, the "stunning experiment" in interracial democracy was yielding
results. In stark contrast to antebellum times, the majority actually ruled.

Thus, the empowerment of blacks in the South turned out to be a way to
empower most whites as well by exposing the con of the ideology of white
supremacy. The Fourteenth Amendment requiring the states to grant equal
protection to blacks—if enforced—would preclude efforts by the elites to
play the white and black working classes off against each other, thereby eas-
ing cooperation to their mutual benefit. The Fifteenth Amendment granting
black men the right to vote—if enforced—was a way to democratize the system for all by breaking the antidemocratic stranglehold of the One Percent.
Despite the cries of "black rule!" these were all biracial governments working
for biracial advantage, with whites still holding most positions of executive
power from the local to the state level.

And of all the places it was working, Natchez may stand above all, as spelled
out in detail by Justin Behrend. It was home to the previously mentioned John
Roy Lynch. It was one of the very few towns in the Reconstruction South that
had a black mayor, Robert Wood, who happened to be the acknowledged
biracial son of the prewar mayor, who was also named Robert Wood. And the
town would produce the first black US senator in American history, Hiram
Revels, who had pastored Zion Chapel African Methodist Episcopal Church
before being drawn into postwar politics. In today's Natchez, a visitor can
walk two miles down St. Catherine's Street between the site of the Forks of the
Road slave market—the second biggest in the Cotton Kingdom—and Revels's
church. A two-mile stretch on one street in one town tracing a path between

the prewar depths of torment, humiliation, and "social death" for enslaved black families and the postwar heights of black political dignity. No other place encapsulates the nineteenth-century black experience so profoundly.

Note the name: "Reconstruction." It should now be plain that the purpose had little to do with the repair of wartime damage. The thing to be worked upon was the constitutional system itself. But the rationale for all reconstructions must begin with a consideration of what was flawed in the original construction. We can't allow our reverence for the Constitution and its authors to blind us to the stark reality of what had happened in 1861–65. The system had failed. It had nearly died. The reason was racial slavery. The system had failed because the founders, for all their virtues, failed catastrophically on this one issue above all.

A slave society had been allowed to metastasize inside the American body politic. A slave society distinctive in sheer scale, in economic centrality, in the degree to which it, and its hierarchical mindset, was "articulated" into the southern and national culture. In light of this, many from the prewar antislavery coalition were convinced that the constitutional system had to be reformed on a far more elemental level. Its areas of faulty construction needed to be reconstructed. New elements needed to be added beyond an abolition amendment. Old elements needed to be reexamined and reinterpreted. According to Eric Foner, nothing less than a "second founding" was required. Frederick Douglass had spoken of "the old dispensation of slavery with its ten thousand evils to both races." The Thirteenth Amendment abolishing involuntary servitude as a legal status was vital. But many of the "ten thousand evils" that slavery had spawned were still alive and well and abroad in the land—most importantly of all, white-supremacist racism. Only if and when these "badges of slavery" were challenged could real and lasting reconstruction be accomplished, could real and lasting democracy be established to the advantage of blacks as well as whites. The former rebels did not need to be executed, imprisoned, or exiled in mass. But simply abolishing slavery and then bringing the prodigal slavocrats back into full citizenship and power was not acceptable either.

But let me make explicit what has already been implied. This extension of rights to more people would require a reconfiguration of the governing bodies charged with protection of those rights. Previously, it had been assumed that state governments, being closer to the people, were the best guarantors of the people's freedoms. But other than protecting the rights of slave owners, states—particularly, but not only, those in the South—had failed in that mission, abdicating their responsibilities to protect even the most basic rights of any, black or white, who opposed the slave society's prerogatives. Henceforth, to protect lives and property from Klan attacks, to ensure the freedmen's right to vote, in this "second founding," the federal government would have to assume the mantle of defender of liberties. Its job was immense.

After the Civil War, there was a need to de-Confederatize the South—but with the understanding that, in deposing Confederate leaders, antidemocratic slavocrats would be deposed in the process. But more, there was a need in this "most thoroughly articulated slave society since Ancient Rome" for a program of what might be called "disarticulation," a concerted effort to disentangle slavery from the various components of southern society. In this system that purposely denied education to almost all blacks and most nonslaveholding whites in order to keep them "docile," there was a need to educate all in the basics so that they could be further educated in their rights and responsibilities as citizens. In this system that reduced humans to legal slavery but also economic dependency, there was a need to grant them not only legal freedom but also the means by which to achieve and maintain economic independence—land ownership with secure titles. In this system in which each master had been a lawless despot on his own plantation and the masters collectively had dominated local and state governments to ensure noninterference with that despotism, there was a need for federal-government enforcement to ensure the rights of citizenship for all. And finally, in this system in which racial prejudice, fear, and outright hate had been systematically and relentlessly created, recreated, propagated, and propagandized for two hundred years, there was a need for systematic, relentless countermeasures. But for how long? For however long it would take.

For most southerners of both races, therefore, the slavocrats' defeat in 1865 represented an enormous opportunity to improve their economic and political prospects. With that old dispensation eradicated, said Frederick Douglass, a "new dispensation of freedom with its thousand blessings to both races" would take its place. But here lies the central question, the one that would shape the future of the South and the nation: Would the majority of whites rejoice in the new dispensation of "blessings," or would they cling doggedly to the old dispensation of slavery and its "evils," particularly that of racial resentment and violence? As of 1865—as delineated in the last chapter—even if the Confederacy had lost the Civil War, the South had won. Would the same be true ten years later?

CHAPTER 20

The Reconstruction and Deconstruction of American Democracy

Given that the white southerners who toppled the Reconstruction governments were known as "Redeemers," doesn't that mean they were in the right?

Lucius Quintus Cincinnatus Lamar—a grand name to match a grand career. Author of Mississippi's Ordinance of Secession, Confederate officer and diplomat, member of the US House of Representatives and the Senate, US secretary of the interior, and US Supreme Court justice. An advocate for sectional reconciliation after the Civil War. In 1874, in his stirring eulogy for the recently deceased Massachusetts senator and abolitionist, Charles Sumner, he called on war-worn Americans to put aside their bitterness: "My countrymen!" he beseeched, "Know one another, and you will love one another." He was one of the men lauded in John F. Kennedy's *Profiles in Courage* (1955).

Lucius Quintus Cincinnatus Lamar—a grand fraud. He was the suave man in the three-piece linen suit who sips smooth brandy and charms you with witty quips as his grimy henchman slips the knife into your back. He provided the respectable façade for the white-supremacist thugs who staged a violent coup against the elected Reconstruction government of Mississippi in 1875. The sectional reunion he advocated was actually only between white northerners and white southerners who, he recommended, should forget their mutual hostility for one another in a rededication of their sacred honors

to their mutual hostility for blacks. His goal was a restoration of "the supremacy of the unconquered and unconquerable Saxon race."

So much for the "grit thesis." According to University of North Carolina
historian Joel Williamson, it is "a persisting myth that manifestations of racial
extremism such as lynching . . . were born of the lower classes ["grits"] and
ran counter to the wishes of the elite." In fact, he says, "Upper class Southern
whites are no more especially sympathetic to black people than are lower
class whites." There was no difference in their racist "assumptions and attitudes," but only a difference of "style." And that stylistic distinction determined appearances, not realities. "Upper class racial prejudice," he continues,
"is often manifested in more subtle forms of economic, social, psychological,
educational, and judicial manipulations. Yes, ownership of land, control of
money and credit, of schools and courts, and domination of the marketplace
can be just as violent . . . as guns, whips and bombs."

In this one sense, race really did turn out to be the great equalizer among
whites in the South. But it didn't raise the worth of those ranked as the worst,
rather it annihilated the pretentions to honor of those alleged to be the best.
On the primary problem plaguing the South, they didn't simply fail to resolve
it, they consistently made it worse. And so it was with the gentlemanly Lucius
Quintus Cincinnatus Lamar, just as before with the sainted Robert Edward
Lee. The true bane of the South—rich white trash.

Men like Lamar were determined to destroy the governments of Radical
Reconstruction but not because of these regimes' failures or their corruption or their incompetence. Though far from perfect, these regimes were
actually succeeding, were not overly corrupt, were ably accomplishing the
people's business—biracial administrations acting to further the biracial
majority's interests. And that—their achievement—is why they had to be
destroyed. With violence, if necessary. As historian Douglas Egerton simply
states, "Reconstruction didn't fail in the South, it was murdered." And let's
be entirely candid about who instigated the murder.

John Dittmer of Depauw University says that the Reconstruction governments' "progress in rebuilding and in fostering a climate of democracy convinced privileged whites that they had to act quickly—and brutally—if they
were to regain political control." Justin Behrend adds, "Because freedpeople's

successful governance aimed at the needs of the majority, not the few, white Democrats resorted to terroristic violence as the only means to unseat their elected representatives." Pay close attention to what is being said here. The brutality was not begun by any and all whites, says Dittmer, but by the "privileged whites." The Reconstruction regimes, says Behrend, were targeted because they prioritized "the needs of the majority, not the few." And so, the "few" directed a terrorist campaign against them. The minority slavocrats may not have had slaves any longer, but they were determined to retain their power and wealth—all the more so since each had been so diminished by the self-inflicted wound of their spectacularly foolish war.

All of which meant that, for the white elite, the dangerous novelty of the Reconstruction governments had always consisted of more than their biracial makeup. They were also democratic—remarkably enough, in both form *and* substance. The now former slavocrats and their new allies among "New South" businessmen were surely offended by the notion of sharing power with blacks, but also by the sharing of power with anyone of any color from among the rabble. This is why, in that fateful period of retrogression in the last quarter of the nineteenth century, Reconstruction had to be deconstructed, but too, Jim Crow would be constructed in its place. As C. Vann Woodward said in 1951, it was never just about white supremacy but about *which* whites would be supreme. And in 2013, Achille Mbembe—Cameroon-born, Sorbonne-educated historian at Columbia University—observed that the tools of oppression originally justified by racial entitlement would inevitably be deployed against the entire working class regardless of color. This was the process he labels the "Negrofication" of whites.

And, after 1865, with racial slavery no longer available to enforce the racial status quo, the white elite stepped up their heated rhetoric. Thus, if anything, after abolition, racism became more intense, not less. In the words of Woodward, the elite sent "signals" meant "to indicate that the Negro was an approved object of aggression." From men of prestige, these "permissions to hate" represented craven assent. Once planted and cultivated, these seeds were sure to sprout and produce violent fruit on their own. No, these gentlemen were less likely to be among the mob on lynching day; they were, however, the inciters and quiet enablers of the mob on every other day. And then, with white venom successfully vented away from their own doors, they were the men who were free to continue their oligarchical plundering of the region and its people of all colors. By no means does this absolve "the grits" of responsibility for their role in racial oppression. They might have refused to be manipulated.

As, at least initially, did Tom Watson, a white Georgian. In 1892, at the height of the Populist fervor, he argued for an alliance between black and white farmers in a truly inclusive coalition of working people. "You are kept apart that you may be separately fleeced of your earnings," he said. "You are made to hate each other because upon that hatred is rested the keystone of the arch of financial despotism which enslaves you both." His orations on this theme of working men's unity, like Frederick Douglass's before him, failed. The fleecing continued. Martin Luther King Jr. returned to the theme in his speech on the steps of the Alabama statehouse after completing the Selma-to-Montgomery march in 1965. He stated, "The segregation of the races was really a political stratagem employed by the emerging Bourbon [white elite] interests in the South to keep the southern masses divided and southern labor the cheapest in the land."

That the diagnosis of Douglass, Watson, and King was essentially correct remains the judgment among historians to this day. Williamson observes that "extreme racism" was the South's way of "not coping with the real problems of the 1890's and afterward." Historian Jeff Forret says that the South's elite ensured their continued dominance by pointing "the electorate's attention away from substantive issues [like education] toward the polarizing issue of race. Flagrant race-baiting, playing to whites' fears and anxieties cemented loyalty to the party of white supremacy. Intimidation, violence and electoral fraud rounded out the arsenal of tactics." Barbara Fields of Columbia University has commented on the well-known "double mission of white supremacy—to hold down black people and white people alike," and George Fredrickson of Stanford notes, "White supremacy was the central rallying cry, . . . to be stressed whenever disadvantaged whites unfurled the banner of class grievance and challenged the elite of planters and businessmen who controlled the party machinery and the state and local governments that served their interests." Paraphrasing Robin Kelley, Walter Johnson notes that "guns and tanks and tear gas are sufficient to control the Black people; white supremacy is necessary to control the white people."

Therefore, it is extraordinarily plain that the ostensibly antiblack politics of 1875 to 1900 was part of a broader, ongoing "anti-democratic political revolution," as Gavin Wright puts it. The post-Reconstruction governments—again dominated by the "privileged whites"—cut spending on public schools, for both white and black children. And they restored the prewar system of grossly regressive taxation, penalizing the majority of whites as well as blacks. In Mississippi's constitutional convention of 1890—in which the avowed aim was to disfranchise blacks once and for all—Woodward comments that the proceedings "actually perpetuated and solidified the Black Belt oligarchy. Its work was therefore doubly undemocratic: it disfranchised the race that composed a majority of the population, and it delivered a large majority of whites into the control of a minority of their own race in the black counties." Wright confirms the opinion, saying, while "wealthy planters allied with other whites to deny blacks the vote," they were "disenfranchising large numbers of poor whites in the process—a not altogether unintended byproduct."

In his 1949 classic, *Southern Politics in State and Nation*, Harvard political scientist V. O. Key, a white Texan, commented on yet another variation of how economic elites "used the race issue to blot up the discontents of the lesser whites." By rousing racist resentments to deny services to blacks, "the governing classes can kill off or minimize pressures for improved governmental services from whites." In other words, it was possible to persuade whites to abandon their own claims to even the most elemental government assistance by associating government assistance with aid to blacks. Whether in the 1870s, the 1970s or the 2020s, the principle remains the same—conspire to turn an alleviation of black grievance into a cause of white grievance. White backlash was thereby guaranteed. Speaking broadly about the tactic through American history, Heather Cox Richardson summarizes, "Thus, at times when it seems as if people of color or women will become equal to white men, oligarchs are able to court white male voters by insisting that universal equality will, in fact, reduce white men to subservience."

But it wasn't enough to destroy the reforms and ideals of Reconstruction; its reputation through history had to be sullied as well. As surely as black schools had to be burned, the "uppity" image of successful biracial governance had to be demolished. That was accomplished by the turn of the century as well by the so-called Dunning School of historiography, actually centered at Columbia University in New York. Out of the reality of heroes and mediocrities and rogues was created the Reconstruction ensemble composed exclusively of venal carpetbaggers, no-count scalawags, and ignorant slaves let loose to ravage southern womanhood's honor and southern manhood's fortunes. The stock characters became the cast of the nation's newest minstrel show, this one, though, masquerading as scholarly history.

And in this theatrical farce, if the "reconstruction" of the South had been so horrid, its original construction must have been virtuous after all. Therefore, the delegitimization of Reconstruction was necessarily accompanied by the relegitimization of slavery and the Confederacy. It's notable that, in the years just after the war, memorials constructed for the Confederate dead were exactly that, memorials for the dead, almost always located in cemeteries. But in this period of racial reaction, particularly after 1890—as in Natchez—far more lavish monuments honoring the fallen but also lauding the virtues of the Confederacy itself began to appear, usually in public parks, on courthouse grounds, on prominent avenues. The young men who had been sacrificed to Moloch slavery between 1861 and 1865 now saw their "honor" sacrificed for Jim Crow so that their sons and grandsons could be fitted for their own shackles.

In reference to the many revolutions across Europe in 1848, the legendary British historian A. J. P. Taylor famously remarked that, "German history reached its turning point, and failed to turn." The country did not join the nineteenth-century trend toward liberal and democratic reforms. Over the next century, a horrendous price was paid. So it was for the American South in Reconstruction. It had reached its historic turning point and failed to turn. Could it have been different?

Emancipation from systematic, totalitarian oppression—whether individual enslavement or the rule of a tyrant—involves far more than a change of legal status. Backsliding into subjugation has been the rule rather than the exception throughout history. Given the acute vulnerability of a person or people just emerging into freedom, efforts must be made to provide them with the means to ensure their continued independence once it has been won. Access to education and economic independence is crucial, but maybe most importantly, for the oppressed to truly escape oppression, the former oppressors have to be prevented from reimposing their rule. In a circumstance in which the enslaver/despot still holds the preponderance of power and wealth, the vulnerable need for powerful friends to take their side, and, if necessary, to match force with force.

Here, the effort to denazify West Germany after World War II is instructive. The original program to rid the military, civil service, judiciary, and big business of Nazis met with only limited results. A few of the most prominent were imprisoned or executed, but most of those purged in 1946 were back at their posts within a couple of years. But crucially, though former Nazis continued to hold many jobs, the Nazi philosophy was not propagandized, the Nazi regime was not restored, Nazi oppression was not resumed, and reparations were paid to the newly established Jewish state of Israel. Though universal justice was not served, West Germany became a fully functioning multiparty democracy with a capitalist economy buffered by a generous welfare state—even with former Gestapo officers in positions of influence. The principal reason for this success is clear—the United States, the most powerful country on earth and among the military occupiers of Germany, would not allow the country to fall under the thrall of Nazism again. Besides this assertion of military/political power, Marshall Plan aid helped Germany to help itself to recovery and beyond, to prosperity. It wasn't only that democratic forms were imposed; it was that the German people saw that this alternative system was working. Whether they extolled the glories of liberty or not, after a few years of postwar hardship, West Germans enjoyed a rising standard of living and an increasing sense of security. Thanks to democracy.

This coupling of a hardline toward Nazism and a rapprochement with former Nazis came at a price, though. There was no real reckoning for the German people with their responsibility in the horrific events of the Adolf Hitler years. The public preferred not to think about it. West German Chancellor Konrad Adenauer explains that they had opted for the "sleep cure." But after that long moral coma, there would be an awakening. The top-down denazification imposed by outsiders in the 1940s had failed, but in the 1960s, a bottom-up self-denazification began. The German "baby boomers" demanded it, insistently asking their parents and grandparents, their teachers and their preachers about their moral compromises in those critical years between 1933 and 1945. This did not, though, lead only to guilt-ridden breast beating about the Holocaust, and it did not necessitate prosecution of, or public shaming rituals for, the entire older generation. Instead, it led ordinary Berliners and Bavarians to see their own history more clearly, to confront their failings more honestly, and to see the destructiveness of Nazism for the world and also for Germany. And to see the ways in which they had conspired in their own self-destruction. They also began to see that, while the Nazi regime lost, the German people themselves were among the winners of the war. If, that is, they took advantage of the opportunity for reform—which they were doing.

In 1955, most Germans still saw Nazi defeat as their defeat, and V-E Day (Victory in Europe Day) was marked by much mourning, little remorse. By 1995, though, over half of Germans saw V-E Day as a day to remember the dead, but also as "a day of liberation," a day of celebration and commemoration. Within two generations, they had not only atoned for the Holocaust, but they were also liberating themselves psychologically from Nazism. Germans call this process *Vergangenheitsaufarbeitung*—"working through the past"—a word that implies the moral struggle of coming to terms with history. It is understood to be a process, not an event. And the process is ongoing.

The contrast with the American South after its defeat in the Civil War is stark and, quite simply, embarrassing, though a good beginning was made. Ex-Confederates were initially expelled from power by the federal government. In 1866–67, when they formed white-supremacist terrorist groups, like the Ku Klux Klan, the federal government responded to their violent force with military force of their own. By 1870–71, the Klan was all but broken. The three Reconstruction amendments were added to the Constitution, and the Freedmen's Bureau was established to aid the newly emancipated in finding family members, in making their way as free laborers, and in acquiring education.

However, the Freedmen's Bureau was never adequately funded or staffed. By 1869, even that spare funding was cut, and in 1872, it was abolished. The freedmen's dream of "forty acres and a mule"—their means to economic independence—never materialized. Also, within a few years, most of the ex-Confederates were back in their positions of political and economic dominance. And, though chattel slavery was not reimposed, their white-supremacist philosophy was propagandized even more vehemently, and white-supremacist oppression of blacks was intensified. With ex-Confederates in many positions of influence, the South's budding biracial democracy was gutted. The primary reason all this happened is simple: the federal government, the most powerful entity in the country and the military occupier of the South, stood aside after 1873 and allowed the region to fall under the thrall of white supremacists once again. It was as if the US government had closed down the death camps but ushered a full-fledged Nazi regime back into power in Germany in 1953.

Needless to say, under these circumstances, the South next partook of its own "sleep cure" regarding its alleged "crimes." There were no misdeeds to acknowledge, southerners insisted—slavery wasn't all that bad, and the slaves were happy, and the formation of the Confederacy and the Civil War weren't about slavery anyway, and since Radical Reconstruction governments were corrupt, incompetent, and abusive, Klan violence was justified in overthrowing them. Those weren't terrorists; they were "Redeemers." Even now, most white southerners see the defeat of the Confederacy as their defeat, when in fact it was—or could have been—their liberation. For over 150 years, then, white southerners have continued to sleep, have refused to wake up. And today, most of these sleepwalking legions rabidly prefer their age-old stupor to any hint of historical alertness, making a virtue of their voluntarily comatose state in their campaign to disparage "wokeness." This, they insist, is essential for regional pride and patriotism.

We white southerners have work to do. It's time to tell ourselves hard truths. To go beyond blathering about honor and to be honorable by being honest. What we need is more than a bit of *Vergangenheitsaufarbeitung*. To be pronounced, though, with a drawl.

CHAPTER 21

When Jim Crow Was Chairman
of the School Board

Why was Brown v. Topeka Board of Education *necessary?*

My mother grew up in the small Mississippi town of Shuqualak—which, to match her idyllic memories, is happily pronounced, SHUG-uh-lock. It is located in Noxubee County in the fertile blackland prairie of the eastern part of the state. It was a place in which she (and I) had and have deep roots. Her great-great-grandmother Delilah Greer McNees had moved there with her husband and her inherited slaves in the 1830s, and it is where her great grandfather Samuel McNees had accumulated substantial land holdings and the forty-one slaves who composed about two-thirds of his net worth. So, this was plantation country, the heartland of the American slave society. Not comparable in wealth to the cotton lands of the Lower Mississippi Valley or the sugar parishes of south Louisiana or the rice lands of the Carolina/ Georgia Low Country but, therefore, more typical of the slaveholding South than those. Having been dependent on slave labor in a slave-majority state, Noxubee retained a large black majority into the twentieth century.

And so, in the year 1930 during the Great Depression, in this tiny, isolated town in one of the poorest states in the poorest region of a country just entering the poorest era in its history, my mother obediently conjugated sentences in the fourth grade at Shuqualak Elementary School. Here, in what she always insisted was an "excellent" public school, she already had her eyes set on a college career. In explaining that quality and her success, it mattered greatly that she was intelligent and studied hard. And I defer to her judgment as to the quality of her teachers. But one has to wonder, did someone else contribute an infusion of plenty amidst the scarcity? Did the upwardly striving schoolchildren of Shuqualak have a charitable sugar daddy? They did. If they were white, that is. His name was Jim Crow.

In 1930, in the racially segregated public schools of black-majority Noxubee County, public spending per pupil for whites was fifteen times higher than for blacks. Yes, that discrepancy certainly should have purchased a bit of quality for my mother's education. Shuqualak was not unique, of course. According to Neil McMillen of the University of Southern Mississippi, "such educational progress as white Mississippians enjoyed after 1890 came directly and quite deliberately at black expense." And Mississippi was not unique either. The same was true across the region.

The Jim Crow era in the South (roughly, 1890–1965) brought black disfranchisement and the lynching mania, but it is probably most associated in the public mind with legally mandated segregation—from drinking fountains to seating in railway cars to cemeteries. And also, in public schools. All of which had been codified by the Supreme Court's ruling in *Plessy v. Ferguson* (1896). The court, by then notably dominated by northerners, declared that racially separate facilities did not violate the Equal Protection Clause of the Fourteenth Amendment as long as those facilities were equal—the infamous "separate-but-equal" doctrine. It was infamous because equality in facilities was almost always a patently obvious farce—from drinking fountains to seating in railway cars to cemeteries. And maybe most obviously in schools. Quite simply, where schools were separate, they were unequal. Some places more so than others.

Mississippi and Noxubee County were not alone in requiring segregation and its inevitable inequities, but of those localities that did, they set the pace. "No state spent less on black education than Mississippi," McMillen tells us. Across the South, for every one dollar spent on a black student, $3.50 was spent on a white student, but here in the highly hospitable Magnolia State, there was a five-to-one discrepancy in spending per pupil. That, though, is the statewide average. Noxubee's fifteen-to-one ratio in spending is extraordinary even by the extraordinary standards of Mississippi.

Given black disfranchisement, inequitable appropriations by all-white state and local politicians were the rule throughout the South. But there was an additional layer of endemic corruption, which accounts for Mississippi's pride of place. According to state law, common school funds from the state were apportioned to local school districts "in proportion to the number of educable children in each." Though the appropriation per black child was less than that for whites, there was nevertheless an appropriation of state monies for each black child. For the white administrators in counties with larger black populations, this proved an irresistible invitation to fraud. McMillen reports that "local officials were free to misappropriate state funds lawfully designated for the black population by simply diverting the greater share of public moneys to white schools." McMillen concludes, "In such a system, plantation county whites benefited handsomely from the Afro-Americans' very presence, managing not only to keep their labor force ignorant, and therefore presumably more docile and dependent, but to educate their own children at black expense." In 1937—the year my mother graduated from high school—sixty-one of eighty-two Mississippi counties dishonestly diverted at least a portion of state money appropriated for black schools to white schools. In Noxubee County—with an 83 percent black majority—almost half of all state funds appropriated for black students were corruptly diverted to the white schools my mother attended. Quite the ill-gotten windfall, which came, let's remember, on top of the already-lopsided legislative appropriations in favor of white schools. But a full 72 percent was embezzled for the benefit of the white schools in black-majority Bolivar County—within which is found the equally tiny town of Merigold, where my father had gotten what he too remembered as a "fine" education.

The black schoolchildren of those counties unwillingly subsidized my parents' educations. The self-confidence provided by a good education and all the promise for the future that it represented—as both went on to graduate from college—were systematically stolen from black children and given to them. As surely as I inherited property from my parents, I also inherited that promise.

But then, white children at least were receiving a quality education, correct? No. Whatever may have been true or exaggerated in the little academic miracles that my parents proclaimed Merigold and Shuqualak to be, education for white students in the state, while vastly superior to that of blacks, was mediocre at best. Bear in mind that those who favored well-funded public education for anyone in Mississippi—white or black—carried a heavy historical burden. While in antebellum times, some had tried to foster public education—and saw some successes—the planter class did what it could to sabotage their efforts. After the war, much of the work for biracial, free public schools during Reconstruction was squandered post-Reconstruction.

Entering the twentieth century, schools in Mississippi—again, for both races—were generally poor. In rural areas—where the vast majority of Mississippians lived—ungraded, one-room schools were the norm. Terms were short and were subordinated to the labor demands of the crop cycle. Teachers were poorly trained and poorly paid. Town schools were better but not by much. Again, nonelite whites had suffered the consequences of Deconstruction right along with blacks.

But then came what historian Albert Kirwan famously called "the revolt of the rednecks." As the century turned, James K. Vardaman (governor, 1904–8; senator, 1913–19) and Theodore Bilbo (governor, 1916–20 and 1928–32; senator, 1935–47) emerged to dominate Mississippi politics. They were chest-thumping advocates for the common white man and, therefore, they said, necessarily advocates for public education. But only for whites. They were rude, crude, vulgar, and violent in their racism. For white schools, though, they ushered in a spirit of reform after 1910, the year of my father's birth. Rural and urban schools in the state began to be consolidated. School terms were lengthened. One-room schoolhouses gave way to graded education. Teacher training and pay were upgraded. Still, though the improvement was real, the state nevertheless woefully lagged behind national standards. In his now definitive, comprehensive history of Mississippi, Dennis Mitchell summarizes the gains achieved by what he tellingly calls the "*attempted* revolt of the rednecks." He observes that, "In the end, all of the noise and excitement of the redneck revolt produced far less than the white farmers wanted." Not unlike the antebellum situation, plain folk could and did win some elections, but they barely dented the entrenched socio-economic system that strangled the state and kept them so painfully plain. The much-ballyhooed revolt failed to deliver for the poor whites it championed precisely because its leaders could not imagine an alliance with "blacknecks," the one strategy that might have broken the One Percent's stranglehold on economic power. "Not one Mississippi leader challenged black oppression," notes Mitchell, "and it never seemed to occur to them that social and economic improvement required raising the living standards for the majority of the population [who were black]." The affirmative of whiteness was one part reality and one part ploy. But the negative of good, old-fashioned class exploitation was wholly and completely real.

We should pause here to acknowledge an exception. Although, it is indicative of the scope of the problem that this glittering exception to the rule in this matter, in the end, was not so lustrous after all. He was Leroy Percy. The great Leroy Percy of Greenville in the Delta, about twenty-five miles southwest of Longshot. He scorned the racist rabble but, too, rose above the blindness of his own class. He was an attorney, planter, investor, personal friend of the high and mighty, and a US senator himself from 1910 to 1913.

But to the point of the moment—in stark contrast to his reviled rivals, Vardaman and Bilbo—he was an advocate for better treatment of and better education for blacks. Amid the hateful rhetoric so common in the day, he didn't abide "permissions to hate" of the sort that C. Vann Woodward noted. But not only did he refrain from race-baiting bombast, he publicly confronted the newly resurgent Ku Klux Klan in 1922. They had wanted to establish a base in Greenville in the flatland. He disapproved and routed them with intellect, scattered them like leaves with a devastating blast of oratory. Greenville remained "his" town. Among those self-identified decent whites of the Delta, Percy was the epitome of the honorable southern gentleman. As a boy, I revered him and devoured the account of his life included in *Lanterns on the Levee* (1941), the book written by his son, the poet William Alexander Percy. He personified the Good, and he was ours.

That is, as long as we ignored the flood and Percy's role in it. In 1927, the lower Mississippi River and its tributaries went on a rampage for the ages, the most devastating flood in the nation's history. Two-thirds of a million people were displaced as waters covered 27,000 square miles of the floodplain. At the command of Delta grandees like Percy, the grueling physical labor of fighting to save the levees was reserved for black men, plantation workers, and convicts forced into the role at gunpoint. When the Mississippi levee broke at Mounds Landing about fifteen miles southwest of Longshot, a one-hundred-foot-high wall of water rushed through a three-quarters-of-a-mile-long crevasse—in volume, double the flow over Niagara Falls. No one knows the exact number, but a hundred or so black men were swept away. Everyone knows exactly how many white men died, though—none.

The relief effort was no more heartening. The federal government and the Red Cross eventually erected 154 camps on higher ground to which the refugees were taken in steamboats. But no blacks from Percy's Washington County made the journey, this despite their better education. Instead, as Leroy decreed and as poetic son Will complied, a "concentration camp" of tents for 13,000 blacks was strung for eight miles along the levee at Greenville. There, black men, women, and children were kept under the watchful eyes, guns, and bayonets of the all-white state National Guard. Atop the levee, just to the north and south of the refugee camp, were two other "camps"—for livestock. The stench was suffocating. The conditions were unsanitary. And the food supply was grossly inadequate. Pellagra, the potentially deadly nutrition deficiency that was an endemic feature of the late-winter lives of the poor in the rural South, became a plague. Many died; no one knows how many. No one kept count. Blacks' lives did not matter.

How can we explain a man who champions black education, stares down the violently racist Klan, and orders the construction of a black concentration camp? The explanation is simple. The common denominator was Percy's mercenary self-interest. His wealth and power depended on cheap black labor. Poor education made blacks want to leave Mississippi; so, he improved their schools. The Klan wanted to chase blacks out of Mississippi; so, he opposed the Klan. The refugee camps beyond the Delta offered blacks an escape from which they would be unlikely to return; thus, he personally prevented refugee evacuation—come hell or high water, life or death. As we saw with cotton planters' cold-eyed balancing of mortality and fertility rates earlier, Percy was deeply concerned with the maintenance of his labor force in the aggregate and astonishingly unconcerned about the life of any given laborer.

Mitchell's judgment of Mississippi's "leadership" applies as surely to the cultured Percy as to the grotesque Bilbo: "The political culture based on fraud and violence endured, marring Mississippi politics for generations. The flawed political system, poverty, and deep racial divisions made progress difficult . . . because none of the leaders made any effort to extend reform to include race relations." In the end, Leroy Percy was not so different from the "grits" Vardaman and Bilbo. The difference was mostly one of appearance and style. Like Lee and Lamar before him, Percy was a "great man" who was a moral Lilliputian on the most singularly critical issue of his time and place.

The Revolt of the Lone Aristocrat had ended in self-inflicted failure as surely as had the Revolt of the Rednecks. No one seemed capable of learning the simplest lesson of all. As has been said by many in many ways, you can't hold another man down in the gutter without getting down in the gutter with him.

Historian Charles Bolton observes the result of Mississippi's low-down living arrangements: "the state actually did not have enough money to construct even one adequate school system." Yet, despite this, it would insist on building and maintaining two parallel systems in all eighty-two of its counties. As a result, in 1939, the state "was spending a greater percentage of its public funds on public education than any other state in the Union," but, says Bolton, it "remained dead last in terms of actual tax dollars used for public education." Even while robbing black Peter to pay white Paul, Paul still didn't have enough. And that was because both were being "plundered" by Judas.

Public monies were scarce not only because Mississippi was poor but also because the members of the wealthy One Percent were able to shield their wealth from taxation. Before the Civil War, owners of agricultural lands were allowed to appraise their own farms and plantations and, therefore, always grossly undervalued them for tax purposes. One of the reasons that taxes went up during Reconstruction is that this practice was ended; appraisals were done instead by public servants on the basis of fair market value. After the deconstruction of Reconstruction, however, the old corrupt, self-serving practice of undervaluation returned and prevailed well up into the twentieth century. There are few better examples of this than that of US Senator James O. Eastland, as detailed by historian Christopher Asch. Eastland owned a plantation of 5,800 acres in Sunflower County. In 1967, it had a market value of about $450 an acre. For tax purposes, though, it was appraised at thirty-two dollars an acre. "Big Jim" pocketed the difference; the public schools of Sunflower County—for both whites and blacks—absorbed the loss.

There was another source of income, however: the newly founded state penitentiary at Parchman, a penal farm just north of Jim Eastland's plantation on which 90 percent of the inmates/laborers were black. After its founding in 1904, it generated extraordinary gains for the state government and any who received benefits from it—like the white school children of Noxubee and Bolivar Counties. It "had become a giant money machine," says New York University's David Oshinsky, one that "annually poured a million dollars into the state treasury." In 1917, the year my father entered the second grade in Merigold, its profits equaled "almost half of Mississippi's entire budget for public education."

And a generation later, it would equal the whole of one of my childhood fantasies.

CHAPTER 22

Mac and Black Annie

Oh listen you men / I don't mean no harm / If you wanna do
good you better / stay off of / Parchman Farm / Well you goes
to / work in the morning / just the / dawn of day / . . . Just at
the setting of the sun that's / when the / work is done.
—**Bukka White**, "Parchman Farm Blues" (1940)

My earliest memory in life is of "the settin' of the sun" at Parchman Farm.
That's the common name of the Mississippi State Penitentiary, which is in the
Delta, about forty miles from Longshot. I was not at Parchman as a prisoner,
mind you, or as a visitor to a family member who was a prisoner. Surely, you
know me and my people better than that by now. That sort of thing didn't
happen to such decent families, so averse to undulations. But even if we
had been a more unruly clan, that would have been highly unlikely. From
its founding in 1904 into the early 1970s, the inmates were over 90 percent
black and overwhelmingly black men. Virtually, the only whites found in
Parchman were the men in charge and, perhaps, their visitors.

That's where I came in. My memory is of a trip my family and I took to
Parchman to get a dog back in the 1950s. Not, mind you, a hound used to
track dangerous, escaped inmates nor one of the "kill dogs" meant to pick up
where the hounds left off. My dog was a puppy whose only job was to be a
family pet. The puppy was a purebred Dalmatian that my father was buying
from his second cousin Marvin Wiggins. Marvin was a casual dog breeder,
but more to the point, he was superintendent of Parchman Farm. We named
the puppy Mac. He was my first best friend. In my mind, the whole experience

of my half-day sentence in the penitentiary floats in a warm, rosy glow of nostalgia for what I remembered to be my very safe, stable, comfortable, middle-class childhood. My white childhood. Others, particularly black men like Bukka White, had/have different memories.

Indirectly but painfully, the farm "off of which you'd better stay" was born out of the Thirteenth Amendment to the Constitution of 1865, the very edict that declared, "Neither slavery nor involuntary servitude . . . shall exist within the United States, or any place subject to their jurisdiction." The devil, in this case, is in those ellipses. Slavery and servitude were banned "except as a punishment for crime whereof the party shall have been duly convicted." That loophole proved to be a black hole of human misery. After the war, southern states, led by Mississippi, immediately passed black codes to govern the conduct of blacks (not whites), and within these codes were included stipulations intended to reinstate racial bondage under the guise of the penal servitude allowed by the "freedom amendment."

The first step was usually to criminalize "vagrancy," which is a vague term in need of definition. Mississippi's code set the parameters of black vagrancy as "all rogues & vagabonds, idle & dissipated persons, beggars, jugglers, or persons practicing unlawful games or plays, runaways, common drunkards, common nightwalkers, pilferers, lewd, wanton, or lascivious persons, common railers & brawlers, & all who habitually misspend their time by frequenting houses of ill-fame, gaming houses, or tippling shops." For those arrested, a fine was imposed. When, as was the rule, the fine could not be paid, the labor of the "convicted criminal" was then leased to anyone who would cover the costs—with preference given to the former master. The reality is that if one person has the power to decree legal prohibitions into existence at will, any person can be made a criminal with the scratch of a pen.

These egregious abuses were made unconstitutional by the Equal Protection Clause of the Fourteenth Amendment of 1868, but neo–black codes were reinstated as soon as the Reconstruction governments were overthrown in the early to mid-1870s. This process of deconstruction corresponded, therefore, with an astronomical increase in the "crime" rate but only among blacks. In Georgia, between 1870 and 1910, the convict population increased ten times faster than the general population. This was, of course, explained by the return of the prolific vagrancy laws, to which Mississippi added a "pig law" in 1876, which redefined petty theft as grand larceny—but again, only for blacks—with a prison sentence of up to five years. But of course, the purpose was not to arrest black desperados for the sake of maintaining public order. The purpose was to coerce labor. Accordingly, says Douglas Blackmon, "The arrest cycle was synchronized with the business cycle, timed to the rise and fall of demand for labor" on plantations but also on railroad construction crews, on lumbering crews, and in coal mines.

It was a privatized penal system on a massive scale, with astronomical profits to be wrung from men whose rights and whose lives were forfeit. Though not only men. David Oshinsky of New York University reports that in Mississippi, by 1880, "at least one convict in four was an adolescent." Economist Garland Brinkley of Cal-Berkeley observes that "when the assets are human beings, duly convicted of racially motivated trumped-up charges and obtained at low cost, the incentive is to work them as hard as possible and to spend little on food, shelter, clothing, medical care, etc., in order to maximize profits." As to that shelter, C. Vann Woodward documents, "The South's 'penitentiaries' were great rolling cages that followed the construction camps and railroad building"—a nomadic Gulag, in other words, with an annual death rate of 12 percent, comparable to those in Stalin's USSR, comparable to those in Dachau concentration camp in Hitler's Germany. In Mississippi, says Oshinsky, "Not a single leased convict ever lived long enough to serve a sentence of ten years." In other words, the criminal justice system had little to do with criminality much less justice. After the demise of slavery, it was a means to restore and maintain racial control. Black lives be damned.

Edmund Richardson lost one fortune when his property of chattel slaves was confiscated at the end of the Civil War but made another, even-larger one in the Delta in the post-Reconstruction era. That fortune came to be spread across banks, steamboat companies, railroads, cotton mills, and, most importantly, cotton plantations. And there, says John Willis of the University of the South, it was made principally thanks to Richardson's "insatiable appetite for convict labor." They cleared the primeval forests, drained the swamps, laid the railroad tracks, and died by the gross as they built his empire, making him—it was said—"the largest cotton planter in the world outside of the

Khedive [Viceroy] of Egypt." His primary residence was Refuge, south of
Greenville. His concentration camps/plantations were located, and so his
crimes against humanity were committed, primarily there in Washington
County, but also in my home county of Bolivar just to the north.

Upon his death in 1886, his eldest son, James Richardson—"an inveterate
gambler and drunk," according to journalist Adrienne Berard—inherited his
father's estate. With that wealth, the heir was determined to found a new town
to be "developed solely as a center of sport" in southwest Bolivar County,
five miles west of the place still so remote it had not yet earned the name of
"Longshot." He personally drew up plans for a racetrack, a Downs to exceed
Epsom and Churchill, and began buying up thoroughbreds. Casinos were
to follow. All to be financed, though, with blood money wrung from convict
labor. He planned to christen his dream "Ingomar" for Ingvi, the Norse god
of fertility, to signify the cotton and gambling profits to sprout from the
alluvium. That name, unfortunately, had already been claimed by another
town, though. And so, Richardson's new settlement settled for "Benoit" in
honor of his company auditor. Only a name, you say. Or was it a harbinger
of things to come?

As an avatar of the Norse deity, "Ingomar" had clearly been destined for
greatness. As the namesake of a bean counter, "Benoit" was destined for
depreciation. Weakened by his life of dissipation, James Richardson died
along with his ambitions in 1898. Benoit did not become Monte Carlo on
the Mississippi, though it was eventually split by US Highway One, "the
Great River Road." Only a Richardson Street remains to honor the founder's
deranged fantasies of baccarat tables and hippodromes to remind all of his
abuse of penal slaves. At the end of that street, though, was built Benoit
Consolidated School—where I started my education. Today, Benoit is another
dying Delta town, dying of its own dissipation and excess, an excess of
inequality. A microcosm of the South, the nation.

Soon after James Richardson's demise, convict leasing was mercifully ended
in Mississippi and, in time, across the South. That "reform," though, was
accompanied by the founding of the state penitentiary at Parchman. It was
a not-so-little piece of hell spread over twenty thousand acres, forty-six
square miles, and housing two thousand inmates. It would be immortalized

in laments by black bluesmen and scarred into black backs by the three-foot long strap named Black Annie, and it would sire puppies for little white boys.

The crime-and-punishment loophole in the Thirteenth Amendment's prohibition of slavery again proved its usefulness. It had allowed southerners to replace chattel slavery with privatized penal slavery, and now it allowed them to replace that with state slavery. The laughably corrupt system of "justice" continued to be a feeder system for the labor needs of Parchman Farm. And those needs were those of a farm. A cotton plantation, specifically. With a labor force that was black and in bondage until the 1970s.

Its founders did not intend for it to be a place of rehabilitation. It might be possible to rehabilitate a criminal into an upright citizen, they thought, but it was not possible to rehabilitate a black man into a white man. And from its founding by Mississippi Governor James K. Vardaman—the rabidly racist "Great White Chief," reviled by Leroy Percy—it was openly intended to be an institution of racial control. It existed to discipline black men into forced laborers on a profitable cotton plantation, with the proceeds flowing into the state's treasury.

The fact that Parchman was a slave-labor plantation rather than a penitentiary meant that penologists need not apply for the superintendency. Only cotton planters were eligible. As was Marvin Wiggins, superintendent from 1944 to 1956 and my father's cousin. In his first mission—to turn a profit—he was spectacularly successful. But he was also known, by Parchman standards, to be a decent warden. Its revealing that this "decent warden" was also a great advocate of the liberal use of Black Annie, even in the face of mounting criticism in the 1950s. So, let's not be deceived. Cousin Marvin was the state-appointed commandant of a state-owned slave-labor camp in the mid-twentieth century. His concern for efficiency sanded off its sharpest edges, but that efficiency then made the trains—and the chain gangs—run on time, assuring the viability of state slavery.

Parchman's reputation for abuse would become even more notorious during the civil rights years. In 1961, several hundred black and white Freedom Riders were sentenced to the farm—their crime being biracial bus-seat sitting. Four years after that, several hundred black Natchezians were sent as well—their crime being "parading without a permit." I'm relieved to report, though, that Cousin Marvin had retired in 1956, no doubt leaving late in the year after the crops had been harvested but thereby escaping whatever credit or blame was owed to the superintendent of those later years. I'm annoyed to report, though, that this presents a complication. The latest date, therefore, on which we could have gone to Parchman to get a puppy from Superintendent Marvin Wiggins was late 1956. But I was born in January 1956. I can be sure that I was less than a year old when the family made its fateful trek. In other words, I was too young to remember it, and yet, I remember it oh so well.

It's called "childhood amnesia": the universal fact that children routinely forget events from the first couple of years of their lives, if not longer. To the degree that I have personal memories of going to Parchman to get my beloved Mac from Cousin Marvin, they are wholly invented. I obviously created them out of later descriptions I heard from my parents and older sisters and out of my desperate desire to be part of the wonderful tale of that family quest. And that magical mystery tour at the age of a few months was my first, my only trip to the prison, ever. I may not actually remember the event, but I grew up with the incredible luxury of making Parchman Farm a setting for a childhood tale of once upon a time.

The Jim Crow years at Parchman lasted into the early 1970s and then were ended only due to federal-court mandates. Black Annie and the chain gangs are gone. But with modifications, the vision of Parchman's founder, Mississippi's Great White Chief, was soon to be reinvigorated.

From the moment of the Thirteenth Amendment's ratification, racial control has been one of the principal aims of the criminal "justice" system in the South, but it is not only there that this has been the case. The black codes of 1866 included "vagrancy." The Jim Crow era had the "pig law." In each, blacks were targeted for arrest and imprisonment for minor crimes or no crimes at all. And where once blacks were subject to police harassment or violence due to offenses such as roguishness, idleness, nightwalking, wantonness, railing, and tippling, they are now arrested or shot for "walking while black" or jogging, driving, playing music, and/or entering their own homes. All within an environment of the "mass incarceration" of blacks and other minorities. Law professor Michelle Alexander of Stanford calls it, with good reason, "the new Jim Crow."

The numbers are staggering. From the mid 1970s to the mid 1980s, the incarceration rate in the United States doubled. In the following decade, it doubled again and continued to rise until peaking in 2007. In total, a seven-fold increase. The United States—with 5 percent of the world's people and 25 percent of the incarcerated—now has the highest incarceration rate in the world, lapping that of every other developed country and eight times higher than Germany. But our rate of incarceration is higher even than autocracies like Russia, China, and Iran. And in this nation of unprecedented levels of imprisonment, Mississippi has the second highest rate in the nation, trailing only Louisiana. This is even though, according to FBI statistics, Mississippi's rate of violent crime is below the national average.

Here, as well as nationally, one might ask why and how this has happened. Primarily, the cause has been an increase in the rate at which black males between age twenty and age forty have been jailed—a rate ten times higher than for the same age range among white males. The United States now jails a higher percentage of its black population than South Africa did at the height of apartheid. And most of this has been the result of arrests for nonviolent crimes, particularly drug possession, and harsh sentences for those arrested.

In the early 1970s, President Richard Nixon declared a "war on drugs." It would be escalated under Ronald Reagan in the 1980s with sentences that were mandatory and longer. To be sure, drugs can be dangerous and were most certainly illegal, so this was not inherently improper. But it is incontestable that blacks and whites use and sell drugs at comparable rates. And still, blacks are far more likely to be searched, arrested, sentenced, and actually imprisoned for any and every category of drug offense. Whites and blacks use cocaine at similar rates, but whites tend to use it in powder form and blacks, in the less expensive crystalline form, i.e., "crack." Nevertheless, convictions for mere possession of crack have not only been far more common, but also sentences have been far harsher than for powder. It is easy enough to understand why blacks are generally more suspicious of, and so, less cooperative with, police.

It is impossible to look at these statistics and not suspect ulterior motives in the waging of the "war." In a 1994 interview, Nixon's Chief Domestic Policy Advisor John Ehrlichman provided one. He admitted, "The Nixon campaign in 1968, and the Nixon White House after that, had two enemies: the antiwar left and black people. You understand what I'm saying? We knew we couldn't make it illegal to be either against the war or black, but by getting the public to associate the hippies with marijuana and blacks with heroin, and then criminalizing both heavily, we could disrupt those communities. We could arrest their leaders, raid their homes, break up their meetings, and vilify them night after night on the evening news. Did we know we were lying about the drugs? Of course, we did" (quoted in Baum).

This quote wasn't made public until after Ehrlichman's death, and its provenance has been challenged. There is no way to verify its accuracy. But its consistency with history is undeniable. It is quite simply impossible to study yesterday's Jim Crow justice and not to see his visage grinning from within the maze of the present. Unless, of course, you're wearing the blinkers of whiteness.

CHAPTER 23

Affirmative Action for White People

No matter the injustices of the past, shouldn't blacks today
be required to pull themselves up by their own bootstraps,
just like white people had to do?

It was "a poor man's promised land," says historian John Willis. Particularly for blacks, and most particularly for freed slaves in the late nineteenth century. Even in this era of rights gained and then lost in Reconstruction, of the dream of "forty acres and a mule" and then that dream denied, of the terror of the Klan and then of lynch mobs, of legally mandated segregation and disfranchisement, it remained a place in which free men and women could aspire not only to land ownership but also to ownership of some of the most fertile land on earth.

No, it was not the prairies in the Land o' Lincoln. Not the independent black republic of Haiti. Not in a "back-to-Africa" utopia in Liberia or Ethiopia. It was the Delta. The Yazoo-Mississippi Delta. After the Civil War, most of the Delta, despite its crazed fertility, remained impenetrable wilderness, a place beyond the reach, or interest, of white commercial planters. Cash-crop agriculture required access to markets, and that required transportation. But for that very reason, the lands at a distance from the watercourses were available to poor men, some white but mostly black, who desired simple subsistence and independence first and foremost and looked to wealth from cash crops only after. Speaking of all these still-remote areas of the Delta, Willis, of the University of the South, observes, "the unsettled nature of the country gave tenant farmers unique prospects for success in the last third of the 19th century. Former slaves were able to work their way up an 'agricultural ladder' toward property ownership. . . . No other part of the South saw comparable black dominance of land owning; nowhere else could ex-slaves reasonably aspire to hold such fertile property." As the twentieth century dawned, two thirds of the farms in the Yazoo-Mississippi Delta were owned by blacks.

Once more, for emphasis—this was true nowhere else than the Delta. The cat's-eye delta. But specifically, the "Longshots" of the region, the backswamps, the bountiful bottomlands, the lands hard as buckshot when dry and gooey as thick-filé gumbo when wet. The seductive lands of subtle undulations and frustrating rebuffs, the lands made rich by the humus of pure cussedness— the lands defined by contradiction. It was a land whose promise proved to be only a proposal, though. Because, as the twentieth century dawned, rough beasts slouched toward the black farmers' Holy Land to be born—white men with money and political connections. The poor black man's place of unmatched opportunity, sure enough, would become the "most southern place on earth," a place to be defined by, doomed by, its extreme inequities of wealth and race.

The transition started slowly, as Californian corporations—often with black convict labor—laid rail lines and as Chicagoan companies cleared the jungle and hauled away the timber. One of their dead-end rail lines into the interior of the forests—called "dummy lines"—reached the unreachable star of Longshot in 1907. In time, a road or two were built, and the eternal commercial cycle began—as small farmers lost out to the middling who lost out to the big who lost out to the bigger who today are being bought out by international corporate conglomerates, rapidly becoming, as Richard Grant judges in *Dispatches from Pluto* (2015), "a foretaste of a dystopian social future, when machines free capital from the burden of labor." But in its early phases, Willis explains that "whites bought, swindled, and crop-liened [*sic*] black farmers loose from their land." By 1920, three-quarters of Delta farms were operated by landless sharecroppers, some whites, mostly blacks. Many others were completely displaced. Some left. Some became itinerates, riding the new rail lines looking for temporary work, conjuring a new form of music as they wandered.

Why were the blues "the deepest in the Delta"? The genre undoubtedly drew on African antecedents and from the musical traditions of slavery days but burst forth at a particular time and a particular place for a reason. Out of all the southern places characterized by hardship, the Delta had become the locus of blacks' dreams and hopes, but now, says Willis, had become the place of "shattered dreams and strangled hopes." The blues expressed "more than anger and sadness; it gave vent to powerful disappointment, the sense of promise betrayed, the knowledge that a unique moment had passed and that the prospects of poor blacks might never soar so high again." Joel Williamson of the University of North Carolina adds, "The early blues was the cry of the cast-out black, ultimately alone and lonely, after one world was lost and before another was found."

It needs to be repeated, though, that this did not happen simply because of market forces. The swindles and debt trickery worked so well because they were officially sanctioned, carried out with a government seal of approval. The swindlers knew they were exempt from prosecution. The debt laws were written by the lenders themselves to give them an advantage over the borrowers. By 1915, the new extension service of the US Department of Agriculture was actively helping bigger farmers at the expense of small landowners, as well as at the expense of tenants and sharecroppers.

But not all whites were directly involved in the swindling, and many of the poorest were scammed themselves. But in other ways, they were still the beneficiaries of government favor. Even those who were least deserving.

There were men who boxed bears and other men who handled venomous snakes. These were among the less well-to-do settlers who came with the money men to Longshot in the 1920s and '30s. The first of these men were well liquored and paid for the privilege of the fisticuffs staged in a "corral" out behind the cotton gin late on Saturday nights. The second group abstained from all spirits but imbibed heavily on the Spirit early on Sunday mornings. The dark of the first and the light of the second seamlessly blended into one another, ever teetering on the cusp of that moment when Saturday night's profligate excess is transformed into Sunday morning's prayerful penance. Such is the union of honky-tonk and "honky-church," that amalgamation of tavern and tabernacle into the goodness-gracious-great-God-A'mighty "tavernacle" that was the white South. The place where "every day's a holy day, and every hour's happy" and to which all pharisaical wastrels were called to their common home on High.

Yes, and then came the Nazis.

From late 1943 to 1946, German POWs were held in many camps around the United States, including four camps in Mississippi. Here, most were from the famed Afrika Corps of Erwin Rommel—the Desert Fox. Some were from the elite units of the Waffen-SS—true-believing Nazis, in other words. Many of these soldiers were then parceled out to one of the fifteen satellite camps in Mississippi to help to alleviate the severe labor shortages caused by the war—with thousands gone to the military and millions more gone in the Great Migration to war work in northern cities. Some of the POWs worked in the lumbering industry in the Piney Woods down south, but most were sent to the Delta to chop and pick cotton. And some of them came to Longshot.

They were housed in a cluster of former sharecropper cabins, about a mile from the Holiness Church of the Snake Handlers and less than a quarter mile from the huge cottonwood tree to which the Boxing Bear was chained between matches and under which, post-bear, I would wait for the school bus every morning some years later—our family home to be built right across the road after the war. Out of this montage of cotton-pickin' Nazis, snake-bit rattler fondlers, and a pugilistic bear sadly gone to seed, I, unfortunately, have no knowledge about comingling, whether untoward or toward. The historical record is struck dumb before the phantasmagoria of bumpkin surreal.

And yet, here in the Delta, these Hitler Youth grown into Hitler *menschen* who had fought in the footsteps of Hannibal in Tunisia, now hoed cotton in the footsteps of black African chattel slaves and penal slaves. Aryan spirituals were bound to have rung out from their quarters. Teutonic angst was given voice in notes as blue as muddy waters flowing down the Rhine. Because surely, for these exemplars of the "master race" in the Third Reich, the Delta of 1944 had become the place of "shattered dreams and strangled hopes . . . of powerful disappointment, the sense of promise betrayed, the knowledge that a unique moment had passed" and that their prospects might never soar so high again.

Though, maybe not. The US military strictly observed the Geneva Convention in its treatment of their German prisoners. If discipline was warranted, it did not take the form of corporeal punishments. This is worth noting since, forty miles up the road from Longshot at Parchman Farm, the state of Mississippi—in fact, if not strictly in law—took advantage of the penal loophole in the Thirteenth Amendment to enslave two thousand American citizens. There, the Geneva Convention was dismissed. It just so happened that the Nazis' arrival in Longshot corresponds to the arrival at Parchman of Cousin Marvin Wiggins, the "kindly" superintendent who was especially fond of meting out the disciplinary tutelage of Black Annie.

Here, a question intrudes: In an area opened up by chattel slaves, developed by penal slaves, enriched by state slaves, why weren't the POWs likewise enslaved? And enslaved for life? Wholly beside the penal exception, capture in war has been the single most common path into enslavement down through history. John Locke, that champion of liberty, cited this fact in his justification for slavery. As he put it in his *Second Treatise of Government* (1689), slavery is "nothing else but the state of war continued, between a lawful conqueror and a captive." The only instance in which enslavement was legitimate, he thought, was as the result of capture of an unjust foe in a just war. Yet, enslaving these German POWs was never considered.

How can we explain the positively bizarre willingness to enslave native-born, English-speaking Christians but not foreign-born, non-English-speaking Nazi SS troopers captured in one of the most just wars ever fought? We, of course, already know the answer. Race. Whites, all whites—regardless of nativity, citizenship, language, religion, or political values, irrespective of intelligence, idleness, poverty, illiteracy, immorality, or criminality—were, and always had been, exempted from enslavement as chattel in English-speaking North America. This immunity was the first and, obviously, the most important of all the affirmative action programs that have defined this country's history.

It was a program that dated to the seventeenth century, long before the affirmative action controversies of the 1970s and '80s. Whites could be and were exploited and abused by their fellow whites, but even if treated as so called "wage slaves," they were not chattel slaves. My cousin Lewis Wiggins, turpentine laborer of North Carolina, was poor, unlettered, and powerless, but he was not subject to sale, did not suffer a "social death," was not forcibly separated from home, family, friends (unless we count his conscription into the Confederate army), did not endure an alienation from his ancestral religion and culture. No, Mississippi planters, like my fourth-great-grandfather Elijah Anderson, never got a chance to tap into the large and growing population of landless whites in the South, like Lewis. The right of nonenslavement was an extraordinarily valuable benefit tied to his whiteness.

And then came the 1930s. In that decade and later, legally mandated racial preferences for whites proliferated. The reason is easy enough to find. The enduring economic wreckage of the Great Depression fundamentally changed most Americans' ideas about the proper role of the federal government. Henceforth, it was assumed by most that it was responsible for maintaining conditions that would yield a certain minimal level of prosperity for the average person. By popular demand, with Franklin Roosevelt's New Deal and then also with World War II, the government became far more active in pursuit of this goal. The unprecedented levels and types of federal assistance did benefit blacks as well, but whites received a grossly disproportionate share.

Sometimes, that was due to barefaced racism. As with the open conspiracy between Federal Housing Administration (FHA) officials, local bankers, and real-estate brokers that maintained an official policy of "redlining"—discriminating against aspiring minority homeowners—from 1934 to 1968. Metropolitan neighborhoods were assigned grades, A to D, from most desirable for loans to least. With areas "infiltrated" by nonwhites given ratings comparable to those near toxic-waste dumps, the FHA essentially refused to guarantee loans to blacks or to whites who lived near blacks, in effect instructing whites to be prejudiced, actually penalizing them if they weren't. The result, even in Boston, Detroit, and San Francisco, was a housing pattern of de facto segregation and, therefore, de facto segregation in schools. This resulted in depressed real-estate values in minority areas and, therefore, lower property-tax revenues from which to fund their now segregated schools.

But sometimes, these New Deal programs produced a racially discriminatory result even when there was no racist intent in their creation. In an era when most families couldn't afford to put aside retirement savings or emergency funds—for potential unemployment, for example—Social Security was created to ease these burdens. However, because of bureaucratic considerations, for the system's first twenty years, farm workers and domestic workers were not eligible to participate. Some whites were therefore excluded but at far lower rates than blacks. In the South, where most still lived, 75 percent of black wage earners fell into the ineligible void.

Sometimes, though, the New Deal program was created with colorblind legislative language, funded with colorblind federal dollars, but then handed off to color-prejudiced state and local officials for implementation. This, for example, was the price demanded for support from southern congressmen in passing the GI Bill of 1944. It was, says Ira Katznelson of Columbia University, "the most wide-ranging set of social benefits ever offered by the federal government in a single, comprehensive initiative," promising veterans' tuition for college and vocational training, loans for homes and for small-business startups. But in the Jim Crow South, whites-only colleges automatically turned away black veterans who applied, and the chronically underfunded all-black colleges lacked the facilities to accommodate most of them. While my father was quickly granted a GI Bill home loan after the war, black veterans who applied for bank loans to buy homes or start businesses were routinely denied, regardless of guarantees from the US Department of Veterans Affairs (VA). In Mississippi in 1947, of 3,229 federally guaranteed GI home loans, two went to black veterans. But too, in New York and northern New Jersey, under one hundred of the 67,000 total VA-insured mortgages went to nonwhites.

For the white beneficiaries of all these programs, the effect was profound, particularly when coupled with the postwar boom. Yes, these people worked hard to get ahead, but the poor (of any color) had always worked hard and, despite the "laissez-fairy tale," had mostly stayed poor. Now, though, their efforts were amplified by government-supplied access to education and job training, low-interest and long-term credit, old-age insurance, and the inheritable equity of home ownership. These federal government programs, says Katznelson, "created the modern white middle class." But not a black or brown one.

This example of the stubborn fact of racial prejudice—north as well as south, among the working class as well as the middle and upper classes—gives the lie to an all-too-common notion that racial exploitation can be reduced to a subcategory of class exploitation. Too often, it is assumed that racial inequality will automatically be alleviated by programs designed to alleviate poverty in general. These programs did undeniably help the poor and, combined with higher taxes and more regulations, narrowed the wealth gap within the American economy. However, during the postwar economic boom of the late 1940s and '50s, notes Katznelson, "the income of Negro men relative to white men declined in every section of this country." And so, he asks rhetorically, "Why did the disparity between white and black Americans widen after the Second World War despite the country's prosperity?" His direct answer: "affirmative action for whites."

Racism has always been designed to oppress nonwhites but has also always been used to limit the rise of the white working class by preventing its alliance with those exploited minorities. It is exquisitely engineered, therefore, to thwart class-based remedies for ending discrimination. Though racial exploitation and class exploitation are not the same, they are linked, with each helping to do the exploitative work of the other. So that, by recommending strictly class remedies, New Deal liberals handed racists their victory, just as their liberal heirs have often done since. "Raceless anti-racism"—as Pulitzer Prize–winning essayist and novelist Ta-Nehisi Coates calls it—is feckless at best.

After three hundred years, white supremacy was finally paying off for the average white person. Not because southern members of the One Percent became more generous. They didn't. Not because state-level Jim Crow became more equitable. It didn't. But because of federal government assistance for whites, but not nonwhites.

CHAPTER 24

The Second Reconstruction of American Democracy

Didn't whites have to give up a lot so that blacks
could get their "civil rights" in the 1960s?

1—10—F—B. That's all I remember.

I was ten when "freedom-of-choice" desegregation arrived in my fourth-grade classroom in 1966. Arrived in the form of one—ten-year-old—female—black. For that year, she represented the totality of token integration at Benoit Consolidated Elementary School—the one on Richardson Street, the street named for James Richardson, the visionary/delusional founder of the town who had dreamed of turning his wealth from privatized penal slavery, i.e., convict leasing, into casinos and thoroughbreds to satisfy the gaming lust of his all-white and wealthy clientele. It was an inauspicious setting for this experiment in minimalist integration.

As for the black girl, I did not call her names. I did not push her. To the best of my memory, no one did—on strict orders from our teacher. We should know that the all-white school board desperately wanted this 1—10—F—B desegregation "plan" to work. It was the means, they hoped, to stave off full consolidation with the town's all-black public school. No taunting, therefore, was allowed. Of course, no one spoke to her either. As she stood alone during every recess and ate alone during lunchtime, she was ignored. I do remember that I made a point to ignore her oh so politely, ever so decently. So, she wasn't physically or verbally abused. No, but she was subjected to unrelenting psychological torture, shunned like a leper. In this white-on-white setting, her blackness shone like a thousand suns, and still, somehow, she was socially invisible.

1—10—F—B.

It is the most elemental and tenacious of white privileges: insensibility, the right not to see, not to hear, not to feel, not to know. For a bourgeois pretender like me, it was a positively regal faux concern. "Let them eat cake," Marie Antoinette is said to have said when told that the common people in France had no bread. "Let them sing Motown," I apparently thought when told that blacks had no rights. Listening to The Temptations certainly seemed to fill my need for atonement on that whole race thing. It was incomprehensible to me that the token of Monroe, Buddhaman, and me harmonizing (?) on "Papa Was a Rolling Stone" didn't appease four hundred years of black grievance. But over time, such studied obliviousness damages the unseer as well as the unseen. Racism also made it impossible for white southerners to see themselves.

I still don't remember her name. No matter. 1—10—F—B didn't come back to class after Christmas holidays anyway.

I had grown up with the civil rights movement; it was with me from infancy. But though constant, it was no more than a vague presence. I was conceived during the arguments before the Supreme Court that yielded the *Brown v. Topeka II* decision, the one ordering desegregation of public schools with "all deliberate speed." Simultaneously, twenty-five miles to the east of Longshot, the Citizens Council—"the white-collar Klan"—was organizing to lead the South's massive resistance to integration. A fault line was opening beneath my white feet before I had feet, before my feet had me. Four months after my conception, fifty miles east in the Delta, Emmett Till was lynched, his murderers to be acquitted after an hour's deliberation, the case to become a national scandal.

I was five years old by the time Freedom Riders were imprisoned and abused at Parchman Farm Penitentiary, just forty miles northeast of Longshot. I was eight when Freedom Summer volunteers established Freedom Schools as near as ten miles away. I was eleven when Bobby Kennedy made his famous tour of poverty-stricken areas of the Delta—spending much of the time within about twenty miles of oblivious me.

But my world and the larger world came crashing together in 1968 with the assassination of Martin Luther King Jr. My parents grimaced and shook their heads but said nothing. The following day, though, none of my father's black tractor drivers showed up for work. Neither did the black woman who did ironing for my mother. Here, at the age of twelve, it was a complete revelation to me that these people that I saw everyday saw their plight as related to the campaigns and sacrifices of MLK. Of course, I hadn't really noticed that they had a "plight." Coincidentally, soon after I realized "the news" had something to do with me, and with my family's position in the socio-economic-political universe, my interest in history began to shift from that of the South to that of modern Europe. Belle Époque France and Weimar Germany and their historical antecedents were fascinating—and distant—from the dramas unfolding in Longshot. I was fourteen when—after fourteen years of "all deliberate speed"—the black and white public schools were consolidated, meaning virtually all the white children in the black-majority Delta, including me, fled to segregation academies.

Be assured that the issue was not race mixing as such, though. Like so many white children in the South, I had grown up playing with black children, after all. Far more was at stake. There is a saying that, in the North, whites don't care how high blacks get as long as they don't get too close. And in the South, whites don't care how close blacks get as long as they don't get too high—"high" as in positions of power. Power over whites. Segregation had never been an end in itself. It was one more means to power. And that, as I heard repeatedly, is why the civil rights revolution would bring doom for whites. A way of life was at stake. The worry was less that blacks and whites would sit next to each other in classrooms or at lunch counters. It was that "they" were "taking over." It was that a cataclysm for whiteness loomed.

"The Civil Rights Revolution turned out to be the best thing that ever happened to the white South." This according to *New York Times* Atlanta Bureau Chief Peter Applebome. I imagine that this assertion comes as news to most Americans, not only southerners, but it is not a controversial statement. The usual assumption is that race relations are a zero-sum game in which black gains have to come at white expense. Sometimes, that was true, but it was not the norm. It's useful to remember that, in the big picture and the long run, black enslavement was bad for most white southerners as well as blacks, and black emancipation and biracial governance during Reconstruction was good for most white southerners as well as blacks, just as Reconstruction's overthrow and the imposition of Jim Crow was bad for most white southerners and blacks. Given this past, Applebome's statement is almost mundane. There are many other journalists, politicians, and historians who essentially agree. The civil rights movement benefitted blacks *and* whites. It was a "double emancipation," the second in our history. Which helps to explain why the civil rights movement is sometimes called the "Second Reconstruction." As with the first, we first have to consider what aspects of the nation's construction needed "reconstruction." In this case, that brings us back to that matchless monstrosity called Jim Crow.

After being part of the historically unprecedented age of emancipation and being the center of the globally unprecedented attempt "to create a biracial democracy from the ashes of slavery," the South then unleashed an unprecedented backlash against racial equality. To be sure, racial prejudice survived in all the societies in which racial slavery was abolished in the nineteenth century, but nowhere else was it taken to such extremes, and nowhere else was it enshrined into a comprehensive body of law such as was created in the postbellum South. There was nothing "traditional" about Jim Crow. In global, historical context, it was unprecedented.

In essence, though the South had not been allowed to secede from the Union, in recompense, it was ultimately allowed to secede from the parts of the constitutional Union it didn't like—specifically the Fourteenth Amendment and Fifteenth Amendment. Jim Crow was à la carte constitutionalism, with clauses, sections, and even entire amendments to be savored or spurned as southerners desired. Even the "inalienable" right to life became optional. From petty points of segregation to state-sponsored terrorism against its own population, race was the point of that sovereignty.

Up to this time, racism had been cultivated to serve the needs of slavery; now, the hate-filled ideological child of bondage would declare its independence, its own neurotic manias proudly displayed for the world to see. At this point, says Arkansas-born C. Vann Woodward, the South completed its total "capitulation to the cult of racism." In service to this cult, many Americans demonstrated again that they were willing to abandon liberty, equality, and democracy. For blacks, of course. But also, for whites. Regarding racial "custom," there was no real free speech or free press for anyone. In the

1940s, the North Carolinian W. J. Cash explained that "dissent and variety are completely suppressed," and there is a "suspicion toward new ideas, an incapacity for analysis, an inclination to act from feeling rather than from thought." Within the open, free society of the United States, the South—most particularly Mississippi—was a "closed society" in the famous phrase of James Silver, longtime professor of southern history at Ole Miss. Silver stresses that "a never-ceasing propagation of the 'true faith' must go on relentlessly, . . . requiring that non-conformists and dissenters from the code be silenced, or driven from the community. Violence . . . enforced the image of unanimity." And thus, says Du Bois, "was built a Solid South impervious to reason, justice or fact."

A regime of unreason, injustice, and delusion is not the recipe for good governance. While shrieking like banshees over the godless communists who, they claimed, were inciting racial unrest, southerners imposed "god-ordained" segregation on themselves—a phalanx of social and economic regulations on such a scale as to make a Soviet commissar blush. Silver speaks plainly: this was "a totalitarian society" functioning within the United States. One defended to their last breath by self-described "conservatives" in the South itself and tolerated by "libertarian conservatives" across the country.

In 1965, right-wing hero Ronald Reagan famously depicted the proposed Medicare reform to be a steppingstone to communism. It would, he claimed, dictate "government control over where Americans were allowed to live" and federal control over "where Americans go and what they do for a living." Regarding Medicare, this was patent nonsense, but of course, this is exactly what Jim Crow did. And still, simultaneously, Reagan and many others were advising against federal interference with this state-government mandated form of totalitarianism. It was a matter of "states' rights," they said.

There were, of course, variations place to place, but the Jim Crow governments, in fact, told people where they could live, where they could go, and what they could do for a living. Citizens in the United States of America were told who to buy their shoes from and to whom they could sell socks. Government mandates dictated where to be born, where to be schooled, where to be hospitalized, and where to be buried. Where to stand in line, where to sip water, where to sit while watching *Beach Blanket Bingo*, where to eat a ham sandwich. And where and with whom one could play checkers in public. The separate schools even had to use separate schoolbooks, which had to be stored in separate book depositories so that the separated schoolchildren would not touch each other even through the surrogate of an algebraic equation on a sheet of paper—before, of course, going home to play with one another. Jim Crow was the King Kong of government regulation. To repeat: support for this tyrannical travesty was called "conservatism." This was the self-destructive and utterly preposterous "way of life" that was so endangered by civil rights "revolutionaries."

To grasp the fantastical extreme represented by this casually accepted status quo, we need to remember that, while racism has been common in many places, there have been only three legally defined racist regimes in history—Nazi Germany, apartheid South Africa, and the Jim Crow South. Of the three, Jim Crow came first. Accordingly, the other two acknowledged their debt to Dixie. Both studied its laws and customs and applied some to their own circumstances. Neither, though, copied Jim Crow wholesale. It's worth pausing to consider that the Nazis—not generally known for their squeamishness on the subject of race—judged some of its features to be too "excessive."

Surely, decent whites in the South saw this as the outrage that it was. But "moderates" insisted that they, as southerners, should be allowed to handle reform for themselves and that those reforms would need to "go slow." It is eminently plain, however, that the South would never have freed itself from the psychosis of Jim Crow—just as it would never have freed itself from slavery. To be freed from the dead hand of Jim Crow, there had to be a second Reconstruction, aka, a civil rights movement. In 1984, former Mississippi Governor William Winter acknowledged this reality. He told Myrlie Evers-Williams, widow of martyred civil rights activist Medgar Evers, that "all the white folks in Mississippi owed you and Medgar as much as black folks. He freed us; we were all prisoners of that system. Because of you, we were able to shake off the bonds that held us."

So, yes, escape from that prison, the unshackling of those bonds, was, in Peter Applebome's words, "the best thing that ever happened to the white South, paving the way for the region's newfound prosperity." Historian Gavin Wright explores the issue in far greater depth in his *Sharing the Prize: The Economics of the Civil Rights Revolution in the American South* (2013). He writes that the movement "invigorated the regional economy by opening it to inflows of capital, creativity, and new enterprises from around the world." And he finds that "southern black employment gains did not come at the expense of white employment, and southern black income gains did not cause southern white incomes to fall." Echoing Applebome, he concludes that "it becomes clear that most white southerners were long-term beneficiaries of this historical change."

Wright acknowledges that there were areas of exception to this rule of achievement—such as desegregation in education. The process was disruptive for all, black as well as white. Here, with some successes, there have been more instances of stalemate and many abject failures. But there would have been a greater chance of a more satisfactory and mutually acceptable outcome if white leaders had been amenable to good-faith efforts at compromise from the beginning, as detailed by University of North Carolina at Charlotte historian Charles Bolton. Instead, though, they adopted "massive resistance." A stone wall of delay, obstruction, and defiance and "permissions to hate." White southern leaders were given a decade and a half to begin reforms for themselves, to exercise the "sovereign rights" that they claimed to value so highly. Fifteen years later, they had essentially done nothing, with examples like that of 1—10—F—B being the exception. Only then did federal courts begin to force the issue. The transition was painful, and in the end, most whites fled to "segregation academies" and/or white suburbs. De facto segregation prevailed in most school districts even after de jure segregation had been outlawed. At which point, and ever since, white southerners have resentfully complained that the federal courts "ruined" their public schools.

Given the judgments of Wright and Applebome, the South's campaign of massive resistance seems foolish. But from the perspective of Jim Crow's champions, was it? In 1962, as Ole Miss was being integrated and the South's fortress of segregation was under assault from every direction, Mississippi Senator Jim Eastland gave an interview to a reporter from the *Chicago Tribune*. At one point, though, he turned the tables and asked the journalist a question: "How long did it take the South [meaning the white-supremacist Confederacy] to win the Civil War?" Taking advantage of the confused pause, he answered his own question, "Eleven Years, wasn't it?" He was referring to what some call the "Long Civil War," which only ended with the murder of Reconstruction eleven years after the Confederacy's supposed "loss" of the war in 1865. Secession had been defeated and slavery ended, but on the issue of race, the white supremacists won in the end. And they did so by means of a tactic of massive resistance, including terrorism. And did so, finally, with the nearly full approval of the federal government. By 1876, most white Americans, north as well as south, had returned to their default position—they were white supremacists. As surely in New York City and San Francisco as in Wetumpka, Alabama. In 1962, says historian Christopher Asch, Eastland expected a similar cycle to turn. He "fundamentally believed that white northerners shared his racial prejudices." Fundamentally, he would be proven right (with exceptions).

"Unreconstructed" despots know how to play the long game. They see defeats as battlefield setbacks in a lengthy war. Tactical retreats are sometimes necessary. They take for granted that their foolish enemies will take every singular victory as a final triumph, another step on the glorious march of progress, a march that is irreversible. The fools will then let down their guard. And that's when the unreconstructed counterattack. By the mid-1960s, another backlash was already underway. This time, to be part of one of the greatest political realignments in our history.

PART 6

THE SECOND DECONSTRUCTION OF AMERICAN DEMOCRACY

CHAPTER 25

The Great Migration of the Yellow Dogs

How did the two political parties come to change "sides"
on the issue of civil rights?

In the presidential election of 1928, the Democrats nominated Al Smith, an anti-Prohibition Irish Catholic from New York City. It was well understood that religious bigotry would be an obstacle for his candidacy and, one would think, perhaps an insurmountable one in the pro-Prohibition, Protestant, and rural South. And sure enough, his Republican opponent, Herbert Hoover, won in a landslide, carrying forty-two states, including the always more bipartisan "Border South." But of the eight states Smith carried, six of them were in the Deep South. In "dry," bucolically evangelical Mississippi, this "wet," big-city Yankee Papist had thrashed the Prohibition-preaching, Iowa-born, Quaker with 82 percent of the vote. How can such a violation of political logic be explained?

A breed of feral "yellow dogs" roamed the southern backwoods. They were curs, mongrels, all judged to be no-count. And so, in the South, to be called a "yellow dog" was to be insulted. It would seem that a man who was equated to a yellow dog was the absolute lowest form of humanity. Not so. There were those who ranked even lower on the region's Great Continuum of Contempt, pestilential varmints inferior even to yellow dogs. As of the 1850s, these were

Republicans. Southern whites proclaimed that they would vote for a despised yellow dog before they would vote for a member of the doubly despised Republican Party. And since the antithesis of a Republican was a Democrat, most southerners were "yellow-dog Democrats." Which meant they would vote for a no-count, lying, thieving, incompetent, megalomaniacal, sexually deviant, dumb-as-dirt Democrat over any Republican opposition, even over the starched-collar Hoover. Therefore, Mississippians hadn't voted *for* the big-city Yankee Papist (the yellow dog); they had voted *against* the Republicans of emancipation and equal rights, the Republicans who yet bore the mark of Cain for their authorship of the Thirteenth, Fourteenth, and Fifteenth Amendments. Today, it's called "negative partisanship." But whatever the label, religion be damned, race hate had conquered all.

Professor Ulrich B. Phillips of Harvard understood. A Georgian by birth and upbringing, he was, at the time, the preeminent historian of the antebellum South. In a famed essay published in the flagship *American Historical Review* in, coincidentally, the presidential election year of 1928, he denied that the essence of southern history was found in the cultivation of cotton. Or, more generally, in its agrarian economy or in its peoples' English and Scots-Irish origins or in evangelical Protestantism. Or even in the legacy of slavery as such. Yet, he insisted, there was, in southern history, "a unity despite its diversity." Throughout, he maintained, the region's "white folk" were "a people with a common resolve indomitably maintained—that [the South] shall be and remain a white man's country." This, he declared, "whether expressed with the frenzy of a demagogue or maintained with a patrician's quietude, is the cardinal test of a Southerner." White supremacy was, as the essay's title proclaimed, "the central theme of Southern history." Race is what gave the region its ballast, rendered it solid or nearly so— pickled in the sour vinegar of bigotry. The election of that year had reiterated his point. In 1928, the tree-toad white Pap Finn had spanked the baby Jesus and made him bawl.

Here, in 2022, the day of dominance by the yellow-dog Democrats is passed. But the days of "yellow doggism" are still with us. In most of the South, whites now vote Republican in the same percentages and with the same blind allegiance with which they once voted Democratic. They do not equivocate; they would sooner vote for a no-count, lying, thieving, incompetent, megalomaniacal, sexually deviant, dumb-as-dirt yellow dog than any Democrat. The yellow dogs live on—as Republicans.

We see the origins of yellow dogs, but what explains their manic migration from blue to red? No, it was not only a matter of race. Economic self-interest did play a role. The New Deal and wartime mobilization had pumped a massive federal stimulus into the South, prompting a transformation of its economy. As predicted by the Texas-born, Harvard political scientist V. O. Key as early as 1947, many in the expanding commercial middle class of the newly emerging "sunbelt" would be naturally inclined to do what their class cousins in the North had been doing since the 1850s: vote for the probusiness Republicans. Also, there is no question that, beginning in the 1980s, cultural-religious "wedge" issues became important in the churchly South. On the basis of these factors alone, the Republican Party would have become at least competitive among whites in the region.

However, the GOP hadn't just become competitive, it had become an object of cult-like blind devotion. Even among Key's expanding class of button-down suburban businessmen and even among the "religious Right," voters had proven willing to opt for a no-count, lying, thieving, incompetent, megalomaniacal, sexually deviant, dumb-as-dirt yellow dog over any Democrat. *That* is the essence of yellow doggism. Clearly, something else was involved, as before, something more elemental than even economics or religion. Race was that something. Party allegiance may have changed, the "central theme" did not.

If southerners' elemental goal was the maintenance of white supremacy, their primary national political goal had to be to keep outsiders in general and the federal government specifically out of their racial business. That meant that the issue of "states' rights" was the means to vouchsafe slavery before the war and Jim Crow after. Of course, enhancing states' power necessarily meant weakening that of the federal government. And, significantly, in the nineteenth century, that small-government philosophy appealed not only to southern slave owners and segregationists but also to the urban working class in the North. This was the era when it was assumed that central government was enthralled to the rich and, therefore, was the greatest danger to the common man's liberty and interests. Therefore, it was argued, the common man should stand against Big Government. And therefore, the immigrant Irish longshoremen of New York City became the political allies of proslavery Mississippi planters in the Democratic Party. Southerners, though, were dominant.

But over the course of the early twentieth century, the Democratic Party underwent a profound change, one reflective of changes in the country. By about 1920, the United States passed over that vitally important threshold between its rural, agrarian roots and its urban, industrial future. The working classes in the cities exploded in size and in their share of Democratic votes. Demographically, the Democratic Party was no longer predominately southern but northern, not rural but urban. These changes in the makeup of the Democratic electorate also dictated a change in their view of the role of government. White workers had feared government in the nineteenth century, but by the early twentieth century, it was becoming obvious that Big Business rather than Big Government was the source of their troubles. And more, Big Government was now seen to be a necessary shield against corporate abuse—most emphatically during the years of the New Deal. Nationally, the Democrats become the primary advocates for the use of federal power for the "general welfare." It could not have been otherwise. From the perspective of rural, agrarian America, the party of the common man was naturally the party of small government. But in urban, industrial America, the party of the common man had to be the party of Big Government. But too, it was becoming the party of the common black man.

Due to the World Wars and the disruptions of the Depression and New Deal, millions of blacks had moved from the rural South to the urban North in the ongoing Great Migration. There, they faced discrimination, but they could and did vote. And when they voted, thanks to the New Deal, they began to shift their votes from the Republican Party of Lincoln to the Democratic Party of Roosevelt. Even though the New Deal helped whites to a much greater degree, it did offer aid to blacks, who judged that the something offered by the Democrats was better than the nothing offered by the Republicans. The now predominately northern, urban, multiethnic Democratic Party was thus also becoming multiracial. By the 1940s, it was possible to envision a Democratic Party not only advocating for federal-government power over state power but also applying that power to the cause of civil rights in the southern states.

Harry Truman, president from 1945 to 1953, was the catalyst. In 1947, his administration pushed for federal action against employment discrimination, lynching, and the poll tax. Each proposal died at the hands of southern

Democrats in Congress. Undeterred, at the 1948 Democratic Party convention, Truman backed a strong civil rights plank for the official platform of his reelection campaign. For many southern Democrats, this was intolerable. Through the Depression and war years, they had fed on Big Government largesse like albino pigs in slop yet professed constitutional horror over Big Government's tentative moves to aid nonwhites. "States' rights!" the delegates bellowed in principled protest . . . as they continued to count their federal-aid dollars, lobbied for still more, and walked out of the convention.

The renegades then formed their own States' Rights Party, unofficially known as the "Dixiecrats." They knew perfectly well that they had no chance of winning the general election; their intention was to punish Truman and the Democrats by siphoning off southern electoral votes and, therefore, throwing the election to the Republicans. Truman didn't blink, however; he doubled down. Less than two weeks after the end of the convention, he ordered the desegregation of the armed forces.

In the November election, the Dixiecrats carried four of the once solidly Democratic states in the Deep South (South Carolina, Alabama, Mississippi, and Louisiana). Significantly, though, Truman won anyway, surprisingly taking both the electoral college and the popular vote by comfortable margins. The Democratic South had cracked, and still, the national Democratic Party had survived nicely. An important lesson had been learned. For many decades to come, local and state offices in the South would still be filled by Democrats who could be counted on to be "right on race," but in presidential politics, white southerners could no longer hold the Democratic Party hostage to their racial demands. As Dixiecrats, they had no future, but a more viable alternative to the Democrats hovered nearby. What if the political equivalent of another New Madrid earthquake were to reduce the rock of the solid South to pebbles, were to make the rivers flow backwards? What if the white South were to go Republican?

By the end of the 1940s and the dawn of the 1950s, some southerners were rethinking the Republican Party. But they were doing so only because the party of Radical Reconstruction had been rethinking itself. Or more exactly, returning to its first principles. In 1854, the Republican Party had been founded as an uncompromisingly antislavery (though not abolitionist) party.

But antislavery was part of the broader probusiness agenda it had inherited from the Whigs and Federalists. It was, then, also the Big Government party of the day, meaning subsidies and other assistance for businesses, both large and small, both railroad corporations and independent farmers. But that also required ever-increasing efforts to break the slavocrats' power over the national government, leading ultimately to abolition and civil rights for blacks, at least for a while.

But by 1873, most Republicans were convinced that the disruptions of Reconstruction and their commitment to black rights had gone too far and gone on for too long, becoming bad for business. They found that they could cooperate quite comfortably with southern white supremacists as junior, rather than senior, partners. And thanks to the careful nurturing by Federalists, then Whigs, and then Republicans over the years, "business" had grown up. It was now Big Business. By the end of the nineteenth century, it had become so big—and potentially repressive—that there were calls for federal-government regulation. In response, most Republicans—once favoring a hands-on policy of aid to business—began to evolve toward a more hands-off, laissez-faire policy, though it was a selective one that assailed regulation while still lavishing subsidies. Where there appears to be an inconsistency, there actually is none. In its first principles, the party was probusiness. When business wanted Big Government subsidies, the party favored Big Government. When business was threatened with Big Government regulation, it opposed Big Government. When the slavocracy had threatened business interests, they had opposed it, but when Big Business reached an accommodation with former slavocrats, most abandoned the blacks' cause.

Republicans of course continued to pontificate mightily about racial justice, and there were always those—consistently, a minority—who were sincerely committed to the issue. But collectively, they acted feebly. Or worse. The prime examples are found on the Supreme Court. In a series of cases between 1873 and 1883, a Republican-dominated court neutered the Fourteenth Amendment, rendering it powerless to stop the erosion of black rights after Reconstruction. And a Republican-majority court sanctified segregation with *Plessy v. Ferguson* in 1896. In twenty-five years, as the party of Lincoln became the party of J. P. Morgan, nonradical Republicans in the judicial branch undid much of what the Radical Republicans in the legislative branch had earlier accomplished.

And so is revealed the path for the Great Migration of the yellow dogs. As national Democrats slowly began to adopt a more hands-on approach to resolving black-white problems, the Republicans' comparatively hands-off approach to state-level racial matters began to look enticing to some southerners. The much-caricatured Democratic demagogue Theodore Bilbo, with his flashy red suspenders, had died in 1947. But old Jim Crow was already being fitted by his Republican tailors for a new gray flannel suit.

CHAPTER 26

The Southern Strategy of the Republican Party

What exactly was the "southern strategy"?

After passage of the Civil Rights Act of 1964, Democratic President Lyndon Johnson, who had engineered its passage, is said to have said to an aide, "We have lost the [white] South for a generation." Some have questioned the legitimacy of the quote, but the point made is not at issue. By late 1964, white southerners were leaving the national Democratic Party (as opposed to, for the time being, their state parties) in droves. But in reality, Democrats had been in the process of losing the white vote in the South for years. Sometimes to a third party but, more ominously, increasingly to Republicans.

My mother, the *W* girl, was one of the first. On her first presidential ballot, she chose Thomas Dewey over Roosevelt in 1944. Losing the vote of the former Miss Scooba was surely distressing for the Democrats, but of greater concern was the tempest brewing in the Old South's once-a-year Brigadoon—Natchez, Mississippi. University of Florida historian Jack Davis, after closely looking at Natchez politics during this era, chronicles some of its earliest stirrings of Republicanism. And here, in this most traditional of southern towns, the political migration was led by the most traditional of southern belles—none other than Katherine Miller, leader of the Pilgrimage Garden Club and matriarch of the Natchez Pilgrimage, the town's annual springtime showcase of its stunning collection of antebellum mansions. The state of Mississippi momentarily remained in the national Democratic column, but with Miller in the vanguard of revolution, white Natchez voted for Dwight Eisenhower, the Republican nominee for president, in 1952 and again in 1956.

Significantly, though, in abandoning the national Democratic Party, Miller never identified herself as a Republican but rather as a "New Republican," one who explicitly rejected the radically activist "Party of Lincoln." Her New Republican Party was the party of laissez-faire—on business regulation but also on racial issues. Though she denied that she had racial motives for making the switch, after she was named national committeewoman for the Mississippi Republican Party, she refused to sit with the regular "black and tan" delegation, which included blacks, and instead took a place among the "lily-whites." When asked why she supported Eisenhower, she said quite simply that he was the candidate who "thinks like we do."

As to Dwight Eisenhower's thinking, he had grown up in Kansas and was by no means a vocal advocate of Jim Crow. But on desegregation, he nevertheless advised a "go-slow" approach, which was understood in the South to be code for publicly applauding the concept while actually doing nothing. He criticized the Supreme Court's *Brown v. Topeka* decision, which mandated desegregation of public schools. He did send federal troops to Little Rock—not to defend civil rights, but rather to defend the rule of law. He did sign the 1957 Civil Rights Bill into law, but it was yet one more toothless attempt to substitute symbolism for substance. Compared to a Dixiecrat's obstructionism, then, Eisenhower paled; but a growing number of white southerners could reasonably conclude that "he thinks like we do" on racial issues, particularly when compared to a Truman Democrat.

But let's not be deceived about the state of affairs in the national Democratic Party at this stage. After Truman's activism, in the next two presidential elections, the party nominated their own go-slow candidate, Adlai Stevenson. And after that, one more in 1960, John Kennedy. This liberal icon did not enter office as a noted liberal on civil rights, seeing them as something of a distraction from his vital work in world affairs. But if he did not naturally gravitate to civil rights issues, those issues would kick down the door of his Oval Office. Facing defiance of federal law on the state level, he and his brother, Attorney General Robert Kennedy, were forced to intervene to protect the Freedom Riders and then to enforce the desegregation of Ole Miss. In terms of coaxing even the slightest federal intervention to protect black liberties in the South, obtuse segregationist governors, like Orval Faubus in Arkansas and Ross Barnett in Mississippi, were the best friends the movement had.

There is a bleak, plain truth here. JFK and RFK, like most white Americans—and still, like most white Democrats outside the South—would have preferred to ignore the discomforting issue of civil rights. But civil rights activists didn't allow them that luxury. The ugly reality of Jim Crow was forced into America's complacent face by the stories and pictures coming out of the South. John Kennedy may have still preferred to immerse himself in the geopolitical intrigue of Berlin and Havana and Saigon, but he could no longer avert his cosmopolitan gaze from Birmingham and Jackson. On the evening of June 11, 1963, he went on national television to call for a new civil rights act, this one to have real bite. And this one, controversially, to move beyond a ban on segregation in government-funded institutions (like public schools) and to ban it in "public accommodations" (privately owned hotels, restaurants, etc.).

As Kennedy spoke, Mississippi was in the midst of a gubernatorial campaign between a Democrat and—of all things—a serious Republican. The GOP's candidate was Rubel Phillips. My mother, the lifelong Republican, was an active supporter of Phillips, dodging cotton pickers while canvassing homes along the gravel roads of Longshot—a Doña Quixote tilting at the windmills of the old Democratic South. She and everyone else knew that Phillips had no chance to win, but the hope was to lay the groundwork for better results in the future. One in which Republicans would lead the white South's defense of states' rights. Phillips didn't criticize Mississippi Democrats' segregationist goals but criticized their buffoonish grandstanding and dangerous flouting of the rule of law. These tactics, he said, were not only embarrassing, though. They had failed abjectly to fend off the integration pushed—however half-heartedly—by the national Democratic Party. But in accepting the economic interventionism of Big Government Democrats, Phillips charged, Mississippians were undermining their own efforts to stop Big Government Democrats' civil rights intervention. Only the laissez-faire Republicans could defend state-decreed segregation and disfranchisement in a logically consistent and constitutionally principled way, he thought. The Kennedy's were "communists" who had "declared war on Mississippi," but even while defending Jim Crow, one must mind one's constitutional manners. My mother (and father) emphatically agreed. Phillips would do better than expected, but on November 5, 1963, he nevertheless dutifully went down to defeat. Another Democratic governor would lead the state's fight against his own party's president. That president, though, would not be John Kennedy. Two and a half weeks later, he was assassinated.

Southern politicians applauded openly. Just as quite a few students in the second grade at Benoit Consolidated Elementary School did. Or at least, that's what I was told; I was out sick that day. In doing so, they were no doubt parroting the vitriol they had heard from their parents at home. My parents had never tried to hide their dislike of Kennedy either, but they quickly corrected any inkling of approval for the assassination I may have shown. My mother, in fact, broke down in tears. Nonetheless, many assumed that Kennedy's death was also the death knell of the fallen president's civil rights bill. On the morning of November 22, the day of the assassination, it was on life support already. And now, Lyndon Johnson, a white southern Democrat—known to be a lewd, crude, corrupt, racial-slur-slinging segregationist—had assumed the presidency. Surely, the "southern way of life" had been saved. It had not.

Against nearly everyone's expectations, the martyrdom of Kennedy and the ascent of Johnson revived the bill. Sympathy for the slain Kennedy's agenda swelled. And the Texan from the Hill Country surprised everyone—most of all, his Dixie kin. Lewd, crude, corrupt, and slur slinging he was, but now he committed himself to civil rights reform with a fervor unmatched by any president before or since. His fervor, though, was more than matched by his brilliant mastery of the legislative process. He manipulated procedure, wheedled, threatened, cajoled, and horse-traded his way to breaking the logjams in both houses of Congress, doing so by garnering Republican votes as well as Democratic. In a last hurrah of the party of emancipation and the Fourteenth Amendment, a number of Republicans from the North not only voted for the bill but played a prominent role in steering it to passage through the months of parliamentary knife fighting that preceded the final vote. With civil rights leader Martin Luther King standing to his left, President Lyndon Johnson signed the bill into law on the July 2, 1964.

The relevant divide of the vote, then, was not partisan but sectional. Almost all southerners, regardless of party, voted "no" on the bill. Almost all nonsoutherners, regardless of party, voted "yes." Crucially, though, one of the few nonsouthern naysayers was Republican Senator Barry Goldwater from Arizona. In light of his vote in opposition, it is frequently pointed out that Goldwater was "not personally racist" and was, in fact, a member of the National Association for the Advancement of Colored People (NAACP). He was, though, a genuine small-government libertarian, dissenting to government mandates of any sort, asserting, "Forced integration [as required by the Civil Rights Act] is just as wrong as forced segregation [as required by state Jim Crow laws]." So, he wasn't in favor of the odious depravity of Jim Crow, he was merely opposed to having government do anything about the odious depravity of Jim Crow. He also believed that government "social engineering" to eradicate racism was futile—though, of course, racism had been the product of three hundred years of "social engineering" at every level of government. He was a ferocious anticommunist, willing to risk nuclear war in the struggle against totalitarianism around the world but was unwilling to muster a single "yes" vote on a civil rights bill to challenge the totalitarian system of Jim Crow within the borders of his native land.

And still, stunningly, in a resounding grass-roots rebuke to the party's pro–civil rights congressmen, Goldwater won the Republican nomination for president only two months later. He would go on to a landslide defeat to Johnson in November, winning only six states. But he swept the white vote in the Dixiecrat core in the Deep South, including in Mississippi. In spite of his attacks on New Deal programs such as rural electrification, the TVA, and farm subsidies—each of which was still benefiting ordinary white Mississippians enormously—he took 87 percent of the popular vote in the state, winning all eighty-two counties. This in a state that had not voted for a Republican for president since 1872, at the height of Radical Reconstruction. To suggest that the Arizonan's civil rights stance was not the source of the hot lava for this political eruption is inane.

Barry Goldwater is sometimes mentioned as a pioneer of what was later dubbed the Republican's "Southern strategy" to win the votes of white southerners. But its self-proclaimed creator was Kevin Phillips, campaign aide to Richard Nixon in 1968 and 1972. The first chess move in this game was not to hold more campaign rallies before white audiences, said Phillips in 1968. Instead, "Maintenance of Negro voting rights is essential to the GOP." The comment was in reference to the Voting Rights Act of 1965, which had provided federal protections for minority suffrage in the South and elsewhere—leading to a 700-percent increase in black voter registration in Mississippi over subsequent years. Northern blacks were already voting Democratic, so, as Phillips well knew, newly enfranchised southern blacks were not potential Republican voters. He acknowledged, "From now on the Republicans are never going to get more than 10 to 20 percent of the Negro vote." But to emerge as the new majority party, he said, Republicans "don't need any more than that." So why were black votes for the Democrats "essential" to the Republicans? It wasn't complicated, he said. "The more Negroes who register as Democrats in the South, the sooner the Negrophobe whites will quit the Democrats and become Republicans."

In other words, black votes were "essential to the GOP" because they would trigger a white backlash in favor of the GOP, one that would translate into two white votes gained for the Republicans for every one black vote gained by the Democrats. Therefore, for the time being, limiting the black vote would be "shortsighted," Phillips said. And in fact, for the next few decades, Republicans faithfully supported extension of the Voting Rights Act (VRA)—self-righteously basking in the Lincolnesque glow every time. Left unsaid was that once southern white loyalty to the Republicans had been cemented, the VRA could be gutted, and black voter suppression could be revived.

Note, too, that he said, "Negrophobe whites . . . will become Republican." Not just "whites." The mark of a "Negrophobe" is not merely a pose of superiority over blacks but, moreover, a fear of them. And a phobia is not simply a fear, but an irrationally exaggerated fear. In this case, one that had been deliberately cultivated over the course of the previous three hundred years and now would be cultivated again. For decades, the Republican Party had tried to lure southern white voters with a promise of passivity, that a federal government under its control would generally let the states handle racial issues as they chose. They remained true to that vow, but now, they began to offer more. Just as Kevin Phillips advised, beginning in earnest with the 1972 election, the party would consciously pursue the racist vote. And more, it would, as the political need arose, completely abandon its traditional passivity and would henceforth weaponize racism by actively inciting white hysteria to its advantage—as it would go on to do in 1972 and 1988 and 2016 and countless other times. But this is what southern Democrats had done in 1861 and 1875 and 1890 and 1955 and countless other times. But too, it is as Virginian planters had done in 1670 and as "patriot" Founding Fathers had done in

1775. As historian Joel Williamson puts it, "from the white point of view, one might say that the Negro-as-scapegoat has been one the nation's most valuable resources. He can be used again and yet again, and never wear out."

But also note that, as Republicans, southerners would shun the more liberal wing of the party, allying instead with the party's archconservatives from the West. Meaning that, as the Republicans took control of the presidency thanks to the votes of southern whites, southern-fortified conservatives would be taking firm control of the party. Which posed a question. Was the essence of this ongoing process the "Republicanization" of the white South or the southernization of Republicanism? And, for that matter, the southernization of all American politics?

On third thought, who did win the Civil War?

CHAPTER 27

The Republican Strategy of the Southern Party

Did the Republican Party take over the white South,
or was it the other way around?

While Alabama Governor George Wallace briefly campaigned for the Democratic nomination for president in the spring of 1964, he ventured into what all assumed would be the hostile ground of the North. Here, nearing the high-water mark of the civil rights movement (the Civil Rights Act would be passed that July), he was defying the tides of history, running as a drawling, Bible-thumping segregationist. And still, running against Lyndon Johnson, a popular incumbent who was on his way to reelection in a landslide, he garnered a third of the vote in Democratic primaries in Wisconsin and Indiana and 40 percent in Maryland. Four years later, running for president as an Independent, he carried five states, all in the Deep South, but also drew enthusiastic crowds of seventy thousand to the Boston Common and twenty thousand to Madison Square Garden in New York.

These cheering Yankees led Wallace to a startling revelation. As journalist Douglas Kiker paraphrases it, he saw that "they all hate black people, all of them. They're all afraid, all of them. Great God! That's it! They're all Southern! The whole US is Southern." With this realization, Wallace was discovering a truth that Malcolm X had already exposed. "Stop talking about the South," he instructed his followers in New York in 1963. "As long as you are *south* of the *Canadian* border, you are *South*." Both Wallace and Malcolm exaggerated for effect. Both cut too close to the bone for comfort. We should remember that while the South's Jim Crow was defined by government-required segregation, in the North, there was plenty of segregation required by individual business owners. The Civil Rights Act would ban both.

And so, at the very moment at which many were declaring the nation's victory over racism, George Wallace was not only leading a long-simmering racist backlash in Alabama, but he also stumbled upon one already brewing among the "southerners" in Sheboygan, Wisconsin, and Staten Island, New York. The entire nation's politics were ripe to be polarized into white versus nonwhite, moralized into a no-compromise, apocalyptic battle between Jesus and Beelzebub, between the Divine Right and the Humanist Left. In short, "southernized."

No, the fuel of this racial reaction would not power Wallace into the presidency, but he was to be, says Emory University historian Dan Carter, "the alchemist of the new social conservatism." It was an ideology that would fuel others' rise to power as it pushed the Republican Party to the Right. This new conservatism, explains Carter, mixed "racial fear, anticommunism, cultural nostalgia, and right-wing economics." But consider that this "new" movement as it evolved over the next fifty years, while novel for the nation, bore a striking resemblance to a brand of old "conservatism"—that which had suffocated the South during the days of slavery and Jim Crow. As Heather Cox Richardson argues, these defenders of "liberty" in the 1960s and later called themselves "Movement Conservatives," though "a century before, their predecessors had called themselves 'Confederates.'" She wasn't being flip. It was meant as thoughtful analysis, with good reason.

An oligarch-friendly trickle-up economics had long been employed in the South. And had long yielded an ever-widening wealth gap between the favored few and everyone else. Such is the product of an agenda of low and lower taxes to underfund low and lower government services, coercion of labor by means of—in succession—slavery, sharecropping, and hostility to unions, and therefore, chronically low "wages" and low consumer buying power. All hermetically sealed away from criticism within the steely carapace of God-ordained racial paranoia and a readiness to assert and defend the "common resolve, indomitably maintained" that this should "remain a white man's country." To lend that hard-edged conviction a gloss of romance, Lost Cause ideologists created one of the most influential of all schools of cultural nostalgia. And, as early as the Radical Reconstruction years—corresponding to those of the Paris Commune—advocacy of racial equity had been routinely equated to sympathy for international communism.

In this "new social conservatism," racial issues were sometimes overt but sometimes covert. It was upfront in controversies over school busing, but it was there behind the mask of many other, supposedly nonracial issues as well, such as law and order and poverty and welfare. The coding of "race" as something else had deep roots. Recall that, regardless of time, place, or race, slaves have been stigmatized with negative stereotypes, such as slothfulness, duplicity, thievishness, and lustfulness. But with the racialization of slavery in the modern Western Hemisphere, these had been deliberately transformed into racial stereotypes. After three hundred years of relentless conditioning, the postabolition American public still faithfully salivated "black" after every ringing of the bell of "criminal," every tinkling implication of "laziness." All long before Pavlov had gained acclaim for his Fido. As Dan Carter puts it, "in reality [i.e., in light of this history], fears of blackness and fears of disorder—interwoven by the subconscious connection many white Americans made between blackness and criminality, blackness and poverty, blackness and cultural degradation—were the warp and woof of the new social agenda" and, he might have added, the interweaving of black issues and the federal government that had, for all its own failures, taken the lead in abolition and civil rights reform. This linkage had the effect of discrediting federal-government programs for any and all purposes, even those benefiting whites in the middle and lower classes. In the "new social agenda," racial resentment was sublimated into resentment against the boogeyman of Big Government. Those proclaiming "states' rights!" had their revenge. And we know this because Republican leaders said so. Said so at the time and afterwards. Like antebellum southerners who explained bluntly that slavery was central to secession, Confederacy-formation, and the Civil War, Republicans explained that race was at the heart of their effort to lure whites into their ranks.

In the last chapter, we saw that Kevin Phillips, strategist of "the emerging Republican majority" in Richard Nixon's presidential campaign in 1972, detailed his southern strategy to lure "Negrophobe whites" to the Republican column. In his diary, Nixon aide H. R. Haldeman said that the president "emphasized that you have to face the fact that the whole problem is really the blacks. The key is to devise a system that recognizes this while not appearing to." In his memoir, Nixon's domestic policy chief John Ehrlichman admits "that a subliminal appeal to the anti-black voter was always present in Nixon's statements and speeches." Nixon's southern strategy survived his fall and became the Republican Party's base strategy. Today, it's commonly called "dog whistling." Dan Carter calls it "soft-porn racism."

With admirable honesty, Lee Atwater, campaign advisor to Ronald Reagan and George H. W. Bush, explains the dog-whistled linking of social issues, economics, and race. The new, polished demagogue does not bellow, Atwater explains, but insinuates, "You start out in 1954 by saying, 'n-----, n-----, n-----.' By 1968 you can't say 'n-----'—that hurts you, backfires." So, to achieve the same effect, "you say stuff like forced busing, states' rights, and all that stuff." And still later, "Now, you're talking about cutting taxes, and all these things you're talking about are totally economic things and a byproduct of them is, blacks get hurt worse than whites. . . . 'We want to cut this,' is much more abstract than even the busing thing, and a hell of a lot more abstract than 'N-----, n-----.'"

Ronald Reagan became quite the master of these abstract arts. In 1980, having just received the party's nomination, he began his postconvention campaign with a speech at Mississippi's Neshoba County Fair. In Mississippi, Neshoba County was famous primarily for its fair, but it was famous nationally exclusively for its murders. In 1964, during Freedom Summer, three civil rights workers had been assassinated by Klansmen. At the time, state and local authorities had either ignored the murders, covered them up, abetted them, or literally participated in them. They then keened woefully over a violation of sacred states' rights when federal officials finally intervened and found the bodies of the murdered men. And still, in his remarks, Reagan not only failed to mention those martyred for constitutional voting rights, but he also made a point to praise the doctrine of states' rights instead.

The "backfiring" n-word, of course, never crossed the ever-genial Gipper's lips. Therefore, those who accused him of racism for his dog whistle were themselves branded as "racists." Of course, this through-the-looking-glass moment when the racist is transformed into offended victim of racism is positively orgasmic for the expert dog whistler. Only willing dupes were deceived, though. In this place of all places, Reagan's omissions as surely as his inclusions made the message of "the Great Communicator" unambiguously clear. In Neshoba County, Mississippi, it cracked with all the eloquence of an overseer's whip.

But in the symbolism of place, another presidential candidate did Reagan one better. Because if there was one other spot that would amplify a speaker's whispered racial message even more it was Stone Mountain, Georgia. It was here that, in 1915, the Ku Klux Klan had been reborn. Here, therefore, the white-supremacist, neo-Confederate Mecca would be established with the commissioning of the largest bas-relief sculpture in the world. Gigantic equestrian images of Jefferson Davis, Robert E. Lee, and Stonewall Jackson were jackhammered into the bare rock across the face of the mount. Until the 1960s, it was the site of the Klan's annual cross burning. Still, it hosts entertainment extravaganzas featuring fireworks and lasers projecting a giant Confederate flag to flap across the beards and brows of the three white knights on horseback, all while, in the background, first faintly, then more loudly, a disembodied, angelic Elvis is heard singing "Dixie." Slow tempo. Holy of holies. It was no coincidence that Martin Luther King's aspirational "I Have a Dream" speech in 1963 included the line, "Let freedom ring from Stone Mountain of Georgia."

Therefore, for a white presidential candidate to stage a speech in this place would not just send a racial message. It would write it across the sky in sulfurous fumes. To stage a racially coded "get-tough-on-crime" scolding at a youth correctional facility—located just off Robert E. Lee Boulevard at Stone Mountain—in which 90 percent of the inmates were black and to have those inmates lined up in formation in white jumpsuits behind the candidate would be a sonic boom of a shriek. That's Bill Clinton, 1992 Democratic nominee for president. And he won.

Whatever Clinton's flaws may have been, he was an excellent election-eer, and his tactics were a response to a very real problem. By 1992, it was clear that the Republicans' southern strategy had paid off handsomely. The party that had lost seven out of nine presidential elections between 1932 and 1964 had won five of six since. White southerners as well as large sections of the white working class outside the South had defected in mass. Some Democrats, such as the Arkansan governor, were determined to take back at least some of that racial ground lost to Republicans. They styled themselves "New Democrats" to distinguish themselves from FDR and LBJ, not unlike the "New Republicans" who earlier had been anxious to separate themselves from Lincoln and the Radical Reconstructionists. (Note that when parties attach the "new" prefix to their names, they are signaling a return to the old-time political religion of racism.) And for the Democrats, who could argue?

The point was to win the next election. Which they would do. But there was an alternative. They might have taken a longer-term approach, acknowledged the hard truth that winning a war sometimes requires the loss of some battles, and pledged ever-greater efforts to build on the still-unrealized ideals of Johnson's Great Society. Instead, rather than mounting another assault on the dragon of injustice, they fed red meat to the beast to persuade him not to devour the party.

And so, as he rang the changes of the racial stereotypes that were as old as racial slavery, Bill Clinton may have tooted his sax on TV, but he was a prodigy on a different instrument—the dog whistle. He vowed to "get tough on crime" but also to "end welfare as we know it" and, later, that "the era of Big Government is over." In his 1992 win, there is no doubt that economic issues were emphasized, but the winning strategy relied on another dictum as well: "It's the thinly veiled racism, stupid."

Clinton was not a reincarnation of Richard Nixon much less George Wallace, but he had poured more of the toxins from centuries of stereotypes into the system. If not "permissions to hate" blacks, in coded language, he gave more permissions for open resentment. But he knew that, however sordid his tactics may have been, most blacks would still conclude—accurately—that "the Republicans are worse." Which all too often had become the pathetic rallying cry of liberal Democrats.

It was, though, just one more verse to the same old song. Blacks had endured such treatment from their white "friends" for generations. There had been the condescension of many white abolitionists in the 1850s. The cold feet of many white Reconstructionists in the 1870s. The cold shoulder offered by white Progressives in the 1910s. The racial loopholes in the New Deal of the 1930s. Lyndon Johnson's snub of the Mississippi Freedom Democratic Party in 1964. And then the shiny, slimy New Democrats' dog-whistling Dixie on their way back into power. There should be no surprise that there is still black suspicion of the good intentions of white liberals. And still, ever redeemed by their by-rote geniality, white liberals respond to that distrust not with self-criticism, but with an eternally uncomprehending dismay.

CHAPTER 28

Trump (and Trumpism) as Mirror

From all this discussion of the past,
are there lessons for the present?

As I mentioned long ago in chapter 1, I am a historian born, raised, and educated in the South, but one who had never been a historian of the South. Nor of slavery. Nor of race and racism. But in the summer of 2010, I began a six-year odyssey of intensive reading in preparation for teaching a series of adult education classes on slavery and the origins of the Civil War, on slavery and the course of the war, on Reconstruction, on slavery in the antebellum South in global perspective, on the origins and development of the concept of "race," on Jim Crow, and finally, on the civil rights movement. It was quite the education for me if for no one else. I came away with an appreciation for the depth and breadth of racism in our history, for the price the entire country—not only nonwhites—paid for this failing, for the vast gap still to be covered. But for all that, I was about to walk away with a sense of progress. After all, throughout this project, the man in the White House was a black man, Barack Obama.

I was finishing up the six years of the series in the fall of 2016, and fatefully, I taught the next-to-the-last session of the last class in this venture early on the night of that year's presidential election pitting Hillary Clinton against Donald Trump. After finishing up, I went to a watch party in the common and complacent expectation of a Clinton victory. I knew the polls indicated a tight race, but I was certain that responsible, mainstream Republicans would not, could not, in the end, vote for the cosmically unfit Trump and would instead quietly select the Libertarian or would abstain. They did neither. The Kiwanis-club yellow dogs turned "yaller," went rabid. And instead of the first woman president, we got, according to author Ta-Nehisi Coates, "the first white president." Of course, all other presidents until Obama had been white, but, says Coates, those others, from Washington to Bush II, had relied on "the passive power of whiteness." That whiteness could be and was taken for granted. But after eight years of a black president, in 2016, it could not. Accordingly, Trump had made race his signature issue from the beginning of his rise to political prominence—from birtherism to anti-immigration and Muslim bans. He ran as a white man, the anti-Obama. He was astonishingly ignorant, corrupt, crude, and deceitful, manifestly unpresidential in every conceivable way except one. He was white.

In turn, he was voted into office by white people. Famously, he won by a large margin among non-college-educated, working-class white men, but he, in fact, won the white vote among all classes. Among those without and with college degrees, among those in every quintile of wealth. He won among white women, even after he bragged about molesting women. He won the majority of white votes, even in some of the bluest of blue states—New York, New Jersey, and Illinois. Of course, Republicans had won the white vote in every presidential election since breaking for Nixon in 1968. But Trump, while losing the total popular vote by three million, won the white vote in a nearly two-to-one blitzkrieg.

To understand 2016, we must begin with Obama's election in 2008. After that signal event, we enjoyed patting ourselves on the back about how his election demonstrated the change in racial attitudes in the country, about the blossoming of our new postracial politics. There was some truth in that analysis, but as should have been evident, Obama's win was no comprehensive proof of whites' transformation on the subject of race. His victory was achieved with a coalition of virtually all nonwhites and a distinct, one-third minority of whites. The proof provided by Obama's election was not that white racial attitudes had changed to a great degree, but that the racial makeup of the country had changed and was in the process of changing even more.

In other words, in the big picture, Obama's win was largely the outcome of an ongoing demographic trend, one that had been causing general unease among many whites in the country long before 2008. Due primarily to immigration, the nonwhite population was growing far faster than the white population. It was universally understood that, if this trend was continued, racial minorities taken together would become the majority of the population by about 2050. Whites would remain a plurality, but collectively, blacks and browns and yellows and reds would outnumber them. But a preview of that future had been provided in 2008. The writing on the wall was indelible: not only did Obama win in 2008 and again in 2012, but many more President Obamas (and/or Garcías, Zhangs, Ahmeds, and Singhs) were clearly to come. The country was ripe, therefore, for another white backlash. What was needed, said many, was a white man on a white horse (or golf cart) to save the country from colorization, to end all nonwhite immigration, to expel those who had previously immigrated "illegally," and to accelerate the suppression of the votes of nonwhites already here.

And so, at precisely the time I was putting a self-satisfied bow on the package of my new and, I thought, profound understanding of our past, that undead past had risen up out of its tomb, given me the finger, and run cackling into the fever swamps of the American political landscape. Just as I was achieving some degree of enlightenment, the country, in its electoral-college wisdom, had made a great display of its self-destructive benightedness. However, even if I had not predicted Trump's victory, my studies over the previous six years had left me better able to make sense of it. Clio, the muse of history, was there to help.

The torrent of images and voices in the present can be confusing. It becomes hard to see patterns, separate cause from effect, symptoms from the disease. But like a special lens enabling us to make sense of an optical illusion, a sense of history can allow us to see form among the contemporary chaos. In the context of the past, the seemingly unprecedented is found to have precedents. Supposed anomalies appear to be closer to normalities. And so it is with this recent eruption of racial politics in America.

Though unprecedented in presidential politics, Trump's campaign was long a staple of American politics. At least in the South during the era of Jim Crow. It went without saying that only white men could run for office, but to win, it was often highly advisable to run *as* a white man, in other words, to run on the issue of race. To be excruciatingly specific, as recounted by Emory

University historian Dan Carter in *The Politics of Rage* (1995), George Wallace once explained that at times, it was necessary to "out-n-----" your opponent. In 2016, this is what Donald Trump did to win the Republican nomination and then the general election. He quite simply outbigoted his competitors, being sure to include Latinos, Asians, and Muslims in the rainbow array of his targets and adding in an occasional foray into thinly veiled anti-Semitism. Amid the incoherence of his positions and innumerable self-contradictions, race was the North Star toward which he oriented. He is often said to have no core beliefs, but white supremacy is his ideology, the central theme of the Trumpian worldview. And his base loves him for it.

This is not just a partisan diatribe. There were a number of issues with which Trump supporters identified: abortion and "culture-war" concerns, economic protectionism, more supply-side tax cuts, etc. But as Emory University political scientist Alan Abramowitz reports, surveys reveal that a high degree of "racial resentment" was the single most common one. With the ever-widening wealth gap of the last fifty years, there was good reason for economic resentment, just not for its racist manifestation. But then, diverting economic resentment away from themselves and toward racial malice had been the specialty of white economic elites since the seventeenth century. In 2016, the plutocrat Donald Trump ran for president as merely the latest in a long line, therefore, of apostles of white victimhood. Here again, the South tutored the nation since nobody can wallow in their own martyrdom like white southerners. In antebellum times, wealthy planters somehow persuaded themselves that they, the enslavers, were the real victims of slavery. Just as whites—as terrorists and their enablers—portrayed themselves as the victims of Radical Reconstruction, just as whites—as vigilante gangs—posed as victims in the Jim Crow era. In white southerners' interpretation, the slavedriver, the Klan arsonist, and the lynch mob were all victims rather than victimizers. And today, it is wailed, "coastal elites" hurt the white South's delicate feelings on a regular basis. But most onerous of all, whites are further victimized in having to listen to blacks lament about their victimization at the hands of enslavers, Klan terrorists, and lynch mobs.

But Trump's racism is not only a danger to nonwhites. It threatens the nation in its entirety. As Ta-Nehisi Coates asserts chillingly—and accurately—"to accept that whiteness brought us Donald Trump is to accept whiteness as an existential danger to the country and the world." Many, I'm sure, will quickly dismiss this notion as an exaggeration. I do not. And after his attempted fascist coup of January 6 (and still ongoing) and with his pose as lapdog for the fascist Vladimir Putin, I fail to see how anyone can disagree. But we must remember that whiteness has threatened the existence of this country once before. Many white Americans were once willing to abolish the country rather than abolish racial slavery. In the name of white supremacy, some whites were willing not only to enslave nonwhites but also to violate the rights of other whites, to corrupt the outcome of elections, to defy the rule of law, to lie, cheat, steal, and murder.

It must also be stressed that the Trumpian enthronement of systematic deceit is a restoration, not a usurpation. Southerners had learned to live with slavery and Jim Crow by living a lie. That method of coping has now been nationalized. The "posttruth society" that is consuming the country today is simply a replay of that of the past. Today, half the country is, again, "impervious to reason, justice or fact," just as W. E. B. Du Bois lamented about the South in 1935. The South made the Big Lie into its Bible long before Hitler "invented" the concept. Trump has simply updated and expanded it. Lying is his truth, inerrant and fundamental.

Which leads me to wonder—as a lifelong resident of the Bible Belt—How can Trump's un-Christlike reality be reconciled with the assumed holiness of the white, evangelical wing of Trump's base? Easily. This bigoted chink in the self-righteous armor of Christian fundamentalists did not begin with Trump. It should hardly need to be pointed out that religion in general and Christianity in particular have been sources of both great compassion and great hate. Most surely, American evangelicalism has not provided any sort of immunization against racial prejudice. Throughout our history, Bible-toting slave owners, Klansmen, lynch mobs, and dog whistlers have always outnumbered evangelical advocates of civil rights. We will remember that most southern evangelicals happily sold their Christlike, egalitarian souls to hierarchical, racist slavery before the Civil War and to Jim Crow after. And their upright reverends, whether seminary trained or Holy Spirit inspired, dutifully sanctified the whole while quoting their "inerrant" scripture. That scripture that musters the moral courage to pronounce judgment on sacred and profane hairdos but not to condemn the atrocity of chattel slavery at any point in its sixty-six canonical books spread over its two testaments written over a span of at least eight hundred years.

Still, as right-leaning evangelicals are happy to tell us, the political phenomenon of the religious Right began decades before Trump and began not
with race, but with abortion, specifically with the backlash to the Supreme
Court's 1973 decision legalizing abortion in *Roe v. Wade*. And there is no
denying that he fulfilled his promise to appoint antiabortion judges to the
Supreme Court, resulting in the landmark reversal of *Roe* in June 2022. But
the religious Right's account of its antiabortion origins is a carefully nurtured
lie, as Dartmouth's Randall Balmer expertly explains.

As the court rendered its decision in *Roe* in 1973, he observes, evangelicals
were silent. And they were silent because, they believed, the Bible was silent
on the matter. In the opinion of evangelicals—defined in large part by their
faith in the Bible as the inerrant, literal word of God—the Bible did not condemn abortion. In 1971—two years before *Roe*—the thoroughly evangelical
Southern Baptist Convention passed a resolution to, "call upon Southern
Baptists to work for legislation that will allow the possibility of abortion
under such conditions as rape, incest, clear evidence of fetal deformity, and
carefully ascertained evidence of the likelihood of damage to the emotional,
mental, and physical health of the mother." But then, too, for all Protestants,
abortion had long been downplayed as a "Catholic issue."

More generally, Balmer explains that, until the 1970s, white evangelicals
had been notably apolitical. Craving "a refuge from the dangers of an increasingly secular society," they had withdrawn into a subculture made up of an
interlocking network of churches, church schools, seminaries, and publishing houses. If they voted at all, they did not do so as a self-conscious bloc.
Quite simply, as long as the fallen world that surrounded them was held at
bay, evangelicals had little interest in involvement with politics. Only a threat
to that self-contained world could rouse them to unified action. In the late
1970s, such a threat emerged. Their schools, they warned, were under assault.

Many of the segregated private academies that had been founded after
Brown v. Topeka in 1954 had been affiliated with white evangelical churches,
therefore sharing those churches' tax-exempt status. But in 1971, federal courts
ruled that such exemptions from federal taxes violated the 1964 Civil Rights
Act, representing inappropriate federal assistance to these private but segregated schools. Delaying tactics held off the IRS until 1977, but in that year, the
tax exemptions of church-affiliated segregated academies were finally denied.
And thus was pierced the dome of the evangelicals' hermetically sealed firma-
ment. Of course, they insisted that race had nothing to do with their sudden

turn to activism. This change in IRS policy, they said, was a sinister attack on their "religious freedom," which of course, it was not. In their churches they were still free to preach whatever doctrines they preferred, and in their own private schools, they would still be free to discriminate as they saw fit. The only difference was that American taxpayers would no longer subsidize them with preferential tax policy while they did so. Deaf to this logic, howls of righteous protest arose. The religious Right of politically committed and partisan Christian "martyrs" was born, led by Jerry Falwell and his newly founded Moral Majority. But it was to be nursed through its early years on the mother's milk of racial prejudice, not reverence for fetal life.

Admittedly, soon after this, abortion did begin to emerge as an issue for evangelicals, and for some, concern over abortion was sincere. But the timing of their transformation on the issue was no coincidence. At the end of the 1970s, advocates of the Bible's literal truth and inerrancy discovered what earlier evangelicals had somehow missed—that the Good Book condemned abortion after all. And this discovery just happened to come just as evangelical leaders discovered the need to rally their congregants to political activism but—in this new age of dog whistling—without racial rhetoric. Abortion filled the bill.

I readily acknowledge that many devout Christians who vote for the racist Trump are not "personally racist." Which simply means, though, that when it comes to race relations, the God they mind is not Lord Jesus but the great and powerful Lord P's and Q's., the god of form over substance. While faithful to civility, they have made their Faustian bargain. They have sold their true faith for a groveling, idolatrous cult of personality, have sold their God-given reason for insane conspiracy theories, and are anxious to sell our Constitution for a Christian, nationalist theocracy. They stand to inherit the political world if Trump returns to power in 2024, but in the process, they will surely lose their own souls. Godly they may be, but they are not masters of the ungodly Trump; the ungodly Trump is master of them.

Please recall that I do not say these things from a perch in Cambridge or Berkeley, Manhattan or Hollywood. I am a lifelong resident of rural/small-town Mississippi—what is now, among whites, fervent Trump country. I have never sheltered myself within an ideological echo chamber—and I have no desire to relocate into one. I do not believe that all who disagree with me are necessarily stupid or evil; I couldn't have lived here for all these years if I did. I have great personal affection for people that I know to be intelligent and moral who nonetheless cast ballots for Trump, who still support *il duce* in his ongoing fascist coup. I would ask the Founding Fathers to forgive them (for they know not what they do), except that, being intelligent and moral, they know exactly what they are doing.

I want to emphasize that this is not a book about Trump, however. It is a book about the congenital national malady that produced countless ills before it produced him. In chapter 2, I quoted historian Howard Zinn's concept of "the South as mirror" of the nation. Let's now reconsider the words but with "Trump" in place of "South." We see that "[Trump] is not a mutation born by some accident into the normal lovely American family. . . . [Trump] contains, in concentrated and dangerous form, a set of characteristics which mark the country as a whole. [Trump] is different because [he] is a distillation of those traits which are the worst . . . in the national character." America, meet your inner demons. "Know your enemy," says the great military theorist Sun Tzu. Well, "we have met the enemy and he is us," reminds the great cartoon possum Pogo.

We will not subdue this enemy by pretending it is utterly alien to our national ethos. The liberals' mantra of "This Is Not America!" which we hear with every new racist and fascistic outrage from Trump is historically obtuse. Trumpism is merely a symptom of racism. To simply "get rid of Trump" as a way to return to "normal" would be political malpractice. An honest reckoning with the entire history of race in America is essential.

CHAPTER 29

The Third Reconstruction of American Democracy

What to do?

It was an October wedding at an old plantation house just north of Natchez in 2015. But this was not your usual "plantation wedding." It was a ceremony in an antebellum mansion that was a repudiation of everything its antebellum origins represented. In a place where masters had once had the legal right to tear enslaved spouses asunder, it was a ritual of union between two individuals who had only recently gained the legal right to marry. Taking place only three months after the Supreme Court's decision in *Obergefell v. Hodges* had legalized same-sex marriage, it was a gay Jewish wedding. There were no hoopskirts, but the many invited guests included gays and straights, Jews and Gentiles, blacks and whites, young and old, locals and out-of-towners, southerners and northerners. In the old river town nicknamed "the Little Easy," it was a very Natchezian sort of event.

The ceremony had been scheduled for the front lawn, and so, of course, it rained. Frantic adjustments had to be made, with the *huppah* (wedding canopy) being hustled up onto the veranda. But in fact, the rain was as welcome as the diversity of the crowd. After a long dry spell, it was very much needed, settling the dust left over from the dog days, cooling the afternoon. Before the wedding ceremony, we were entertained with an operatic recital with each selection celebrating togetherness, and afterwards, at the reception, the dance band played several encores of Sly and the Family Stone's effervescent "Everyday People": "There is a yellow one that won't accept the black one / That won't accept the red one that won't accept the white one / And different strokes for different folks." Thanks to the anointment of the rain, the seven traditional blessings of the nuptials, and Sly's refrain, "We gotta live together," this old fallen and falling world was briefly given the sheen of new life and hope. Celebrating the unity and dignity of all in the human family, it was a joyous occasion. For one day, it was spring in fall.

Earlier that day, however, I had attended a different sort of event—the fiftieth-anniversary commemoration of the Second Reconstruction in Natchez. In other words, the local civil rights movement's tragedies and triumphs of 1964–65. Dorie Ladner had returned—very reluctantly. At the age of twenty-two, she had been the Student Nonviolent Coordinating Committee (SNCC) project director for its Freedom Summer campaign in Natchez, enduring numerous death threats for her trouble. The threats had not been idle. This part of Mississippi and the neighboring parishes of Louisiana had become a "virtual Klan nation," according to historian Lance Hill of Tulane. Five murders in the area are attributed to one of its splinter groups for the year 1964 alone.

At the commemoration, a man described some of the terrorists' handiwork—the bombing that nearly killed Adams County NAACP President George Metcalfe, also, unfortunately, a very Natchezian sort of event. He recalled that as a teenager he had helped to pull the victim's mangled body from his smoldering pickup. The protest marches that arose from these events led to the imprisonment and abuse of several hundred peaceful demonstrators in Parchman Penitentiary, two hundred miles to the north. For all attendees, the morning had been a gut-wrenching experience. For one day, the not-so-old scars—psychic if not physical—were again on display. But then, for me, on to the festive wedding.

How to process these experiences? To be blunt, no matter how effusive, the symbolism of the afternoon's ceremony couldn't erase the still-living legacy of the events recalled in the morning. But neither could the distress of the morning overwhelm the elation of the afternoon. The two then commingled, became blended into one inexpressible emotion. Words failed, so the images from the morning and the music from the afternoon filled in my blanks. While hearing the heavenly "Flower Duet" from Léo Delibes's *Lakmé*, I was seeing the hellish horror of the bombing playing on an endless loop in slow motion in my head. The obstinately tangled splendor and anguish of Natchez was, there and then, made cinematic. For me, the former has remained the soundtrack for the latter. As Yeats said of sublime, tortured Ireland, "A terrible beauty is born."

Maybe that is all that can be said. Maybe this is the place where historians humbly surrender the field to the subtle verities of art and poetry. But historians can at least contribute truth as reason and evidence allows us to know it. To have any hope to reconcile our mornings and our evenings, we need to agree on one truth above all; we need to agree about our identity as a nation, about who we are, who we have been, and who we want to be.

In recent years, we have observed a number of American commemorations. A procession of events from the Civil War years have had their sesquicentennials. And those of the civil rights era have had their semicentennials. But have we Americans actually commemorated anything? To "commemorate" is literally to "remember together." But to remember together, people have to remember the same thing at the same time. To a large degree, we as a nation have not been doing that over the last several years. Generally speaking, on the subjects of slavery, the Civil War, Reconstruction, and the civil rights movement, we are not all singing from the same hymnal of remembrance. If the cacophony of clashing voices was only grating, it would be bearable. But this chasm in historical understanding is much more than a nuisance.

Whether for individuals or for nations, memory is the superstructure on which hangs our sense of self. Note that we describe the condition of personal amnesia, the loss of memory, as to "not know who you are." No memory equals no identity. It follows, then, that historical amnesia is not to know who we are. We Americans are not amnesiacs, though; we have historical memories. But they are vastly different from one race to another. We live in parallel historical universes and exist as parallel nations, with contradictory notions of who we are, contradictory notions that play themselves out in present-day conflict. The danger, I believe, is very much real. To paraphrase our greatest president, a house divided against itself in memory, in its very sense of self, cannot stand.

This is not a uniquely American problem. French historian of religion Ernest Renan confronted this very issue in 1882 in his famous essay, "What Is a Nation?" Citing the United States as an example, he pointed out that a nation did not have to be identified with any particular language, religion, or ethnicity. But whichever of these characteristics predominated in the nation, its "legacy of memories" had to receive "present consent," had to inspire "the desire to continue to invest in the heritage that we have jointly received." But what if—as was so often true—separate groups within the nation had different, even conflicting, memories? How could they be reconciled? Renan's answer was simple: by deceit. Far from truth leading to a reconciliation in a common nationhood, the reconciliation of memories required untruth. "Forgetting, I would even say historical error," he declared, "is an essential factor in the creation of a nation."

To constitute a single soul, to be a nation, he thought, we *must* lie to one another and, so, to ourselves, must evade rather than confront the inherent contradictions of our history. We must cite self-serving delusions rather than footnotes, compile bibliographies made up of nostalgic fantasies rather than primary sources. As to academic history's fetish for facts, he said quite bluntly that it "often poses a threat to nationality." All the more reason, then, for scholars to be actively recruited into this great jingoistic charade. Soldiers are asked to die for their country. Historians, like diplomats, are beseeched to lie for theirs. And through the nineteenth and early twentieth centuries, most did. In the United States, our formal history reflected the sociopolitical reality of the white man's country. North, South, East, and West, its "legacy of memories" was as segregated and discriminatory as its society. In our original "cancel culture," its historical recall, as surely as its system of laws, actively suppressed ethno-racial minorities and women. Scholars have labored tirelessly to correct these lapses over the past half century or so, but changes in the public's perceptions have not kept pace. We are still a forgetful people. We have forgotten because we wanted to forget. We ignore because we prefer ignorance to knowledge, coma to wakefulness.

In light of the history recounted above, colorblindness is simply blindness. So says Harvard's Drew Gilpin Faust: "Not to see color, its legacies and its enduring effects on our society is not to *see*." Treating everyone the same in one's personal life—not to "see color"—is a worthy ambition, but as a public policy, it allows us to ignore, she says, "the broader cultural, structural, historical forces that perpetuate inequality and injustice in the US—inequality and injustice for which we all, sheep and goats alike, bear responsibility." There are those—many of them white liberals—who are admirably openminded in their personal interactions but are narrowminded in their political comprehension. They are so busy "not seeing color" in the people within their conscribed circle that they refuse to see the consequences of color prejudice in the broader society around them. There is a reason for black annoyance with whites who will make a great show of public comity and racial solidarity but then make no effort to understand the structural obstacles that cripple their community.

Here in 2022, we should commemorate yet one more one-hundred-fifty-year anniversary—that of the high-water mark of Radical Reconstruction, called by Eric Foner a "stunning experiment to create a biracial democracy from the ashes of slavery." It was an experiment without precedent before or since in the annals of mankind. And it was far more than an effort to aid the freedmen after centuries of bondage. It was, as the term indicates, far more radical than that.

The word "radical" scares people, though. It implies something on the fringe, far from the norm. But a corrective to that notion can be found in the fact that, in origin, "radical" is related to "radish." They come from the common Latin root word for "root." This tells us that a genuinely radical solution is one that tries to go beyond surface symptoms and to get at the source of a problem. From the same cognate, to "eradicate" something, thus, is to tear it out by its roots. It is in this sense that Radical Reconstruction sought not only to transition the nation out of civil war, not only to oversee the end of slavery as a legal institution, but also to remake American democracy itself, the American democracy that had been so perverted by the slave society that had articulated itself into its core. Reconstruction aimed to emancipate blacks from slavery as well as the "badges of slavery" and also to emancipate whites and the entire nation from its corruptions. Measured by that goal, it was making progress.

This is something, therefore, worth commemorating. And as we remember this together, we must take account of Frederick Douglass, one of the seminal figures of this Radical Reconstruction. In a speech given in 1869, he struggled with the problem of nation creation that Ernest Renan would consider later. Douglass acknowledged that the United States was "a tangled network of contradictions. . . . a country of all extremes, ends and opposites; the most conspicuous example of composite nationality in the world. Our people defy all the ethnological and logical classifications." And prior to the Civil War, how had the United States dealt with its profusion of ethno-racial groups? Douglass noted, "Heretofore, the policy of our government has been governed by race pride, rather than by wisdom."

But Douglass offered wisdom as an alternative—the one that was being actively implemented all around him in the Radical Reconstruction year of 1869. He declared that the only principle that could resolve this conflict "and give peace, strength and security to the Republic [was] the principle of absolute *equality*." A principle that would commit us to the "mission" to respect the rights of "the people of all races and of all creeds." And, he might have added, both genders, since he was a vocal advocate of women's suffrage. Our unity, then, would not be based on color or religion, but on our common humanity since "Man is man the world over. . . . A smile or a tear has no nationality. Joy and sorrow speak alike in all nations, and they above all the confusion of tongues proclaim the brotherhood of man." We could achieve wonders, he said, as "the most perfect national illustration of the unity and dignity of the human family that the world has ever seen."

To those who would demand that we identify with a "tribe," as Edward Wilson told us we must, and to engage in the "Us/Them-ing" that Robert Sapolsky told us is so engrained in our genes, he was proposing an "us" consisting of all those who welcome everyone to their tribe in contrast to a "them" consisting of "the narrow and bigoted." Crucially, therefore, in forging this vision, Douglass offered a rebuke to Renan. Our nation's unity would not be based on language or religion or, crucially, forgetting. In his lifetime of struggle against slavery and racism, Douglass forgot nothing, edited nothing, redacted nothing in his past or that of the country. He himself had lived out, and written extensively about, the nightmares that had composed a significant part of the memory of the nation. And he refused to repress them.

This was a man whose white father fathered him by raping his enslaved mother, whose mother was sold away from him while he was still an infant. Placed with his grandparents, he was then taken from them at age six. He was whipped repeatedly for insubordination, then turned over to a "slave breaker" for his "finishing school." On escaping to the North, he found more prejudice in these states that had abolished slavery but certainly not white supremacy. All of these offenses had been committed against him within the laws and accepted customs of the United States of America, land of the free.

And still, after war and emancipation, he granted his "present consent" to this nation above all others. That choice is no mystery. He knew America's terrible beauty in his bones. It was *because* Frederick Douglass had endured our worst that he held all the more fiercely to our best. There are no higher expressions of Americanism than the prose arias to our founding ideals composed out of his suffering, endurance, and triumph as a self-emancipated slave. But then, as Orlando Patterson explains, "those who most denied freedom, as well as those to whom it was most denied, were the very persons most alive to it." Meaning that the slave owner Thomas Jefferson cherished freedom but did so because, by personally denying it to others, he saw its value for himself. Douglass cherished it for himself and all others because he himself had experienced the travesty of its denial. Jefferson wrote the Declaration of Independence on a piece of paper. Douglass lived a declaration of independence and had its painfully won ideals written in the scars on his back. Jefferson was congenitally incapable of living the universalist ideals expressed in his rhetoric. In his devotion to universal human rights, Douglass reached notes of transcendence in his rhetoric surpassing any that could have been penned by the slave owner Jefferson or, for that matter, by the pragmatic emancipator Lincoln.

And for all that, the extraordinary Douglass's extraordinary Reconstruction was destroyed by enemies of biracial government, but more exactly, by enemies of real democracy of any pigmentation. The cold-blooded tactics of the anti-Reconstructionists highlight the ways in which the Reconstructionists themselves were at fault. Too many lacked the will to stay the course for the long term. In addition, though radical in ways, their goals were ultimately too moderate in others. Frederick Douglass was disheartened by the fall of the Reconstruction governments, but his experiences had steeled him for a long-term battle. His life had been a continuous quest for justice, but he also knew that entrenched power had to be countered by power. "The whole history of the progress of human liberty shows that . . . if there is no struggle there is no progress. Those who profess to favor freedom and yet deprecate agitation are men who want crops without plowing up the ground; they want rain without thunder and lightning. They want the ocean without the awful roar of its many waters. . . . Power concedes nothing without a demand. It never did and it never will." That meant activism, not just good will and biracial pleas for divine intervention. "I prayed for freedom for twenty years," said the runaway slave, "but received no answer until I prayed with my legs." He knew that the "narrow, bigoted people" will always be with us, will always have to be overcome. There would have to be a second Reconstruction, and now, hopefully, a third.

A century and a half ago, a small minority of slavocrats took their racism wrapped in religion and deceit, weaponized it, and used it to manipulate a larger minority of ordinary people into open defiance of the rule of law, into an embrace of violence and a rejection of majoritarian democracy, and a treasonous effort to destroy the constitutional union. Only the bloodiest war in our history stopped them. Only a "radical" postwar Reconstruction had any hope of repairing the flawed system. Its successes were "stunning," but many of its gains were then squandered as reformist energies lagged and the inevitable revanchist backlash surged. A century later, another Reconstruction was required. More successes followed; though, over the last fifty years, much has been squandered again.

Today, a small minority of plutocrats are again weaponizing their ugly brand of racism prettified with religion and armored in deceit. They are doing so in order to, once again, manipulate a larger minority of ordinary people into open defiance of the rule of law, an embrace of violence and a rejection of majoritarian democracy, and a treasonous effort to destroy our constitutional system. In this time of crisis, a war à la 1861–65 is highly unlikely. But a third Reconstruction of American democracy is desperately needed. This time to be sustained. This time to be truly "radical."

In this effort, polite nonracism must give way to aggressive antiracism—the relentless Big White Lie must be challenged relentlessly with Big Truth. A plan of reparations must be implemented, but not only for slavery and not to be limited to a one-time monetary restitution. The racism that was articulated into the institutional structures of America long ago must be taken out by their roots. But also, it must be remembered that the cause of civil rights and the cause of democracy are mutually reinforcing. Therefore, we must work to make our system more truly majoritarian, less minoritarian. The electoral college and the senatorial filibuster must be put out of our misery. Federal enforcement of voting rights must be restored to end state-level voter suppression. Hyperpartisan gerrymandering can no longer be tolerated. The Supreme Court must be expanded and reformed to the end, among many other things, of reversing the Supreme Court's ruling in *Citizens United v. FEC* (2010), which has allowed "dark money" billionaires to poison our politics.

But then, amid this wave of uprooting and reconstruction, we individual white Americans must also reconstruct ourselves. Our race problem is not caused by the physical presence of people who are not white, but by self-consciously white people who are hostile to their presence and/or by the merely white people who are always liberal in mind and quick with symbolic gestures but inclined to be inertial in deed. Our race problem is not a black problem or a brown problem; it is a white problem. A problem on display in the mirror every morning.

Edley, the Mirror, and Me

Just at the point when I thought this manuscript was finished, I accidentally exhumed Edley from his grave, that grave of family memories found at the back of the bottom drawer of old filing cabinets. He was my family's "dog-hair moment" from a century ago, my father's father's first cousin—my first cousin, twice removed. And he served a four-year sentence in Leavenworth Prison for the offense of "seditious conspiracy." The federal authorities who convicted him said that this small-town Mississippi boy had grown up to conspire to overthrow the government of the United States of America. And that he had done so in a moment of great peril for that nation, in August 1917, only four months after United States entry into the Great War against the German legions of Kaiser Wilhelm II. However, he proclaimed his innocence, and the evidence, then and now, confirms it. He was not a seditionist. But he *was* a "Wobbly," an organizer for the radical and racially egalitarian labor union, the Industrial Workers of the World (IWW). And for the powers that be, that was crime enough. A few years after his release, though, he returned to Mississippi only to be murdered in 1929. So said the fifty-year old genealogical form I had excavated from the filing cabinet. But to append a flourish, the document added that he was murdered "near Moorhead," that crossroad on the maps of the Mississippi Delta where the Southern Railroad intersected another nicknamed the "Yellow Dog." But in the primeval lyrics of the antediluvian Blues, where cold-blooded menace ever-intersected desperate hope, it became the mythic spot where "the Southern cross the Dog." Still, after such a momentous life, such a portentous death, he was buried in obscurity and has moldered there ever since.

His legal name was James Edley Wiggins, but he had many identities. He was called Edley by his family, a tribute to his Confederate grandfather. He was stamped with the cipher 13843 by his jailers. But among his Wobbly brethren and among the newspaper men who wrote about this "most dangerous man unhung," he went by an alias. In the world of grand affairs, he was known by the fearsome nom de guerre of "Hobo Wiggins."

He was born in 1879 into the eminently ordinary household of an ordinary doctor in the hills of east Mississippi, though the family's predictable routines had soon been upended. Edley's mother died when he was six. His father remarried when he was eight. A stepbrother was born when he was nine. His father then died when he was ten. And finally, at sixteen, it is said that he impregnated a girl named Lila to whom he pledged undying love and marriage, only to be rejected by her father. Distraught, he ran away from home, not to return for thirty-four years. While acknowledging the psychological toll of losing his parents and leaving his siblings, this trauma could help to explain the young man's unusual course in life. Escape from his conventional home in 1895 Mississippi was, potentially, an escape from the then-emerging regime of Jim Crow. It was a brutal system that inflicted a violent police state on blacks but that also cauterized the minds and consciences of southern whites, rendering them, as Du Bois says, "impervious to reason, justice or fact." Edley, now alienated from the comforts of such a "home," had a chance, at least, to become pervious to each.

But also, a chance to experience poverty. In 1895, the country was in the throes of depression, one of a series it endured between the Civil War and the Second World War. Edley initially moved west into the Mississippi Delta but ultimately joined the throngs of men across the country travelling from one job to another in timber camps and mines, railroad construction camps and large commercial farms. In the parlance of the times, he had become a "hobo." Which means that, it must be stressed, hobos were not bums. As Ben Reitman famously put the distinction, "The hobo works and wanders, the tramp dreams and wanders, and the bum drinks and wanders" (quoted in Anderson). Hobos were, by definition, migrant *workers*. Though ones who did not conform to the dictates of employers. They were by no means lazy and were more than willing to work and to work hard, though only on their own terms. They mocked the stereotype that mocked them with the satirical lyrics of "Hallelujah, I'm a Bum." It became their unofficial anthem, their "Yankee Doodle." Some took to the road of necessity, but some had done so by choice. With their easy mobility and their scorn for consumerism, they were thus able to reclaim a bit of the independence lost in submission to wage labor.

To be a hobo, then, was to roam freely through society's mores as well as its geography. We need not exaggerate their triumph over racial convention, but to a degree, hobos even defied the dictates of segregation in their "jungles"—isolated hobo camps outside of city limits where they themselves made the rules of interaction. It is impossible to know how much of this racial iconoclasm Edley had absorbed in his early years of wandering. But by 1910, he had moved on to the timber camps of southwest Louisiana. And here, definitively, he received his revelation.

After the Civil War, lured by the South's cheap labor, in both white and black, and by the lavish inducements offered by the South's political elites, northern corporations had set about strip mining the South's natural resources, including the vast forests of yellow pines that stretched across the Gulf coastal plain. The camps were operated as feudal domains with hired gunmen—and a consciously promoted racism—ensuring "peace," i.e., profits. White workers were goaded into exhausting their anger about poor pay and working conditions in the fight to keep blacks beneath them. Meanwhile, blacks were lured into acting as scabs should white workers threaten to strike over those grievances. For all workers, it functioned as a perpetual motion piston of biracial self-destructiveness—with blacks helping to keep whites poor and poor whites striving to keep blacks poorer. For the plundering owners, it was a profit-making machine. But then, as the great labor historian Philip Foner puts it, "racism had always been used by the ruling class to divide black and white to the injury of both."

The solution was as obvious as it was radical. The exploited of both races had to work together to end their common exploitation. And in southwest Louisiana and east Texas, in 1910, they began to do precisely that. With the active support of many in the local community, workers formed a biracial union, the Brotherhood of Timber Workers (BTW). As to the con of white supremacy, the BTW proclaimed, "As far as we, the workers of the South, are concerned, the only 'supremacy' and 'equality' they [the employers] have ever granted us is the supremacy of misery and the equality of rags." Edley Wiggins became a charter member of the brotherhood.

Then, in 1912, understanding their plight to be only a local variant of a far-wider problem, the BTW formally associated with the Industrial Workers of the World, the alternately reviled and romanticized "Wobblies." Though some other unions had made overtures to this notion, labor unity across lines of race, ethnicity, gender, and skill level was a core principle of the IWW. The antidote to workers' woes was, they announced, "One Big Union" in which all were equal. A commitment to equality, therefore, was not a matter of charity from whites; it was a matter of self-interest for whites.

For all this, it should come as no surprise that the Wobblies' racial practice did not match their theory. Three centuries of ingrained prejudice could not be completely erased by a few years of rhetoric, however inspired. But we can admit the Wobblies' shortcomings and still recognize their virtues. Even if the whole truth of that man-made witchery called "race" remained murky to them, they had at least begun to see the lies that lay at its heart. Most crucially, long before the notion became common among social scientists, they saw that "race" was a social construct, one not inherited but created, carefully cultivated, and propagandized to enhance the power of economic elites. And since racism had been deliberately imbedded into the foundations of American capitalism and electoral democracy, Wobblies insisted that it could therefore be deliberately unimbedded. This systemic problem, therefore, would require systemic change, specifically a change to a classless society. Not to Soviet-style communism, though. Rather, to anarchism.

This is not the place for a longwinded explication of this long-caricatured doctrine. It is enough to say that anarchist Wobblies advocated the creation of a "cooperative commonwealth" of highly decentralized and noncoercive governance, distinguished by direct democracy and a socialist economy emphasizing community well-being rather than private profit. This goal was not to be achieved through armed insurrection, however, but by "the mighty power of folded arms," a general strike of all workers—made possible by the One Big Union. For this agenda, anarchist Wobblies were and are often condemned as calamitously wrongheaded, more often dismissed as woefully impractical, and virtually always stereotyped as violent. No, I am not now a convert, but I will insist that their anger was right-minded; their critique of capitalism's defects was eminently sensible; their resort to violence was in response to violent attacks by corporate goons. Their faults were real enough and have been broadcast far and wide, but their virtues, too, were real. They have lessons to teach.

Whatever our evaluation today, however, hobos like Edley found these doctrines attractive, and the feeling was mutual. In fact, Wobblies were convinced that hobos—i.e., rootless, migratory proletarians—were the true revolutionary vanguard. Thoroughly alienated from the social-economic-political-religious status quo, these "floaters" were the exemplars of class consciousness, the Chosen People of the labor movement in what truly became a secular religion, complete with a revivalist style, the apocalyptic imagery of the general strike, and even a nod in song to "the hobo carpenter of Nazareth." In the roiling archipelago of urban hobo districts, the IWW recruited heavily, opening assembly halls and bookstores where they scheduled films, concerts, plays, lectures, debates, and discussion groups to entertain and edify. In these "Hobohemias," one would also find newspapers like the *Hobo News* and "hobo colleges" offering informal classes in English composition, public speaking, economics, and law. If hobos were not lazy, neither were they ignorant.

It was here in the vibrant culture of the IWW, that James Edley Wiggins found his higher education as well as the higher calling of union organizer. And his alias. When the Mississippi hobo became a Wobbly, he became "Hobo," Wobbly incarnate. This was, then, no mere casual nickname among friends. It became his identity, a declaration of independence from traditional religion, traditional notions of private property and mainstream politics. And a counterdeclaration of commitment to the IWW. On his admittance form at Leavenworth, it is noted that he did smoke but did not drink or use drugs. His residence was given as "none." His formal religion was "none." He is listed with no family. It speaks volumes that his contact "in case of illness or death" was not a Wiggins in Mississippi but a Wobbly in Chicago. The brotherhood of the hobohemian One Big Union had become his family, the highways to recruiting new members had become his home, its doctrines were his religion. In this hierarchy, he rose to the rank of comparatively anonymous captain rather than general. But if hobos were—as they liked to boast—the "Knights of the Road," Hobo had taken vows to be a holy warrior in their Knights Templar.

Now committed to his mission, Edley left Louisiana in 1913 for the then-socialist hotbed of Oklahoma, there to organize white, black, and Native American sharecroppers—as nonwage workers, ineligible for IWW membership—into a "Working Class Union" (WCU). That accomplished, in 1916, the IWW sent him to work among miners and railroad workers in Montana. But whether in the Gulf South, the southern Plains, or the northern Rockies, he churned the capitalist waters at every stop, just as his Wobbly cohorts were doing across the continent. Meanwhile, business and governmental elites seethed and schemed.

It's vital that we remember why, out of all of America's leftist groups, these elites were so fixated on the threat posed by the IWW. They certainly judged any manifestation of socialism to be an abomination, but they knew from long experience that as long as its unions and political parties were kept fragmented into mutually hostile ethno-racial tribes, it would never pose a serious challenge to their lucrative status quo. Which is why American elites had been doggedly stoking race hatred since the seventeenth century. Conversely, says Dean Strang, "What made the IWW different is that it tried, at least fitfully, to unite men and women of different races and languages." That "difference" was its death sentence. Ad hoc repression had failed; the IWW had to be destroyed.

Vexingly, though, the IWW's ideals and rhetoric may have been radical, but its activists, like Hobo, were not actually doing anything illegal. However, if that rhetoric could be criminalized—First Amendment be damned—the elite's plans of destruction for the One Big Union could move forward. Conveniently, one big war would provide them with their opportunity. In April 1917, with the US declaration of war on Germany, a jingoistic mania seized the country. Government propaganda immediately began to portray mere antiwar and antidraft opinions (like those routinely voiced by the IWW) as anti-American or even as pro-German sabotage. Senator Henry Ashurst of Arizona alleged—only half-jokingly—that IWW stood for "Imperial Wilhelm's Warriors" (quoted in Dubofsky). By June, Congress had codified these hysterics into law as the Espionage Act. With a scribble, the radical but lawful IWW had been transformed into a criminally seditious enterprise.

Under the virtuous cover of wartime patriotism, then, the authorities unleashed the most sustained, extensive, and violent repression of a labor union in American history. IWW offices were raided, documents were seized, and its leaders of all ranks, from general secretaries to hobos, were arrested

and brought before kangaroo courts in which guilty verdicts were foreor-
dained. In the primary Wobbly trial, held in Chicago in 1918, almost one
hundred men, each charged with one hundred crimes consolidated into four
charges against each, were tried in the same courtroom at the same time.
Chaos reigned. and still, all the defendants were convicted—four hundred
determinations of guilt by the jury in less than one hour. The other legal
charades in Sacramento, Omaha, and Wichita followed the same pattern.

Edley, however, would be tried separately in Tulsa and for a very specific reason. Members of the sharecroppers' union (WCU) that he had
organized in Oklahoma in 1913 actually did hatch a seditious conspiracy to
overthrow the federal government. This was the woefully misguided Green
Corn Rebellion of August 1–2, 1917, in which a few hundred armed tenant
farmers set out to march on Washington, intending to gather a few million
converts along the way, to overthrow the federal government, and thus, to
end the war. It was, of course, a pathetic failure, comical if not for the four
deaths. The rebellion's WCU leaders were arrested and prosecuted, but the
mysterious IWW activist "Hobo Wiggins" was accused of being the "moving
spirit" behind it all, the man who had intimidated others into the plot to plant
bombs and kidnap government officials. Unfortunately for the prosecution,
Hobo had left Oklahoma a year before the uprising. In the summer of 1917, he
was in fact 1500 miles away in Butte, Montana, helping to organize the IWW
strike against the Anaconda Copper Company and haranguing angry crowds
after the judicial murder of IWW executive board member Frank Little. The
lynching occurred on August 1—a date that made Hobo's alleged role in the
Oklahoma insurrection on August 1–2 problematic. Numerous witnesses corroborated these facts, but fortunately for the prosecution, nine of the Green
Corn rebels accepted a plea bargain to testify to Hobo Wiggins's leadership
in the conspiracy. In the end, the innocent Edley was hunted down in Seattle
and, after nineteen months in jail in Muskogee, was finally convicted in 1919.
As the nine guilty Green Corn rebels who helped to frame him were promptly
released, the ulterior motive to target Wobblies was plain. At this point of
reckoning, though, Edley was steadfast. Offered a lesser sentence if he would
confess, he refused, saying that to do so would be to "commit a crime against
myself" by lying. Declaring to the end, "I am an IWW and will die one!" he
was condemned to four years "at labor" in Leavenworth.

There is no question that the incarceration took its toll on Edley—whether
it was the stonework, the rough treatment meted out by guards for one

labeled a "traitor," or the sheer monotony of prison life. His dedication to
his cause, though, continued undiminished. After his release, in 1923, he
published his magnum opus, *Workers' Non-Profit Cooperatives,* in which he
reiterated his commitment to the principles of anarchism and workers' unity
across racial lines and again proclaimed the injustice of his imprisonment.
And then, again, he disappears from the record. When we next hear of him
in 1926, he had returned to Mississippi. And only two and half years later, he
would die, we are told, there where "the Southern cross the Dog." In the Delta.

First, a point of reclarification. This was the Yazoo-Mississippi Delta, the one
shaped like the pupil in a cat's eye. The one that historian James Cobb calls
"the most southern place on earth," southernness double distilled, where its
beauties and its horrors soared to new heights of fancy. In 1900, when Edley
had lived there, it was certainly no racial utopia, and it was in the initial
stages of its great transformation, but the region was, for the most part, still
an unsettled bottomland of insanely rich soil but without the transportation
infrastructure on which commercial agriculture depended. Thus, wealthy
whites who had their choice of the best, most easily exploited lands, for the
most part, had not chosen it, particularly not the backswamps, the buck-
shot/gumbo lands, the "Longshots" of lore. Not yet. By default, therefore,
over the last third of the nineteenth century, its profligate fertility had been
available for poor whites, but it was even more important to black freedmen who placed a priority on self-sufficient independence in the wilderness over dependent debt in the white man's market. With this in mind, as
mentioned a few chapters ago, historian John Willis has called it the "poor
man's promised land."

But time passed, and the hurricane of civilization made landfall. Corporate
agents arrived. Railroads were built. The backwoods were clear cut for timber.
The backswamps were drained for cotton. The planters arrived in force. By
the 1920s, when Edley returned there, the promise was no more. The Delta
had become, says William Pickens, field secretary of the NAACP, part of the
"American Congo," invoking a comparison to the Congo Free State in central
Africa (quoted in Woodruff). The comparison was not a compliment. Earlier
in the century, the colony had been the site of a regime of forced labor, torture, and pillage on a massive scale, all in service to exploiting black labor

and African resources for the booming profits of white Europeans. Now, the Delta that had been a haven for the formerly enslaved had become the new template for grotesque inequalities of class and race. It had become *the* Delta in all its gory glory.

During these gold-rush years of the early twentieth century, the flatland's "gold" came in two forms. One was the fertile soil, but the other was cheap black labor. Labor without which the precious land was worthless, labor kept cheap with the constant threat of violence sanctioned by both state and local governments. This was the region's mother lode. These exploited workers produced wealth for the "miners," of course, but also, in turn, for those who swarmed into the Delta to serve the miners' needs—the snake handlers but also the lawyers who codified the planters' legally devious land grabs. The bear boxers but also the merchant/bankers who provisioned sharecroppers year by year and shackled them with debts for a lifetime. And the doctors who poulticed the bites and the clawings and, too, the diseased consciences. Like the Delta-bound lawyers, doctors, and merchant/bankers of Edley's family, my family.

From 1895 to 1926, while Edley had been hoboing across the country, fighting timber barons in Louisiana, organizing sharecroppers in Oklahoma and railroad hands in Montana, being arrested in Seattle, being falsely convicted in a show trial in Tulsa, serving four years in prison in Kansas, and finally, having a book published in Chicago, his relatives had been otherwise engaged. Profitably engaged. To name a few: Edley's first cousin (my grandfather) had moved his medical practice to the Delta where he was eventually to open the first hospital in Bolivar County. Edley's older brother (who lived a block from my grandfather) was a merchant who had turned crop liens into foreclosures and, ultimately, into planter status for himself. By the 1920s, he was serving as the chairman of the county board of supervisors. Edley's younger half-brother, Marvin, similarly a highly successful merchant/planter but in neighboring Sunflower County, was later to be appointed superintendent of the Mississippi State Penitentiary, the infamous Parchman Farm, birthplace of my first puppy. (A pause to gawk is allowed here. In this fraternal linkage of Leavenworth Wobbly and Parchman warden, we find a conjunction of criminal-justice planets seen once a millennium, if that.) But one thing is certain. To succeed, the Delta Wiggins of the early twentieth century had to be dutifully obedient to Jim Crow's demands and so to be—even with their medical degrees and honorific titles—"impervious to reason, justice or fact." And then, into their entirely straightlaced midst plopped Hobo

Wiggins, their racial integrationist, labor agitating, hobohemian, anarchistic, socialistic, "seditious," ex-con kinsman. Ointment, meet fly.

Which led me to wonder—had Hobo the Wobbly returned to revolutionize his home? Here, could I find the motive for his murder? Surely, not by a relative but, perhaps, by thugs, whether Klannish or corporate?

No, I could not. On several research trips back to the Delta, confoundingly, I found nothing at all even hinting at the high, homicidal intrigue I had anticipated. For that matter, I found nothing that would explain why anyone of note would have bothered to assassinate Edley the Wobbly since I turned up nothing about the Wobbly activity that I assumed Edley had renewed on his return to Mississippi. More, his official death certificate says that he did not die of a shooting, clubbing, stabbing, strangulation, or poisoning but of an "acute dilation of the heart," a condition complicated by pleurisy. The murder apparently didn't happen. There was no murder because there was no motive. And no motive because there had been no agitation. I made a point to travel to Moorhead where I stood astride the exact spot where the Southern really had crossed the Dog, but there, Hobo Wiggins had crossed swords with neither man nor beast.

The real reason for his return is simple and heartbreaking. It seems that he had nowhere else to go. Government repression had accomplished its task—by 1922, the IWW had been gutted. Edley's 1923 treatise on anarchism in action—a few sparkles shy of "scintillating," to be honest—had not inspired a rebirth. The golden age of hoboing was over as well. But too, blacklisted for employment, he couldn't find another job. And too, though only forty-seven, his health was already failing. Therefore, in 1926, he had swallowed his pride and surrendered to his past. He had turned to that "place that when you go there, they have to take you in." Home, to his family. Which was now in the Delta. Like an old, sick dog crawling off into the bushes, he had come home to linger and then to die. Which he did on February 29, 1929.

On his passing, the world took no notice. For this man whose arrest, trial, and conviction only a decade earlier had made headlines across the country, I could find no press reports of his death. It was early 1929, after all. Capitalist Wall Street was roaring. That delusional house of cards would implode the following October, but in February, few cared to hear about has-been Wobblies.

True to form, however, his fine southern family followed all the basic protocols of a "decent burial," no more. A death announcement appeared in the local newspaper, though the proclamation all but ignored Edley himself, dwelling on the achievements of his brothers instead. On his headstone, there was no attempt at a grand summation of his life's meaning in either psalm or militant rhetoric. There is simply his name and dates of birth and death. The eccentric nomad was then hidden away in a correctly flat, rectangular, and treeless cemetery, his monument lost among those others lined up in a conformist phalanx of the dead as if assembled to protect the tomb of a Chinese emperor. Though here, the intent was to bury him beneath a mound of anonymity.

Beyond his closest kin, many in the family seem to have completely ostracized him from the beginning. That certainly appears to have been the case with Edley's first cousin, my grandfather Dr. J. P. Wiggins, who lived a few houses down from Edley's eldest brother in Merigold. And it was also the case with my then-sixteen-year-old father, who—one would think—would have taken an interest in his notorious ex-con cousin just down the street. And yet, in the 1970s, when a descendent of Lila—the girl with whom Edley had fathered a child out of wedlock in 1895—contacted him for information, he swore that he had no memory of any cousin by that name. Edley had been airbrushed from the recall or notice of that branch of the Wigginses' lineage. And so he should remain, thought my perpendicular father. Having no reason to doubt his recall at the time, I too promptly forgot. Until I came across the few genealogical forms that Edley's grandson had sent my father, the one that had begun my own pursuit for information. But no one else followed up on his queries, and the rest of his grandson's apocryphal gospel of Hobo Wiggins has apparently been lost.

Amid this willful forgetting, I decided, the least I could do was remember. But in Cousin Edley, I not only found someone to remember but someone to admire. He was a small man of small account who turned out, though, to be a more honorable southern gentleman than the commonly lauded grandees we are told to revere. He was wrong often enough, but he was mostly right about the one transcending issue that they all got wrong: race. So self-destructively, damnably, hypocritically wrong. In seeing that wrong and trying—fitfully, futilely—to make it right, he paid a high price. And from the parable of his life, we see the fate of those who actually struggle to live the ideal of honor instead of merely posing in seersucker finery for the ceremonial portrait. For his efforts, fate rewarded him only with heartache, hard toil, hard time, and a lonely death.

In compensation, we can at least reward him with our attention—Hobo Wiggins still has lessons to teach. Included in his prison file that I received from the National Archives were his fingerprints. Mere black smudges on white pages, they are still somehow the most mesmerizing item in the cache. Personal and intimate and unsettling, they reach out like painted hands on prehistoric cave walls, commanding us not to commit a crime against ourselves by lying. Here, in this age, when we are harangued to see no evil, speak no evil, hear no evil about the systemic evils of our racial past (and present), we should heed the message they send to us in sign. It may be that no "Ballad of Hobo Wiggins," no "Wobblyman Blues" were sung to mark his death, but even now, out in the roughhewn opera houses veiled within the cypress breaks, the cicadas still whang their wings like diddly bows to accompany a spare *Le Hobohème* to his memory. The defiant words of the libretto still hang there from the limbs like forbidden fruits. Ripe for the plucking for any who care, or dare, to join the chorus.

As I have obsessively chased after the meager motes of Edley's life and death floating through history's ether, one thing, if nothing else, has become clear. This journey is not really about Hobo. It is about me. This dawned on me in a fit of dejection while driving back to the hotel after one more long and fruitless day of searching through jaundiced documents for the man to match the myth of my own making. I saw that it is a story about the absurdly gaping abyss between what I urgently needed to believe about Edley and what can be known about him. I chased after him so doggedly because I needed him to be my salvation. Selfish and lazy as I am, I reveled in the revelation that he had gone to prison for my and my family's sins. I wanted him to have died for them, too. But that is too much to ask of the hobo carpenter of Nazareth much less of the Hobo Wobbly of Merigold.

He did not, could not die for my sins. They are still mine. He cannot be my redeemer, my guru, my spirit guide. No one else can hand me a box of enlightenment to pop into my spiritual/ethical microwave for a two-minute meal of uplift. Intellectually, I know that I am not responsible for the errors of my ancestors, though I feel the burden emotionally. But my personal iniquity has not been enslavement, sexual abuse, kidnapping, lynching, nor even racial rudeness. While dutifully disapproving of all of the above, I have been guilty of the ever-polite, self-satisfied indifference of the white boy emperor in his ever-new clothes, those pieced together out of the "rags of facts and fancies" that Du Bois critiqued three generations ago. I set out to write a book "explaining" race and America, and in that, I have clearly failed. As any white man would. But I have succeeded in writing a book about my struggle to tame that historical beast. The image in America's mirror has turned out to be me.

As I write this during the centennial of James Edley's release from imprisonment for telling the truth about our lies, we are nearing another anniversary worthy of commemoration: the semicentennial of my own refusal to listen to the truth divulged to me by six-year-old Danny when I was sixteen. Fixing me with his child's wise eye, he had asked me why white folks, like me, had floppy dog hair instead of people hair, like his, and beneath it, white dog skin instead of people skin. "Why that?" he asked in honest wonder, boring a jagged hole into the core of my sense of self-worth. After a moment or two of flummoxed stammering, I, of course, dodged the issue and then dodged it for many more decades. But if I had thought more deeply about what the question implied, I could have saved myself a lot of eyestrain. Now, fifty years later, I have read a small mountain of books on the history of the South and race and spent countless hours pondering while staring into the distance, and my level of comprehension has finally arrived approximately back to where I was at that fateful moment on the edge of a soybean field in Longshot, there on the dizzying precipice of enlightenment in the smack-dab middle of adolescence in the cat's-eye delta of Mississippi, the South's south, America's America, the crushingly centripetal black hole of our historical gravitation. Danny didn't realize it—he was only six, after all—but his inquiries had been prodding me to doubt not only my sense of racial superiority but the entire concept of racial identity. But somewhere in that sunstroke of self-examination, James Baldwin's challenge was waiting to pounce: "As long as you think you are white, there's no hope for you."

For me, now, maybe there's hope. Slowly climbing out of a four-hundred-year-deep hole, I think that I am beginning to think that I am beginning to become less white. Part of the reason for hope, though, is that I know I'm not there yet. For all that I know now that I did not know then, I know that I cannot, therefore, just "get over it" and "move on." I am, and will remain, a work in progress, no doubt, until my dying day. As for America, though, here in the fraught days of September 2022, one thing is plain: as long as it thinks it is a white man's country, there is no hope for it.

To which Hobo Wiggins says, "Amen."

Acknowledgments

This was not an easy lift. Without the help and forbearance of many others, there would be no book. Bill Ferris, Vincent Joos, and Alan Woolf read parts of the manuscript and buttressed the resolve of an author at times unsure of his course. Richard Grant took time he did not really have to read the whole, offering constructive criticism, insight on the publication process, and wise recommendations on the medicinal uses of "writer's tears." At the University Press of Mississippi, thanks to Craig Gill, Diane Bunch, Lisa McMurtray, Valerie Jones, Laura Vollmer, and June Pulliam. Zahn Dawson gave me a huge head start in the mysteries of genealogy and added her learned guidance throughout. A special thanks, though, goes to my good friend, Peter Buttross, poet and scholar and gentleman. He has been my most faithful supporter in this entire endeavor, reading and counseling on the composition of every revised version and giving invaluable advice on the book's direction and organization. And then, there is my wife, Judy. I am fully capable of generosity, charm, and wit but can be moody and withdrawn on any given Wednesday. Over the gut-wrenching years of writing this book and then the frustrating wait for its publication, any given week has all too frequently had many such Wednesdays. She put up with me even when I could barely put up with myself. Through it all, even though this difficult subject was not her chosen topic of obsession, she was reading my drafts, advising, and encouraging, always the better angel whispering in my ear to quell (hopefully) my excesses.

Bibliography

Abramowitz, Alan. *The Great Alignment: Race, Party Transformation, and the Rise of Donald Trump.* Yale University Press, 2018.

Alexander, Michelle. *The New Jim Crow: Mass Incarceration in the Age of Colorblindness.* New Press, 2012.

Alford, Terry. *Prince Among Slaves: The True Story of an African Prince Sold into Slavery in the American South.* Oxford University Press, 1986.

Allen, Theodore. *The Invention of the White Race.* 2 vols. Verso Books, 2012.

Amar, Akhil Reed. *America's Constitution: A Biography.* Random House, 2006.

Anderson, Nels. *The Hobo: The Sociology of the Homeless Man.* University of Chicago Press, 1923.

Applebome, Peter. *Dixie Rising: How the South Is Shaping American Values, Politics and Culture.* Times Books, 1998.

Aristotle. *Politics.* Translated by Ernest Barker, revised by R. F. Stalley. Oxford University Press, 2009.

Asch, Christopher. *The Senator and the Sharecropper: The Freedom Struggles of James O. Eastland and Fannie Lou Hamer.* New Press, 2008.

Baldwin, James. *Collected Essays.* Library of America, 1998.

Baldwin, Joseph. *The Flush Times of Alabama and Mississippi: A Series of Sketches.* Louisiana State University Press, 1987.

Balmer, Randall. *Bad Faith: Race and the Rise of the Religious Right.* Eerdmans, 2021.

Baptist, Edward. *The Half Has Never Been Told: Slavery in the Making of American Capitalism.* Basic Books, 2014.

Barry, John. *Rising Tide: The Great Mississippi Flood of 1927 and How It Changed America.* Simon & Schuster, 1998.

Baum, Dan. "Legalize It All: How to Win the War on Drugs." *Harper's Magazine,* April 2016. https://harpers.org/archive/2016/04/legalize-it-all/.

Beckert, Sven. *Empire of Cotton: A Global History.* Knopf, 2014.

Beckert, Sven, and Seth Rockman, eds. *Slavery's Capitalism: A New History of American Economic Development.* University of Pennsylvania Press, 2016.

Behrend, Justin. *Reconstructing Democracy: Grassroots Black Politics in the Deep South after the Civil War.* University of Georgia Press, 2015.

Berard, Adrienne. *Water Tossing Boulders: How a Family of Chinese Immigrants Led the First Fight to Desegregate Schools in the Jim Crow South.* Beacon Press, 2016.

Bergad, Laird. *The Comparative Histories of Slavery in Brazil, Cuba, and the United States.* Cambridge University Press, 2007.

Berlin, Ira. *Generations of Captivity: A History of African American Slaves.* Harvard University Press, 2003.

Blackburn, Robin. *The Making of New World Slavery: From the Baroque to the Modern, 1492–1800.* Verso Books, 2010.

Blackmon, Douglas. *Slavery by Another Name: The Re-enslavement of Black Americans from the Civil War to World War II.* Anchor Books, 2008.

Blake, William. *The Complete Poetry & Prose of William Blake.* Edited by David V. Erdman. University of California Press, 2008.

Blassingame, John. *The Slave Community: Plantation Life in the Antebellum South.* Oxford University Press, 1972.

Blight, David W. "A Doubtful Freedom." *New York Review of Books,* January 16, 2020. https://www.nybooks.com/articles/2020/01/16/fugitive-slaves-doubtful-freedom/.

Blight, David W. "Introductions: Why Does the Civil War Era Have a Hold on American Historical Imagination?" Lecture on Open Yale Courses, 2015. https://oyc.yale.edu/history/hist-119/lecture-1.

Blight, David W. *Race and Reunion: The Civil War in American Memory.* Harvard University Press, 2001.

Bolton, Charles. *The Hardest Deal of All: The Battle over School Integration in Mississippi, 1870–1980.* University Press of Mississippi, 2005.

Bolton, Charles. *Poor Whites of the Antebellum South: Tenants and Laborers in Central North Carolina and Northeast Mississippi.* Duke University Press, 1994.

Boyd, James. "Nixon's Southern Strategy: It's All in the Charts." *New York Times,* May 17, 1970, 215.

Brinkley, Garland. Review of *One Dies, Get Another: Convict Leasing in the American South, 1866–1928,* by Matthew J. Mancini. H-Net Reviews, October 1999. https://www.h-net.org/reviews/showrev.php?id=3523.

Carson, Clayborne. *In Struggle: SNCC and the Black Awakening of the 1960s.* Harvard University Press, 1985.

Carter, Dan. *From George Wallace to Newt Gingrich: Race in the Conservative Counterrevolution, 1963–1994.* Louisiana State University Press, 1996.

Carter, Dan. *The Politics of Rage: George Wallace, the Origins of the New Conservatism, and the Transformation of American Politics.* 2nd ed. Louisiana State University Press, 2000.

Cash, W. J. *The Mind of the South.* Vintage Books, 1991.

Clark, Charles. "Governor's Message." *Journal of the House of Representatives of the State of Mississippi* (February–March 1865). DocSouth. https://docsouth.unc.edu/imls/msfeb65/msfeb65.html.

Coates, Ta-Nehisi. *We Were Eight Years in Power: An American Tragedy.* One World, 2017.

Cobb, James. *The Most Southern Place on Earth: The Mississippi Delta and the Roots of Regional Identity.* Oxford University Press, 1992.

Cobb, James. *The Selling of the South: The Southern Crusade for Industrial Development, 1936–1990.* University of Illinois Press, 1993.

Cooper, William J., Jr. *Jefferson Davis, American.* Knopf, 2000.

Cooper, William J., Jr., *Liberty and Slavery: Southern Politics to 1860.* University of South Carolina Press, 2000.

Dalberg, John Emerich Edward (Lord Acton). *Acton-Creighton Correspondence.* Online Library of Liberty, [1887] n.d. https://oll.libertyfund.org/title/acton-acton-creighton-correspondence.

Daniel, Pete. *Breaking the Land: The Transformation of Cotton, Tobacco and Rice Cultures since 1880.* University of Illinois Press, 1985.

Daniel, Pete. *Dispossession: Discrimination against African American Farmers in the Age of Civil Rights.* University of North Carolina Press, 2013.

Davis, David B. *The Problem of Slavery in the Age of Emancipation.* Vintage Books, 2014.

Davis, David B. *The Problem of Slavery in the Age of Revolution.* Oxford University Press, 1999.

Davis, David B. *The Problem of Slavery in Western Culture.* Oxford University Press, 1988.

Davis, David B. *Slavery and Human Progress.* Oxford University Press, 1984.

Davis, Jack. *Race against Time: Culture and Separation in Natchez since 1930.* Louisiana State University Press, 2001.

Davis, Jefferson. *The Rise and Fall of the Confederate Government.* 2 vols. Da Capo Press, 1990.

Davis, Ronald. *The Black Experience in Natchez, 1720–1880.* Natchez National Historical Park, 1994.

DePastino, Todd. *Citizen Hobo: How a Century of Homelessness Shaped America.* University of Chicago Press, 2003.

Dew, Charles. *Apostles of Disunion: Southern Secession Commissioners and the Causes of the Civil War.* University of Virginia Press, 2001.

Dittmer, John. *Local People: The Struggle for Civil Rights in Mississippi.* University of Illinois Press, 1995.

Donald, David. *Lincoln.* Simon & Schuster, 1995.

Donald, David. *Why the North Won the Civil War.* Simon & Schuster, 1996.

Douglass, Frederick. *Autobiographies.* Library of America, 1994.

Dubay, John. *John J. Pettus, Mississippi Fire-Eater: His Life and Times, 1813–1867.* University Press of Mississippi, 2008.

Dubofsky, Melvin, *We Shall Be All: A History of the Industrial Workers of the World.* Abridged ed. University of Illinois Press, 2000.

Du Bois, W. E. B. *Black Reconstruction in America, 1860–1880.* Free Press, 1992.

Du Bois, W. E. B. *Du Bois: Writings.* Edited by Nathan Huggins. Library of America, 1986.

Egerton, Douglas R. *The Wars of Reconstruction: The Brief, Violent History of America's Most Progressive Era.* Bloomsbury Press, 2014.

Ehrlichman, John. *Witness to Power: The Nixon Years.* Simon & Schuster, 1982.

Eltis, David, ed. *Atlas of the Transatlantic Slave Trade.* Yale University Press, 2010.

Eltis, David, ed. *The Rise of African Slavery in the Americas.* Cambridge University Press, 2000.

Etheridge, Robbie. *From Chicaza to Chickasaw: The European Invasion and the Transformation of the Mississippian World, 1540–1715.* University of North Carolina Press, 2009.

Evans, William McKee. *Open Wound: The Long View of Race in America.* University of Illinois Press, 2009.

Faust, Drew Gilpin, ed. *The Ideology of Slavery: Proslavery Thought in the Antebellum South, 1830–1860.* Louisiana State University Press, 1981.

Fehrenbacher, Don. *The Slaveholding Republic: An Account of the United States Government's Relations to Slavery.* Oxford University Press, 2001.

Fields, Barbara J. "Ideology and Race in American History." In *Region, Race and Reconstruction,* edited by J. Morgan Kousser and James M. McPherson, 143–77. Oxford University Press, 1982.

Fields, Karen E., and Barbara J. Fields. *Racecraft: The Soul of Inequality in American Life.* Verso Books, 2014.

Finley, Moses. *Ancient Slavery and Modern Ideology.* Chatto & Windus, 1980.

Fogel, Robert William, and Stanley L. Engerman. *Time on the Cross: The Economics of American Negro Slavery.* W. W. Norton & Company, [1974] 1989.

Foner, Eric. *Free Soil, Free Labor, Free Men: The Ideology of the Republican Party before the Civil War.* Oxford University Press, 1995.

Foner, Eric. *The Second Founding: How the Civil War and Reconstruction Remade the Constitution.* W. W. Norton & Company, 2019.

Foner, Eric. *Reconstruction: America's Unfinished Revolution, 1863–1877.* Perennial Classics, 1989.

Foner, Philip. "The IWW and the Black Worker," *Journal of Negro History* 55, no. 1 (January 1970): 45–64.

Forret, Jeff. *Race Relations at the Margins: Slaves and Poor Whites in the Antebellum Southern Countryside.* Louisiana State University Press, 2006.

Foster, Gaines. *Ghosts of the Confederacy: Defeat, the Lost Cause, and the Emergence of the New South, 1865–1913.* Oxford University Press, 1987.

Fredrickson, George. *The Arrogance of Race: Historical Perspectives on Slavery, Racism, and Social Inequality.* Wesleyan University Press, 1987.

Fredrickson, George. *Racism: A Short History.* Princeton University Press, 2002.

Fredrickson, George. *White Supremacy: A Comparative Study in American and South African History.* Oxford University Press, 1981.

Freehling, William. *Prelude to Civil War: The Nullification Controversy in South Carolina, 1816–1836.* Harper & Row, 1966.

Genovese, Eugene. *Roll Jordan, Roll: The World the Slaves Made.* Vintage Books, 1976.

Genovese, Eugene. *The Southern Tradition: The Achievement and Limitations of an American Conservatism.* Harvard University Press, 1994.

Genovese, Eugene. *The World the Slaveholders Made: Two Essays in Interpretation.* Wesleyan University Press, 1988.

Grant, Richard. *The Deepest South of All: True Stories from Natchez, Mississippi.* Simon & Schuster, 2020.

Grant, Richard. *Dispatches from Pluto: Lost and Found in the Mississippi Delta.* Simon & Schuster, 2015.

Gutman, Herbert. *The Black Family in Slavery and Freedom, 1750–1925.* Vintage Books, 1976.

Gutman, Herbert. *Slavery and the Numbers Game: A Critique of Time on the Cross.* University of Illinois Press, 1975.

Haldeman, H. R. *The Haldeman Diaries: Inside the Nixon White House.* Berkeley Books, 1995.

Hartz, Louis. *The Liberal Tradition in America.* Harvest Books, 1991.

Helper, Hinton. *The Impending Crisis of the South.* Burdick Brothers, 1857.

Hill, Lance. *The Deacons for Defense: Armed Resistance and the Civil Rights Movement.* University of North Carolina Press, 2004.

Hopkins, Keith. *Conquerors and Slaves.* Sociological Studies in Roman History 1. Cambridge University Press, 1978.

Hyde, Sarah. *Schooling in the Antebellum South: The Rise of Public and Private Education in Louisiana, Mississippi and Alabama.* Louisiana State University Press, 2016.

Ingraham, Joseph Holt. *The Southwest by a Yankee.* 2 vols. Readex Microprint, 1966.

Inikori, Joseph, ed. *The Atlantic Slave Trade: Effects on Economies, Societies, and Peoples in Africa, the Americas and Europe*. Duke University Press, 1992.

Jefferson, Thomas. *Jefferson: Writings*. Edited by Merrill Peterson. Library of America, 1984.

Johnson, Samuel. "Taxation No Tyranny: An Answer to the Resolutions and Address of the American Congress." The Samuel Johnson Sound Bite Page, [1775] n.d. https://www .samueljohnson.com/tnt.html.

Johnson, Walter. *River of Dark Dreams: Slavery and Empire in the Cotton Kingdom*. Harvard University Press, 2013.

Johnson, Walter. *Soul by Soul: Life inside the Antebellum Slave Market*. Harvard University Press, 1999.

Johnson, Walter. "To Remake the World: Slavery, Racial Capitalism, and Justice." *Boston Review*, February 20, 2018. https://www.bostonreview.net/forum/walter-johnson-to -remake-the-world/.

Jordan, Winthrop. *Tumult and Silence at Second Creek: An Inquiry into a Civil War Slave Conspiracy*. Louisiana State University Press, 1993.

Jordan, Winthrop. *White over Black: American Attitudes toward the Negro, 1550–1812*. University of North Carolina Press, 1968.

Judt, Tony. *Postwar: A History of Europe Since 1945*. Penguin, 2006.

Kakel, Carroll. *The American West and the Nazi East: A Comparative and Interpretive Perspective*. Palgrave Macmillan, 2013.

Karp, Matthew. *This Vast Southern Empire: Slaveholders at the Helm of American Foreign Policy*. Harvard University Press, 2016.

Katznelson, Ira. *When Affirmative Action Was White: An Untold History of Racial Inequality in Twentieth Century America*. W. W. Norton & Company, 2005.

Key, V. O. *Southern Politics in State and Nation*. University of Tennessee Press, 1984.

Kiker, Douglas. "Red Neck New York: Is This Wallace Country?" *New York*, October 7, 1968, 25–27.

Kirwan, Albert. *Revolt of the Rednecks: Mississippi Politics, 1876–1925*. University of Kentucky Press, 2005.

Kolchin, Peter. *Unfree Labor: American Slavery and Russian Serfdom*. Harvard University Press, 1987.

Ladd, Donna. "Evers, Winter: Mississippi Moving Forward, But . . ." *Jackson Free Press*, September 28, 2012. https://www.jacksonfreepress.com/news/2012/sep/28/evers -winters-mississippi-moving-forward-but/.

Levin, Kevin. *Searching for Black Confederates: The Civil War's Most Persistent Myth*. University of North Carolina Press, 2019.

Lewis, Bernard. *Race and Slavery in the Middle East*. Oxford University Press, 1990.

Lincoln, Abraham. *Speeches and Writings: 1832–1858*. Library of America, 1989.

Locke, John. *The Second Treatise of Government and a Letter Concerning Toleration*. Dover Publications, 2002.

Loewen, James, ed. *The Confederate and Neo-Confederate Reader: The Great Truth about the Lost Cause*. University Press of Mississippi, 2010.

Lynch, John R. *Reminiscences of an Active Life: The Autobiography of John Roy Lynch*. Edited by John Hope Franklin. University of Chicago Press, 1970.

MacLean, Nancy. *Behind the Mask of Chivalry: The Making of the Second Ku Klux Klan*. Oxford University Press, 1995.

Majewski, John. "Why Did Northerners Oppose the Expansion of Slavery? Economic Development and Education in the Limestone South." In *Slavery's Capitalism: A New*

History of American Economic Development, edited by Sven Beckert and Seth Rockman, 277–98. University of Pennsylvania Press, 2016.

Marable, Manning. *Race, Reform, and Rebellion: The Second Reconstruction and Beyond in Black America, 1945–2006*. 3rd ed. University Press of Mississippi, 2007.

Martin, Bonnie. "Slavery's Invisible Engine: Mortgaging Human Property." *Journal of Southern History* 76, no. 4 (November 2010): 817–66.

Marx, Karl. *Critique of Hegel's Philosophy of Right*. Marxist Internet Archive, [1844] last modified 2009. https://www.marxists.org/archive/marx/works/1843/critique-hpr/intro.htm.

Mbembe, Achille. *Critique of Black Reason*. Duke University Press, 2013.

McCurry, Stephanie. *Confederate Reckoning: Power and Politics in the Civil War South*. Harvard University Press, 2012.

McDonald, Forrest. *States' Rights and the Union: Imperium in Imperio, 1776–1876*. University Press of Kansas, 2000.

McMillen, Neil. *Dark Journey: Black Mississippians in the Age of Jim Crow*. University of Illinois Press, 1990.

Merritt, Keri Leigh. *Masterless Men: Poor Whites and Slavery in the Antebellum South*. Cambridge University Press, 2017.

Miers, Suzanne, and Igor Kopytoff. *Slavery in Africa: Historical and Anthropological Perspectives*. University of Wisconsin Press, 1977.

Mississippi Black Codes. MIT, [1865] n.d. https://web.mit.edu/21h.102/www/Primary%20 source%20collections/Reconstruction/Black%20codes.htm.

Mitchell, Dennis. *A New History of Mississippi*. University Press of Mississippi, 2014.

Montagu, Ashley. *Man's Most Dangerous Myth: The Fallacy of Race*. 6th ed. Altamira Press, 1997.

Morgan, Edmund. *American Slavery, American Freedom*. W. W. Norton & Company, 2003.

Morgan, Jennifer. *Laboring Women: Reproduction and Gender in New World Slavery*. University of Pennsylvania Press, 2004.

Natchez National Historical Park. "Visit Forks of the Road." National Park Service, last modified June 11, 2021. https://www.nps.gov/thingstodo/about-forks-of-the-road.htm.

Neem, Johann. *Democracy's Schools: The Rise of Public Education in America*. Johns Hopkins University, 2017.

Neiman, Susan. *Learning from the Germans: Race and the Memory of Evil*. Farrar, Straus and Giroux, 2019.

Nelson, Stanley. *Devils Walking: Klan Murders along the Mississippi in the 1960s*. Louisiana State University Press, 2016.

Newman, Simon. *A New World of Labor: The Development of Plantation Slavery in the British Atlantic*. University of Pennsylvania Press, 2013.

Nichols, Shaun S. "Conference Report: 'Slavery's Capitalism; A New History of American Economic Development.'" Harvard University, last modified July 15, 2015. https://scholar.harvard.edu/snichols/publications/ conference-report-slavery%E2%80%99s-capitalism-new-history-american-economic.

Oakes, James. *The Ruling Race: A History of American Slaveholders*. W. W. Norton & Company, 1998.

Oakes, James. *The Scorpion's Sting: Antislavery and the Coming of the Civil War*. W. W. Norton & Company, 2014.

Oakes, James. *Slavery and Freedom: An Interpretation of the Old South*. Knopf, 1990.

Orwell, George. *1984*. Harcourt, 1949.

Oshinsky, David. *"Worse than Slavery": Parchman Farm and the Ordeal of Jim Crow Justice.* Free Press, 1996.

Oxford English Dictionary. s.v. "peculiar." n.d. https://www.oed.com.

Painter, Nell Irvin. *The History of White People.* W. W. Norton & Company, 2010.

Parish, Peter. *Slavery: History and Historians.* Harper & Row, 1989.

Parkinson, Robert. *The Common Cause: Creating Race and Nation in the American Revolution.* University of North Carolina Press, 2019.

Patterson, Orlando. *Freedom in the Making of Western Culture.* Vol. 1, *Freedom.* Basic Books, 1991.

Patterson, Orlando. *Slavery and Social Death: A Comparative Study.* Harvard University Press, 1982.

Perlstein, Rick. "Exclusive: Lee Atwater's Infamous 1981 Interview on the Southern Strategy." *The Nation,* November 13, 2012. https://www.thenation.com/article/archive/exclusive -lee-atwaters-infamous-1981-interview-southern-strategy/.

Phillips, Kevin. *The Emerging Republican Majority.* Princeton University Press, 2015.

Phillips, Ulrich. "The Central Theme of Southern History." *American Historical Review* 34, no. 1 (October 1928): 30–43.

Pomeranz, Kenneth. *The Great Divergence: China, Europe and the Making of the Modern World Economy.* Revised ed. Princeton University Press, 2001.

Ransom, Richard. *One Kind of Freedom: The Economic Consequences of Emancipation.* 2nd ed. Cambridge University Press, 2001.

Renan, Ernest. *What Is a Nation? And Other Political Writings.* Edited by M. F. N. Giglioli. Columbia University Press, 2018.

Reséndez, Andrés. *The Other Slavery: The Uncovered Story of Indian Enslavement in America.* Mariner Books, 2017.

Richards, Leonard. *The Slave Power: The Free North and Southern Domination, 1780–1860.* Louisiana State University Press, 2000.

Richardson, Heather Cox. *How the South Won the Civil War: Oligarchy, Democracy and the Continuing Fight for the Soul of America.* Oxford University Press, 2020.

Richardson, Heather Cox. *To Make Men Free: A History of the Republican Party.* Basic Books, 2014.

Roediger, David. *How Race Survived US History: From Settlement and Slavery to the Obama Phenomenon.* Verso Books, 2008.

Roediger, David. *The Wages of Whiteness: Race and the Making of the American Working Class.* Verso Books, 1991.

Rosenthal, Caitlin. *Accounting for Slavery: Masters and Management.* Harvard University Press, 2018.

Rothman, Joshua. *Flush Times and Fever Dreams: A Story of Capitalism and Slavery in the Age of Jackson.* University of Georgia Press, 2014.

Rothman, Joshua. *The Ledger and the Chain: How Domestic Slave Traders Shaped America.* Basic Books, 2021.

Rutherford, Adam. *A Brief History of Everyone Who Ever Lived: The Human Story Retold through Our Genes.* The Experiment, 2017.

Saikku, Mikko. *This Delta, This Land: An Environmental History of the Yazoo-Mississippi Floodplain.* University of Georgia Press, 2005.

Sapolsky, Robert. *Behave: The Biology of Humans at Our Best and Worst.* Penguin, 2017.

Scott, Rebecca, ed. *The Abolition of Slavery and the Aftermath of Emancipation in Brazil.*
    Duke University Press, 1988.
Seidule, Ty. *Robert E. Lee and Me: A Southerner's Reckoning with the Myth of the Lost Cause.*
    St. Martin's Press, 2021.
Silver, James. *Mississippi: The Closed Society.* Harcourt Brace, 1966.
Snowden, Frank. *Before Color Prejudice: The Ancient View of Blacks.* Harvard University
    Press, 1991.
Sparks, Randy. *On Jordan's Stormy Banks: Evangelicalism in Mississippi, 1773–1876.*
    University of Georgia Press, 1994.
Stampp, Kenneth. *The Peculiar Institution: Slavery in the Ante-Bellum South.* Vintage Books,
    1956.
Steckel, Richard H. "A Peculiar Population: The Nutrition, Health, and Mortality of
    American Slaves from Childhood to Maturity." *Journal of Economic History* 46, no. 3
    (September 1986): 721–41.
Strang, Dean. *Keep the Wretches in Order: America's Biggest Mass Trial, the Rise of the Justice
    Department, and the Fall of the IWW.* University of Wisconsin Press, 2019.
Tadman, Michael. "The Demographic Costs of Sugar: Debates on Slave Societies and
    Natural Increase in the Americas." *American Historical Review* 105, no. 5 (December
    2000): 1534–75.
Tadman, Michael. *Speculators and Slaves: Masters, Traders, and Slaves in the Old South.*
    University of Wisconsin Press, 1996.
Taylor, A. J. P. *The Course of German History.* Routledge, 1961.
Thornton, John. *Africa and Africans in the Making of the Atlantic World, 1400–1800.*
    Cambridge University Press, 1998.
Twain, Mark. *The Adventures of Huckleberry Finn.* W. W. Norton, 1999.
van den Berghe, Pierre. *Race and Racism: A Comparative Study.* Wiley, 1967.
Van Evrie, J. H. *The Negro and Negro "Slavery": The First an Inferior Race; the Latter Its
    Normal Condition.* Van Evrie, Horton and Company, 1861. Internet Archive. https://
    archive.org/details/negroslaveryoovane/mode/2up.
Waldstreicher, David. *Slavery's Constitution: From Revolution to Ratification.* Hill and Wang,
    2009.
Wallerstein, Immanuel. *World Systems Analysis: An Introduction.* Duke University Press, 2004.
Wertenbaker, Thomas. *The Planters of Colonial Virginia.* Russell and Russell, 1959; Project
    Gutenberg, 2010. https://www.gutenberg.org/files/32507/32507-h/32507-h.htm.
White, Booker. "Parchman Farm Blues." In *The Blues Line: Blues Lyrics from Leadbelly to
    Muddy Waters,* edited by Eric Sackheim, 236–37. Da Capo Press, 2003.
Whitman, James. *Hitler's American Model: The United States and the Making of Nazi Race
    Law.* Princeton University Press, 2018.
Williams, Eric. *Capitalism and Slavery.* University of North Carolina Press, 1994.
Williamson, Joel. *The Crucible of Race: Black-White Relations in the American South since
    Emancipation.* Oxford University Press, 1984.
Willis, John. *Forgotten Time: The Yazoo-Mississippi Delta after the Civil War.* University of
    Virginia Press, 2000.
Willoughby, Christopher. "Running Away from Drapetomania: Samuel A. Cartwright,
    Medicine, and Race in the Antebellum South." *Journal of Southern History* 84, no. 3
    (August 2018): 579–614.
Wilson, Edward O. *The Social Conquest of Earth.* Liveright, 2013.

Woodruff, Nan. *American Congo: The African American Freedom Struggle in the Delta.* University of North Carolina Press, 2003.

Woodward, C. Vann. *Origins of the New South, 1877–1913.* Louisiana State University Press, 1971.

Woodward, C. Vann. *The Strange Career of Jim Crow.* Oxford University Press, 2002.

Wright, Gavin. *Old South, New South: Revolutions in the Southern Economy since the Civil War,* Basic Books, 1986.

Wright, Gavin. *The Political Economy of the Cotton South: Households, Markets and Wealth in the Nineteenth Century.* W. W. Norton & Company, 1978.

Wright, Gavin. *Sharing the Prize: The Economics of the Civil Rights Revolution in the American South.* Harvard University Press, 2013.

Wright, Gavin. *Slavery and American Economic Development.* Louisiana State University Press, 2006.

Zinn, Howard. *The Southern Mystique.* Alfred Knopf, 1964.

Index

About the Author

James Wiggins was born in 1956 and grew up on a farm in "the most southern place on earth," the Yazoo-Mississippi Delta. This during the turbulent years of the 1960s and early '70s. He earned a BA in history from Mississippi State University with an emphasis, though, on modern Europe rather than the South. After a semblance of a hobo year, during which he worked as a deckhand on a Mississippi River towboat, tended bar in a Delta dive, and backpacked through Germany, France, and Ireland, he took an MA in history. Again, modern Europe was his area of specialization, with the social and cultural milieu out of which fascism emerged as his thesis topic.

In 1981, he accepted a teaching position at Copiah-Lincoln Community College in Natchez, Mississippi, an old river town that was a showplace of antebellum mansions that had been built out of the clotted blood and congealed sweat of enslaved Africans. However, as with the historical drama bubbling around his childhood home, he was happily blind to such things. He was certain that Natchez would be only a short-term stopover on his path to a PhD in modern European history. He was mistaken.

In Natchez, he met his soon-to-be wife, Judy, and, as it happened, found his job and surroundings congenial. The advanced degree gradually slipped down the list of priorities. They moved to a house deep in the woods—a great success. He wrote a novel—a nonsuccess. But to the present point, he was ever so slowly enticed into an interest in the history of slavery and race in the South, the topic that had been buzzing around his historian's head since adolescence. Interest became fixation. He created semester-long special-interest classes for the general populace of Natchez. And wrote a regular column on race in the local newspaper. This book is the result.